Stunted:
My 20 Years at 12

Jonathon Sims

abstinence NOW Publishing
Bellingham

ISBN: 978-1-4801-8057-4

To both my wife and my mother,
who obviously deserve more thanks than I can give.

Preface

At thirteen, I began a list of the young ladies I'd kissed. Over the next couple years, it came to include girls I'd been in any way romantic toward, whether she realized it or not. It's still a surprise to me, thirty years later, that I foresaw my impending memory problems as a teen. Had I known then the extent to which the mercury from a broken thermometer I'd handled as a youngster would sap my ability to recollect even some of the major events in my life, I surely would have kept more extensive notes.

While I have kept a few journals throughout my life, I've done a miserable job keeping them current. Months, sometimes years, passed without a single event documented. As a result, the accounts detailed here are as accurate as I can recall and to some degree, verify.

As this tome developed, I was advised to remove several stories which didn't critically move the story forward yet were entertaining on some level, if only to me. To this end, more than 100,000 words have found their way onto the cutting room floor. I have, however, kept many references to the removed stories in the book you now hold in your hands and vice versa. Do keep in mind the bits found at the repository, http://stunted2012.com, haven't had the luxury of time in bed with an editor and as a result are somewhat less polished.

All of the names, as well as some locations, have been changed to protect the anonymity of those involved. To reduce the number of overall characters, I've also merged several friends into composites. While blurring the overall factual make-up presented, it has also helped to obscure people's identities. As many of the people who have figured prominently in my life aren't aware I've written about them, I sincerely apologize for the fictionalization of our friendships.

On a lighter note, I've been able to contact some of those who have starring roles in my life, thanks to Facebook. A few of the ladies have even been gracious enough to offer their own pseudonyms for this book, knowing full well what I was creating. I haven't managed to burn every bridge I've made in my life, just most.

The list of those to thank is massive and shall certainly not be fully realized here. Massive thanks to Anders, Jadon and Kenneth from Bellingham, eternal love to Gayle from Tacoma, sincere gratitude and apologies to Nikki from Tacoma for her patience and guidance, a big hug to Dave from Seattle for goading me, a humble nod to Troy from Bellingham for sticking with me, a kiss on the forehead to Kevin from Issaquah for his help with some of the little things, a big grab of the ass for Marty from the creeps for support and ever-present humor, an emphatic handshake to Kristine and Lance at Greene's Corner for continued support and food, a big thanks to Scott at Red Robin for always asking about my progress and the smiles, a monstrous thanks to Amy at Video Extreme for covering my ass more times than I can count while I got the ball rolling, a pinch on the cheek for Laurie at Boeing for listening and advising, smilies to family Kreft for insisting on the first copies to keep me motivated and a sincere man-hug for my cousin Nick for laughing with me and at me.

Twelve:
August 17, 2001 (Real World, Year 9)

"Enh?" I asked Ezra, when he walked into the deli next to my girlfriend's workplace. I lifted my arms before turning a three-sixty.

Ezra, prematurely graying but still a strikingly handsome man at an athletically-built six feet, gave me a once over. "Not bad. What excuse did you give her for wearing a tux?"

"Back in May, I told her I'd been hired to emcee a charity auction today. Said I'd stop by so she could see me in my monkey suit."

"What about the ring?"

"I already gave it to Lucy, a gal she works with. She's going to put it on a piece of velvet in her cash drawer while she's at lunch."

Ezra nodded toward the café's pastry-covered counter. "You want anything?"

"No, thanks. My stomach's doing back flips."

"You'll be fine. Not getting cold feet, are you?" Lowering his voice, barely audible over the traffic noise, "You know you don't have to go through with this."

"No, no, nothing like that. I really want everything to come off okay." A white limousine crawled past outside. "Shit, he's early."

"I got it," Ezra said. "I'll keep him out of sight until you guys come out of the bank." He stepped outside and flagged down the limo.

I sat. *Is this the right thing? Can't imagine life without her. Broken up twice already. What if it doesn't work? She loves me. It was empty without her. Both times. Why I went back. Funny, kind, puts up with all my bullshit. Doesn't care about the store.*

My mom sure loves her. She never liked Mallory. Rebekah didn't want kids. Do I want kids? She'll be a great mother.

Can't stay away. Don't want to. Need to be with her. She's the one.

Ezra returned. "He's going to wait in the parking lot across the street until I wave to him. Not enough room for him to wait on the street." *Dammit.* "When will you know to go in?"

"Lucy's going to call my cell when the coast is clear."

"You look like you're going to puke or pass out."

"That would certainly be endearing," I replied.

My phone rang. *Shit. Shit. Shit.* I answered. Lucy whispered, "She's back from lunch. Everything's set."

"On my way," I managed.

I stood up. Something released in my pants. *What the hell?*

"Good luck," Ezra said.

"My pants just broke."

"How can you break your pants?"

"Shit, I don't know. The waist got all huge. They're trying to fall off."

"Here." Ezra reached into the waistband of my trousers. "Need to pull this tighter." He yanked. "Better?"

"Not really. I got to go." *Shit. Why right now? Damn pants.*

"It's next door. Thirty feet. You can keep your pants on for thirty feet. Once you're in the limo, you can take them off."

"Ezra," I said, starting to mist up. "Thanks for everything. I couldn't have done it without you." While hugging him, I whispered, "This would be a little less gay if my pants weren't falling down."

"Breathe." He patted me on the back. "You'll be fine."

Hands in my pockets holding my pants up, I walked the twenty yards to the bank's main doors. Lucy wore a huge grin, but my girlfriend wasn't at her station.

I folded my hands on the chest-high countertop, my mouth dry. *Where is she? What's taking so long? What if she says no in front of all these people? Can't ever come back here. Why would she say yes? She won't. Too much of a gamble. I've fucked up every relationship I've ever had.*

One:
February 1982 (Eighth Grade)

Friday night, I sat with my friends Hunter and Jake on the bleachers in the gym of Mason Junior High School watching our shoeless classmates dance. Hunter, my doppelganger save his brown hair curled into a fluffy faux 'fro, elbowed me in the right side. "You should ask Justine to dance."

I should. I shrugged. "If she likes me so much, why hasn't she talked to me?"

"Girls don't do that. You've got to make the first move. Be a man," Hunter said. "Wendy already said she likes you."

"That's what you said. But I've never seen her look at me. Why would I ask her to dance?" *What if she says no? Is Kenna here?*

"She's right over there," he pointed, smiling.

"I'll wait for a slow song."

Leaning close to Jake on my other side, I whispered, "You haven't told anyone about me and Valerie, have you?"

Jake, an inch taller than me, two inches wider, with straight, sandy blond hair that fell to the middle of his ears, guffawed. "Of course not. It's your business if you want to mash on tramps like her."

Didn't know she was a tramp when she came over. "What do you think about Justine?" *Please don't think she's a slut too.*

"Wendy's friend? Seems nice, I guess. She next on your list?"

She's okay, then? "Hunter said she liked me," I said. "Thinking I'll ask her to dance."

"Open Arms" by Journey played and faded, my friends and I still rooted to the bleachers.

Isaac, my best friend, a tall, skinny drink of water with strawberry blond hair and pale as the moon from stem to stern, was dancing with a couple of gals. He insisted Hunter, Jake and I join him on the dance floor when Billy Idol's "Dancing With Myself" began. The group danced there until another slow song started.

Justine approached me on my way back toward the bleachers. *You're taller, aren't you? And skinnier? Still kind of cute, though. And you like me, right?*

"You want to dance?" she asked.

"Sure." Her hands on my shoulders, I clasped mine above her butt. *Pretty green eyes, lovely smile.* Neither of us spoke.

The song ended and Justine hugged me tightly. "Thank you." She kissed me on the cheek before disappearing into the masses.

She kissed me! That was cool. She really does like me.

Hunter nudged me. "Nice job."

"She asked me," I admitted.

"Then you're still a pansy."

A huge grin crossed Jake's face as we left the concession stand at the far side of the gym. A tap on my shoulder. Valerie, the first girl I'd ever kissed, a few weeks prior, stood there. "Hey, Jon. How you doing?"

"Good," I replied. "What about you?" *Where'd Jake go? Shit. Where's Justine? Don't let her see me with the tramp.*

"Not bad," Valerie said. "Did you know today's my birthday?"

"Really?" I replied. "Happy Birthday."

She smiled. "I think I deserve a birthday kiss."

I gave her a quick peck on the cheek.

"How about a real kiss?" Valerie pressed against me, opened her mouth, exploring my mouth with her tongue. "You should call me."

Everyone thinks you're a slut. "Yeah, I will. For sure." *Justine must have seen that. Please, oh please, don't let her have seen us.*

Justine found me as "Keep On Loving You" by REO Speedwagon began. "One more dance?"

She wouldn't ask if she'd seen Valerie, would she? "Absolutely," I replied.

My fingers ran through her hair as we made lazy circles on the dance floor. The music faded. Justine looked up, kissed me, a light touch on the lips.

Delightful.

"You should call me this weekend," Justine said.

"I will."

Justine grabbed her friend Grace by the hand, and the two of them, heads together, walked away.

"What was that with you and Valerie?" Jake asked me on the way to retrieve our shoes from the ancillary room off the gym.

"I have no idea. It was really weird."

"Looked like something," he said.

"I'm sure, but it was all her. She tried to swallow my face."

"Justine didn't see you, did she?"

"Don't think so," I said. "She kissed me after the last dance."

March 1982 (Eighth Grade)

Saturday night after my mother had gone to bed, Justine and I were on the phone for the sixth night in a row. An hour into our conversation I asked, "What color are your nipples?"

"What color do you think they are?"

You could show me. "Um, medium pink. You're too light skinned to have dark brown nipples."

"Wow, you're right, they're kind of a lighter pink. What about yours?"

"Brown," I said. "Average, I guess. What about Grace?" Grace was Justine's best friend. A seventh grader, she was both taller and skinnier than Justine, plus markedly more outgoing.

"Much darker than mine. Dark brown."

You've seen Grace's boobs? Awesome. "What color's your pubic hair?" I asked. *Grace's is black, isn't it?*

"Sort of a light brown. What about yours?"

Pulling down my jeans. "Kind of two tone. It's lighter on my balls than anywhere else."

"Really? That's weird."

"I know," I said. "When you spread your legs, does your vagina open up?" My pants now off, I started stroking myself.

"I don't know."

"You've never looked?" *How can you have something as cool as a vagina and never look at it?*

"No."

"Would you?"

"You really want me to?" Justine asked.

"Aren't you curious?"

"Not until now. Hold on, I'll look in my mirror." She set the receiver down. She returned a couple seconds later. "Yeah, it kind of does."

"That's pretty cool," I said. "Do you ever masturbate?"

"Eww, no. Why, do you?"

"Uh, yeah...I'm kind of touching myself right now."

"You are not!"

"Okay, I'm not," I said. "You've never touched yourself?"

"Not like that," she said. "Are you really touching yourself?"

"Yeah. I already had my pants off. Is that all right? I can stop if you want."

"No, it's fine," she said. "Would it be okay if Grace and I stopped by your house tomorrow afternoon?"

Will you let me touch your boobs again? Or your pussy?
"That'd be great," I said. "My mom's going shopping around one."

# # #

"After we drop your shit off," Hunter yelled to the girls, "let's go to the swings over at Grant." Isaac, Hunter and I followed Justine, Wendy and their friend Grace toward Wendy's house, two blocks away from school.

Wendy turned around. "I can't. I'm grounded."

Why are we going to your place then? "Is your mom home?" Wendy shook her head. "Then she'll never know. C'mon."

"She's called the past couple days to make sure I was home," Wendy said. "She said I can have Grace and Justine over for an hour to study, but that's it."

Hunter scoffed.

The girls went inside Wendy's house, leaving us boys on the front porch. I asked Isaac, "Why didn't you come to the meet yesterday?"

"My mom wanted me to do some shit around the house."

Hunter shook his head. "Why do you go to those meets, anyway?"

"A couple of the girls are really hot," I said.

"They're all flat," Hunter said.

"Yeah," I replied, unable to stop a grin.

"Gymnasts don't do a thing for me."

The front door opened. "I can do better cartwheels than the girls on our gymnastics team," Grace said.

"I can do better cartwheels than you," Hunter said.

"Ha!" Grace countered.

Justine returned, Wendy right behind her. She set her phone in the doorway, leaving the front door ajar. "Don't any of you answer it, okay?"

"What makes you think we'd do something like that?" Isaac asked.

"Don't!" Wendy insisted, her eyes boring into me.

"There's no way you can do a better cartwheel than me," Grace said to Hunter.

"I'll show you."

Justine and I watched the other four on the front lawn from the porch. "I meant to ask, what happened in home room yesterday morning?" *Never saw you to ask.*

"God, it was so embarrassing," she began.

As Grace tumbled on the front lawn, her shirt lifted, revealing a taut, pale belly. *Damn. Grace looks really good under her clothes.*

"I started having my period after I got to school and didn't have any pads with me. All anyone had was tampons and I've never used them before."

Don't tuck your shirt in. Dammit.

Justine continued, "Well, they were all too big. I couldn't get one in."

"It wouldn't fit?" After Hunter flailed his way through an abortive attempt at a cartwheel, Isaac tried one. With his lanky frame and shaggy blond hair, Isaac looked like a faulty Catherine Wheel.

"No. I didn't know what to do, so I had someone get our teacher."

Remaining focused on our friends in the front yard, I asked, "What happened?" *Why isn't Grace on the gymnastics team? Such a great butt.*

"Well, she tried to talk me through it, because there weren't any smaller tampons."

My focus returned to Justine. *Smaller? There's different sizes?*

"I finally got one in, but it hurt so bad, I started crying. Our teacher sent me home to get some pads and after all that I couldn't come back to school." *From a tampon?*

"How do you feel now?"

"Better. But I'm still sore down there."

"It's been a day. How long did you have it in?"

"Half an hour." *From a tampon?*

Wendy screamed from the lawn, "Don't touch it, Jon!" as the phone rang.

Throwing my hands in the air. "What?"

After a quick discussion with her mother, Wendy told all of us we had to leave.

"See you guys tomorrow," Grace said, before hugging Isaac. Then Hunter. Justine followed suit, quickly embracing Isaac.

Moving to me, Grace pressed herself firmly into me. *You feel great. You didn't do this to Isaac. Do you like me? You're holding me longer than them. You must like me, right?*

"Bye," Grace said, moving away.

Later that night, on the phone again with Justine, our conversation ran into silence. Justine, "Um, th-there's something I want to tell you."

"Okay, what?"

"Well, I don't want you to freak out, but I want you to know I love you." *Love me?*

"Uh huh."

"I know we haven't been going out very long, but I wanted you to know."

"I like you a lot," I said. *How can you love me already?* "And I love you as a friend. But, I can't say I'm in love with you."

"Oh, yeah, that's okay," she replied. "That's more of what I mean. Not in love, but love you as a friend. So when I say I love you, that's what I mean."

"You'll know what I mean if I say I love you, then?" I asked.

"Yeah, so we can say it and not mean actually in love."

Our call ended with mutual "I love you's."

April 1982 (Eighth Grade)

Justine, Grace and Isaac came over to my house Thursday afternoon of spring break. "If you two want some alone time," Grace said, shortly after arriving, "Isaac and I can entertain ourselves out here for a while."

I looked to Isaac. "You sure?"

"Don't be all day..." he replied.

On my bed, Justine lifted the covers over us. *Can I touch your pussy again?* Lying next to her, I undid her pants and pulled them off. *I can? Awesome. Since you love me, you'll fuck me, won't you?*

My San Francisco™ jeans and bikini briefs worked their way off. Justine continued kissing me. She raised her butt off the mattress as I tugged her panties down.

On top of her, I wriggled between her legs. *My dick just goes in, right?* I pressed my dick against her and felt resistance. I pushed again. No give.

Should I stop? "You okay?" I asked.

"Yeah, I'm fine," Justine replied.

A couple more fruitless efforts, then right hand reached down to help. *Ah, wet. There.* I pushed again. Justine writhed away. *Wait, that was it. Where are you going? Try something else.*

Onto my back, pulling Justine with me. *Wouldn't be like that if she didn't want to keep trying.* Positioning her with my hands, I placed her in my cock's path. A slip, a slide, a flop then... *Got to be it.* My dick stopped waggling about. Applying hip pressure, dick stopped moving.

Justine, "Stop."

"What's the matter?" I stopped pushing.

"Stop. It hurts worse than a tampon."

You're kidding, right? There was a tear in the corner of her eye. *Dammit.* I backed out.

"Sorry. You going to be all right?"

"Give me a minute," she said.

My clothes back on, I handed Justine her pants.

"That was quick," Isaac called upon hearing my bedroom door open.

"Did you think we'd leave you out here for hours?" I asked.

"You never know," Grace replied.

#   #   #

Two days later, I picked up the phone. *Worse than a tampon? Christ. Grace has been flirting with me all the time. If Grace didn't want me, why'd she kiss me yesterday? Bet she masturbates. And she's cuter than Justine. She'll probably fuck me. But she won't if I'm with Justine. But if we're not going out any more...*

Justine answered on the third ring. "Hi, Jon. What're you doing? Grace and I could come over, if you're going to be around. What's Isaac doing?"

"Uh, I don't know. Look, Justine, I've been thinking..." I began.

Long pause. "What about?"

"We should stop seeing each other," I said.

"Oh, God. Why?"

I can go out with Grace. "Well, since we're not in love with each other, it's probably better if we break up."

Her voice trembled. "But Jon, I could fall in love with you..."

"Uh...well...." *Is she crying? Oh lord, she is. What do I do?* "Uh, well, uh... I don't think I could fall in love with you, so the best thing to do would be to break up, yeah?"

A sniffle was her response.

Why doesn't she hang up? "Um, then, well, I should probably let you go."

Justine whispered, "Are you sure about this?"

Yes. No. "Yeah. I think it's for the best."

May 1982 (Eighth Grade)

Watching music videos on MTV, alone at my house after school, the last piece of a Totino's Canadian bacon pizza on my plate. My mother, Mary, returned from her job as a halfway house cook at 6:40pm. Her shoulder-length brunette hair slightly disheveled, she wore casual clothes and no trace of a smile. Mary asked as she walked through the living room, "Have you already had dinner?"

"Pizza," I said, nodding to my plate. "Work all right?"

"Nothing interesting. Need to make up next week's menu.

"I spoke to your aunt today. She's going to check in on you and take you grocery shopping while I'm in Spain." Mary was visiting relatives the first three weeks of June.

"I'm pretty sure I can handle shopping by myself," I said. "I'll only be getting pizza, soup, and mac and cheese."

"But how will you get the bags back here?"

"Hadn't thought of that."

From the kitchen, "Where's your little friend been lately?"

"Who? Justine? Uh, well," I said. I got up, plate in one hand, slice in the other, joining my mother in the kitchen. "We broke up a few weeks back. She hasn't talked to me since."

"You must've done the breaking up, then?" Mary asked, shutting the oven door, setting the timer.

"Yeah. She was all telling me she loved me and it was all way too much. I couldn't handle it." *And her best friend likes me.*

"Well, girls at her age do tend to do that," she said. "Did you two sleep together?"

That wasn't sleeping together. I hesitated before answering. "No."

She closed the refrigerator door and glared at me. "Okay. Well, there's something we need to discuss." She took a deep breath, passed me on the way to the dining room and sat down.

"You may not believe this now," Mary began. "But you always remember the person you lose your virginity to. Regardless of whether it's good or bad, you will remember that first person forever."

Forever? "You remember yours?" I asked, sitting across from her.

She scoffed. "For all the things I've forgotten over the years, I remember my first time quite clearly.

"I know it's not as big a deal for boys, but it's a huge thing for girls."

It's a pretty big deal.

"Before you get intimate with someone," Mary continued. "You should take some time and seriously think about whether or not you want to be the person they're going to remember the rest of their life."

"Okay," I said. "Do you remember your second at all?"

She paused. "Some. Not anything like the first, though. That first guy ended up not talking to me. He was an asshole so I'll remember him, forever, as an asshole. Simply because he was my first.

"The second, I think he was an all right guy, but he was second. You can only have one first time."

And only one second. "Sooo, I shouldn't be anyone's first?"

"Is that what you're getting?" She shook her head. "Listen, Jon. Please keep in mind, everything you do before and after will be permanently etched onto that girl's memory. It's a big responsibility."

"But it's okay if I'm second?" I asked.

"I suppose," she sighed. "Not really the point I'm trying to make here."

June 1982 (Eighth Grade)

Before making our way outside after school, a girl, who had attended school with me since first grade but I'd never really spoken to, caught up to Isaac and me and pulled me aside.

Isaac rejoined me three minutes later when she disappeared through the main doors. "What was that about?"

"Wanted me to know Justine's been talking a bunch of shit," I replied. "Said Justine was saying I'd used her and dumped

14

her and I should talk to Justine and clear things up before things got out of hand."

Isaac and I stepped out into the warm spring sunshine. "Don't you actually have to fuck someone in order to use them?"

Isaac began to answer, "Uh..."

"I mean I tried, but we didn't have sex."

Isaac laughed. "Maybe she thought it was sex?"

"Fuck you. And now she's saying I used her? Used her for what? Blue balls?"

Continuing toward Chalet Bowl for a couple games of Ms. Pac-Man, Isaac slowed his pace. "Is there anyone you think is hot but wouldn't want people finding out about?"

"Um..." I hesitated. *Big time.* "Like who?"

Isaac looked back over his shoulder. "Well, I've got a thing for Jen Smith," he confessed.

I stopped. "How would that work? She barely comes up to your belly button. She's pretty cool, though."

"True, but she'd never go out with me. She's always hanging out with the popular kids." He gazed off into the distance. "I love imagining a little midget-type girl like her on top of me."

We burst out laughing. "Her big ol' titties a jigglin' all over the place and her tiny hands around my dick. It'd look huge."

I fell over on a patch of lifeless grass next to the Methodist Church parking lot, unable to catch my breath. A minute later, wiping the tears from my eyes and debris from my pants, I stood back up. Isaac continued, "Seriously though, I kind of have a thing for Nicole."

She's so plain. And never talks.

"When she stands up in French to recite, I get hard."

"Seriously?" I asked.

"Practically. I imagine her whispering naughty things in French in my ear. But you know how she is."

Quiet, boring. "She talks in class?"

"When she has to," Isaac said.

After getting quarters for Ms. Pac-Man at Chalet Bowl, I said, "All right. But you've got to promise to keep this secret."

"Of course. You already know about Nicole."

"Yeah, but mine's worse. Not a word. Not even Hunter."

Isaac shrugged. "How much worse could it be?"

"Kenna Anderson," I mumbled.

"Anderdisease?" Isaac stopped, his eyebrows raised. "Wow. Okay, it is worse."

"Ever since our first day, last year. When she walked into Algebra, I couldn't stop watching her. Hell, I go out of my way to walk past her locker to see if she's there."

Isaac stared at me. "But Christ, she's annoying. So stuck up."

"I know," I agreed. "That's why you can't say anything. Hunter would give me shit forever.

"But think about how flexible she must be, being a gymnast like that. Prop her up against the wall, hold one leg over her head and go to town." We started laughing again. "And all that red hair. Could roll around in that for hours." *Beautiful.*

"You couldn't really roll around in her tits," Isaac chuckled.

"More than a mouthful's a waste."

"Couldn't fuck her outside," Isaac continued. "Skin that white, she'd spontaneously combust."

Two:
March 1983 (Freshman Year)

A sunny Saturday, walking home from the 7-11 on 6th Avenue when I saw shoulder length, curly red locks atop a slender frame ahead of me. "Hey, Kenna!"

She turned. "Oh, hey Jon."

You know my name? "Where you heading?" I asked.

"Toward UPS."

Totally out of my way. "Me, too."

Our conversation covered mutual teachers at Mason before I asked, "What kind of music do you like?"

"King Crimson, Lene Lovich, Adam and the Ants, Siouxsie and the Banshees."

"Hmm, I'm a big fan of Adam and the Ants."

"But isn't Adam's latest solo album awful?"

No, not at all. "Uh…"

"I mean, the strings? And the lyrics? 'Give me some chili sauce.' Garbage."

You care about the lyrics? Don't you have to like everything a band's done if you like one thing?

"This is me," Kenna said. I walked her to her door.

Please invite me in. Want to see your house. Get to know you. Kiss you.

"See you Monday," Kenna said, closing the door behind her.

Dammit.

# # #

A mutual friend gave me Kenna's phone number over the weekend, but her father railroaded me on Monday night, something about Kenna being busy doing homework. He did, however, assure me he would give her the message I'd called.

Tuesday evening: "Hey, what's new?" Kenna asked.

You called me? "Not a whole lot. Working on some history stuff," I replied. "What about you? You finish everything?"

"More or less. I want to go over the English paper, clean it up."

"When's it due?" I asked.

"Monday," Kenna said.

No wonder you get better grades than me. "What're you taking next quarter?"

"Washington State History, English, Art, Trig, and more French."

"What period you taking Art?"

"Fifth. You have Art next quarter?"

We're going to be in the same class again? Sweet. "An independent study fifth period," I said. "You still doing gymnastics?"

"No. I don't have the time I used to put into it, with school and all."

"How much were you practicing?"

"Five days a week, an hour and a half to two hours a day, depending when meets were scheduled. I was perpetually sore, especially my back. It's been a treat walking without pain the last few months."

"I give good backrubs, if you ever need one," I said.

"Really, now? And you'll have Crisco and a tarp?"

What are you talking about? That's about sex, isn't it? "Absolutely. Any time," I replied. *Crisco?*

"How about tomorrow after school?"

You'd come over here? "Sure, my mom won't be home until about six." *Tarp and Crisco? She wants to get naked and slide around on it, right? Naked? Love to see her naked.*

# # #

Three thirty, Kenna knocked on the front door. *You weren't joking. You're here. There's no tarp. Or Crisco.*

"Let's see your room," Kenna said.

Kenna bounced onto my bed. I sat next to her. A dry, closed-mouth kiss followed. *She let me kiss her. She does want to fuck!* I kissed her again. She kissed me back. My left hand went from her belly to her boob.

Firmly, she shoved my hand away, sprang to her feet. "What else do you have in your music collection...?"

Crisco's okay, but I can't touch you?

She flipped through my LP's. "'Slow Children'? 'Altered Images'?" Kenna asked.

"You didn't listen to KYYX?"

"No, not really."

How do you know Adam and the Ants? "What stations do you listen to?"

"Classical, if I'm listening to the radio at all," she answered.

"You want that backrub?" *That's what you wanted, right?*

"I guess."

"Go ahead and lay on the bed," I said.

"Too soft. How about the floor?"

"Wherever."

She stretched out face down on the floor and I sat on her butt. After a quick once-over on top of her shirt, my hands weaseled underneath. Kenna didn't react. *Thin and firm, smooth and soft. Perfect.*

I worked her neck, shoulders, to her shoulder blades. *Reach around for her boobs like with Justine. Unfasten her bra? Let her do it. Or ask me to.*

Both hands crept toward Kenna's sides. As soon as my thumbs left her shoulder blades, Kenna jumped. "Stop that! I'm ticklish."

Back to either side of her spine, I rubbed lower until I hit the top of her jeans, far above her lower back. I scooted off her, to her side, continuing the massage with solely my right hand, inching downward.

Panties!

Kenna twisted, squirming away. *Why not?* Hand went back to her lower back, remaining below the waist of her jeans. After a calm couple of minutes, hand again ventured toward Kenna's butt.

Panties!

Kenna struggled, forcefully bucked her hips. "No, no, no," she said. Right hand retreated to her lower back.

What the hell?

Sitting on her bottom, I massaged my way back to her shoulders. "How's that?" I asked. *Can we kiss more?*

Kenna said, "I'm going to go."

"Uh, okay." *What the hell is going on? You're the one who brought up tarp and Crisco. Now you won't let me touch you? You kissed me.*

At the front door. "I'll talk to you later?" I asked.
"Oh, yeah." A smile on her face.

# # #

A week later, the first day of spring quarter, Kenna was sitting at the table in the middle of the Art room by the time I arrived. She was finishing a perspective painting, tiny, delicate strokes of the brush across the piece. The long, slender fingers of her left hand fanned apart, holding the paper to the table. *What gorgeous hands.*

"Hey, Jon," she said.

"Hi, Kenna." *Why haven't you called me? Pissed I tried to touch your butt?*

Looking toward the classroom door, Kenna said, "The mural turned out well. What are you working on now?"

"Thanks. Nothing big, yet. Going to see if our teacher will let me paint a mural outside the door with the other stuff out there."

Hunter passed behind me, moving toward the table where we'd been sitting all year.

"You got something in mi--" she began.

Our teacher interrupted. "Take your seats, everyone. Jon, you too."

I nodded to Kenna, taking the seat next to Hunter. His hand over his mouth. "What are you and Anderdisease discussing?"

"She asked about the mural."

Kenna caught up with me as we walked out of class. "You haven't called me."

You're mad at me, aren't you? "You haven't called me either," I replied.

"Fine. Will you be home tonight?"

"All night."

"Then call me," she said.

"I will."

Seven o'clock, on the phone with Kenna. "How was spring break?" I asked. "Do anything exciting?"

"It was all right. Went to the Seattle Art Museum for the day, but not much else. You?"

"Hung out with Isaac and Jake. Helped Hunter with his paper route. That's about it." *Why are you acting normal now?* "How does the new quarter look?"

"About the same. Washington History doesn't seem too tough. Speaking of, I should get going. I've got a couple things to finish up before I go to bed."

"Uh, okay." *For four hours? Why'd you want me to call?*

"I'll see you in Art then," she said.

"Okay, bye." *What the hell?*

# # #

Friday, Kenna called me at 8:32. "Hey, haven't talked to you in a while," she started.

"The Art teacher keeps me on a short leash," I said. "I think I had more free time when I wasn't independent study."

"You could've called me," Kenna said.

You want me to call you? "You're always seem busy with homework," I said. "Didn't want to bug you."

"I'll tell you if I'm too busy to talk," she replied. "Are you mad at me or something?"

Something. "No, Kenna, I'm not mad. It's just..." I paused. *What happened over break? Don't know where I stand with you from minute to minute. Feel like a complete idiot around you. If you didn't want me to touch you, why'd you talk about tarp and Crisco? Never would've tried anything if you didn't want to.*

"It's just..." I hesitated again. *I really, really want to kiss you again but you don't want that, do you?* "No, I'm not mad at you. I'm having a hard time being around you."

"A hard time? Why?"

Because you drive me crazy. Because you obviously don't know you're doing it. Because my friends hate you. "Because of the way you are," I said. "I can't explain it better than that. You're just being you, but I'm having a hard time with it."

"O-kaay," she said. "That's pretty vague. Could you help me out here?"

"If I could explain it better, I would."

"So we're done talking?" she asked.

"For a while anyway."

She sniggered. "It doesn't make any sense to me, but if that's the way you feel..."

"I'm sorry, but for now it is," I said.

"I guess I'll talk to you sometime, then." She hung up. *Dammit.*

May 1983 (Freshman Year)

Friday, in Art class, I was searching for Cadmium Yellow acrylic paint in the cabinets at the far side of the Art room. A commotion behind me. "Oh my God!" I turned to see half the class surrounding Kenna's table.

The teacher had left the room and the hullaballoo continued. "You're lesbians!" someone cried out.

"Dykes!"

"What's going on?" I asked one of my friends next to the table.

"One of the guys dared Kenna and that other girl to kiss each other. He kept saying, 'Kiss her. It's no big deal. Just kiss her.' So they did and got all into it, using their tongues and everything."

What the hell? Kenna kissed a girl? I missed it?

Kenna's face was red as our teacher walked back in the room. "Enough, everyone! Back to your seats. You've got plenty to do." The crowd dispersed.

I returned to my seat, nodding toward Kenna's table. "Hunter, you see any of that?"

"I caught the end," he said. "Anderdisease is a dyke now, huh?"

"I don't think so." *Tell him she kissed me. No. What if she is a dyke? I'll look like an idiot.*

"You didn't see them?" Hunter asked.

"Not at all," I said. "By the time I looked over, it was done."

"There were going at it until they realized where they were. Then they got all embarrassed and stopped."

"Hmph." *She likes girls now? Because I tried to touch her butt? Call her tonight. Ask her what's going on. Why would she tell me?*

# # #

Mary plopped down a basket of laundry next to the overstuffed chair in the living room where I was sitting. "It's time for you to start doing your own laundry and putting your own clothes away."

I turned my attention from the television. "Um, okay."

"I found the magazine in your sock drawer," she continued. *Oh shit.*

"Well, I, um," I stuttered. *Should've put it under my mattress.*

"I'm not mad, Jon. I understand you're at the age where these things happen." *You're going to make me throw it away.*

"Okay..."

"I want you to understand that what's in those magazines isn't the way sex really is."

Yeah it is. Penis in vagina. Sex. How is it different? "How do you mean?"

"It's not real. Women don't really behave like that. It's pretend. You know that, don't you?"

They don't like fucking? "Yeah."

"I don't want you to expect the girls that you're dating to act like the women in those magazines." A lengthy pause. "Have you already had sex?"

"No," I replied. *Justine keeps telling everyone we did.*

"I know this doesn't mean much to you now," she said. "But if you can, you should wait until you're older."

"Like sixteen?"

"At least," she said.

Another two years? Can't wait that long. No one else is.

"Um, why?"

"A few reasons actually," Mary said. "There's nothing to look forward to once you've had sex. It's the last big mystery. What if you get the girl pregnant? You wouldn't be able to take care of a baby at your age. You don't want kids, do you?"

"No. No, of course not. I plan on being careful."

"I hope so. I'm not interested in becoming a grandmother any time soon."

June 1983 (Freshman Year)

The last day of classes after I'd gotten home from a visit to Chalet Bowl with Hunter, Isaac and Jake, I flipped through my yearbook again. On the inside cover I discovered an upside-down paragraph from Kenna Anderson. *How'd she get my yearbook?*

> 'Remember the last time we talked on the phone? You told me that you couldn't say why, you just didn't want to be around me. Just because of the way I am. That hurt a lot. really a <u>lot</u>. But one day I understood what

you meant and saw the stupid way I was acting. I'm learning to be myself now. Don't ask me why I wasn't myself before because I don't know. But I was being stupid. Call me over the summer

Love
Kenna

P.S. If you ever run out of girlfriends invite me over, I'll bring the salad oil and the plastic tarp. You can find my G-spot.'

Next to her signature, a bright red lipstick-kiss.
What the hell does that mean? She still wants to fuck me?
I reread her note. *If she's changed so much, why didn't she talk to me? Why'd she sneak around writing this in my yearbook instead of talking to me?*
Run out of girlfriends? No one I've kissed the past couple months even go to our school.
She wouldn't let me touch her when she was here. Why would she ask me to find her G-spot? Couldn't her girlfriend do it?
She didn't start wearing lipstick until she kissed what's her face. Looked so much better without it.

Three:
May 1986 (Senior Year)

After school, in the parking lot, Isaac was talking to Virginia, a chunky sophomore with short blonde hair, a red bandana around her neck. *Why is he talking to her?* A skinny girl, two inches taller than Virginia, sporting bobbed, bleached blonde hair and overstated red lipstick appeared from behind Isaac. *Who's that?* I bumped Isaac's shoulder. "What'cha guys doing?"

Virginia answered, "Kayley's here checking out Lincoln," she nodded toward the blonde. "She's thinking about coming here next year."

"Where do you go now?" I asked.

"Bethel, but it sucks," Kayley replied. "Virginia's mom said I could stay with them if I end up coming here. I sat in on a couple of Virginia's classes. They were all right."

"What're you doing now?" I asked Isaac.

"Going back to my place," Virginia spoke up. "My mom's not home. You guys want to come over?"

Kayley's hot. Little boobs. Nice n' skinny. "Okay."

Isaac showed me around the house while the girls went upstairs. "Check out the view from the kitchen."

When did you start coming over here?

Over the sink, the windows looked out over the Tacoma Waterfront, to Brown's Point and the lighthouse. "You can see all of Vashon Island from upstairs."

"Damn," I replied.

Smiling, Virginia walked into the study. "Did Isaac show you the sewing room already?"

"Oh yeah," I said. "Great view."

"Thanks. My mom bought this house from my grandfather who helped build it when he was in high school."

"Wow. Where's Kayley?"

Virginia's expression fell. "On the phone with her mom. You want something to drink?"

"Sure, what'cha got?"

"Milk, water. Maybe some lemonade." Isaac and I followed her to the kitchen. "The glasses are in that cupboard, help yourself." Virginia returned upstairs.

"I've had better times," I said as I sat down in the living room with a glass of water.

"You want to split?"

"If they're both going to hang out upstairs..."

We waited for two minutes, then five. Kayley's muffled voice got louder. Virginia returned. "My mom's going to be home soon. You guys should leave."

"All right." Isaac and I went to the front door. "See you tomorrow then."

"Yeah. Thanks for the ride home," she replied, as she closed the door.

In my mother's white hatchback Tercel, I asked Isaac, "Is Kayley seeing someone?"

"Couldn't tell you," he said. "Looked like Virginia might be into you."

"Oh no no no. Not my type in the least."

"I thought they only had to be breathing," Isaac joked.

"Ha ha. She's far too much woman for me," I said.

"Not nice. But true. Kayley seems like a bitch."

"Yeah, but she's seriously hot."

"She's okay. Kind of thin though."

"Yeah," I said, followed by an evil chortle. "Snap her in half while I'm fucking her."

#   #   #

"Wondering when you were going to call," Kayley answered, after being handed the phone from her mother.

"Huh?"

"Virginia told me Isaac was probably going to give you my number and I should expect a call from you."

"Uh, is that okay?" I asked.

She laughed. "Yeah, but you know, Virginia doesn't have many nice things to say about you? Warned me to stay away from you. Says you use girls."

Bitch. I ought to sock her in her fat face. "Guess you should ask the girls," I replied in monotone.

"But I'm asking you."

"Well," I paused. "Has she mentioned anyone specifically or is this what she's picked up from the rumor mill?"

"Not saying. I'd like to hear your side of it."

She can't know about Parker or Miranda. Maybe a couple girls from Lincoln. How many have there been? Fourteen the last time I counted. That was before Miranda last summer. Five or six since then. But that's only the ones I've slept with... "I've dated a couple gals this year. Neither for a very long time, a couple weeks probably. When we realized we didn't want to keep going, we stopped. How's that?"

"Yeah, okay. What about last year?"

Fuck me. Fifteen or something. Don't tell the truth. "Last year? A few girls, but nothing serious."

"What's a few?" Kayley asked.

"Four or five." *That went to Lincoln, who Virginia might know about.* "I don't keep track." *Can she tell I'm lying?* "I think the longest lasted about a month, but I certainly wasn't using anybody."

"Five girls in a year..."

"A girl every couple months. I'm guessing Virginia heard something from my ex, Justine. She's been saying I used her for sex since we went out in eighth grade."

"Did you?"

"We never had sex. So no, not really."

"Oh," her tone softened. "Why did she say that, then?"

"You should ask her. I don't have any fucking idea. But I'm sure that's where Virginia got her information about me."

The conversation swung to more pleasant topics. Kayley told me she was probably going to be moving into Virginia's at the start of summer because she wasn't getting along with her mom, and their counselor had suggested taking some time off from each other over the break. I ended the conversation asking if Isaac, Hunter and I could stop by on Saturday.

# # #

Hunter drove Isaac and me out to Kayley's Saturday. They dropped me in front of a filthy, weathered beige house, easily mistaken for a double wide trailer, while he and Isaac continued on to a mutual friend's house.

"Let's go to my room," Kayley suggested. "My mom's getting ready to go over to a friend's. We should stay out of her way."

Nine pictures of Kayley with assorted people lined the edges of her vanity, a lone poster of Public Enemy over the bed, the other three beige walls empty. A limp, brown teddy bear sat propped against the wall on her single bed next to a solitary pillow. "I meant to ask you," I began after she'd closed the door to her room. "Do you have a boyfriend?"

"Depends on what you mean."

What do you think I mean? What could I mean? "What are my options?"

"I'm not seeing anyone seriously, if that's what you're asking."

"No, that wasn't what I was asking."

"I didn't think so." She waited a moment. "I'm going to the movies with a guy from school tonight, and I don't know where things are with us."

"Hmm."

"You should ask me tomorrow."

Fat chance.

She stepped to me. "Unless you'd rather kiss me now."

Yeah. My fingers cupped her face, into her hair.

A latch clicked, Kayley jumped back. Her mother called from the hallway, "I'm taking off. See you later."

Kayley stuck her head into the hallway. "Bye, Mom."

"My buddy Hunter is having people over next weekend, you think you can make it?" I asked her.

"I'll see if I can spend the night at Virginia's. There's no way my mom would let me go, but Virginia's mom doesn't care."

"Virginia can come." *If she has to.*

"I'll see if she wants to. What about Willow?"

Who?

"Any chance you could get us some wine coolers?" Kayley asked. "I don't like beer."

"See what I can do."

A knock interrupted us. Kayley broke our embrace. Isaac stood at the front door.

"He wasn't home," Isaac said. "Hunter wants to head back."

Dammit.

"Did you fuck her?" Hunter asked after the car door shut.

"Didn't give me enough time," I replied.

"You had ten minutes."

"Maybe that's enough for you."

#   #   #

Virginia darted to Isaac and pulled him aside as soon as our group arrived at Hunter's house. Hunter, Jake and a few other people milled about. I grabbed coolers for Kayley and Willow, a beer for myself.

"Who's that?" Hunter asked me, pointing to Willow. *Ugh, that hair.* Willow's brunette hair spiked up on top though not uniformly, as if she'd recently woken up, cropped closely on the sides. The three shirts she had on revealed little of her form. Neither did her baggy brown slacks.

"Willow? Met her on the way over here."

Hunter left to chat her up.

I tugged Kayley's hand. "What's up?" she asked.

"There's something you should see." I led her through the kitchen, to the backyard.

"What's out here?"

"Not them." I kissed her. A moment later, Virginia's face filled the kitchen window.

"Shit," I whispered.

"What?"

"Virginia's glaring at us."

"Oh, Christ. I'll be right back." Kayley hurried back inside.

Isaac joined me on the porch a couple minutes later. "You think Kayley's coming back out here?" I asked him.

"Nope. She's talking to Virginia out on the front stoop. Virginia looked seriously pissed."

"What the fuck does she care if Kayley and I do anything?"

"What? Besides the fact that she hates you and Kayley's her best friend?"

"Hates me now, huh?" *Hate her too.*

"Strongly disapproves of you?"

"Hate works," I said. "Is that what she was talking to you about?"

"Yeah. Can't believe Kayley likes you even though she's warned her about you."

"Maybe she should live her own life."

"Good luck." We returned to the party, grabbing another beer on our way through the kitchen.

Hunter and I discussed rerecording one of the songs we'd put together the year before. "Should make it the extended dance mix," he joked.

"I could write a couple more verses," I offered.

Isaac interrupted us. "Virginia wants to go home, so I'm going to take her."

"You coming back?" Hunter asked.

"Nah. Thanks for having me over. We're painting our fence tomorrow starting at eight, so I should get to bed. Jon, you good with Willow and Kayley? Virginia wants to make sure."

"She did? Really? But she's going to leave them here?" Pause. "Yeah, I got them."

In the car an hour later. "Where do you live, Willow?" I asked.

"A little way past Virginia's, down Stevens, by the cliff."

"That funky intersection?" I asked.

"Couple blocks from there."

Pulling away from Willow's, Kayley turned to me. "I can't show up at Virginia's like this, I'm too drunk. I don't have to be there for another hour. Can we go to your place so I can sober up?" *And we can get naked?*

"I guess."

She stumbled getting out of my mom's white hatchback Toyota Tercel. I steered her to the door of our new apartment on North Pearl Avenue. Once inside Kayley said, "I think I should lay down."

"C'mon." She slumped onto my bed. *We going to fuck now?* I squeezed between the wall and Kayley. I ran my hand across hers. No response. A snort. *Guess not.*

The clock read 11:38. *Half an hour, then home.* A deep, masculine belch. Kayley rolled toward the edge of the bed. Another belch. *Oh no. No no no. Don't hurl in my room.*

Kayley bolted up, clutched the windowsill and retched.

Goddammit! All my clean clothes are on the floor. "C'mon, Kayley. Let's get to the bathroom," sliding my arm around her.

She vomited again.

Mary stood in the hall wearing a nightgown, curlers, and a look of concern.

Once Kayley was facially connected to the commode, Mary asked, "Has she been drinking?"

"Yes."

Mary scowled with the disapproving parental face.

"She threw up on my clothes," I said.

Mary and I examined my room while Kayley wrecked our bathroom. *Not as bad as it sounded.* "It's your mess to clean up," Mary stated. "Unless you think she's going to do it."

Not a chance.

I mopped up the puke on the wall with a couple barf-drenched shirts. My mother tossed me a wet towel. "There's some on the floor right there."

While Kayley rinsed out her mouth, Mary hissed at me, "You need to take her home. Right now."

Leading Kayley by the hand toward the front door, I said, "C'mon, let's get you back to Virginia's."

"Back to Virginia's?" Kayley slurred.

"Yeah. We got to go."

I guided Kayley up the stairs to Virginia's front door, she stared into my eyes.

No way I'm kissing you.

#   #   #

"What did her parents say when you brought her home like that?" Mary asked me immediately upon my exit from the bathroom in the morning.

"She's spending the night with her friend," I said. "I got her to the front porch and watched her go inside. That's all I know."

"Okay. What do you think her parents would say? Do you really think they'd be happy with you bringing their daughter home fall-down drunk?"

Is this a trick question? "Um, no. I didn't force her to drink anything."

"It doesn't matter. She was with you."

I'm not responsible for her. "But..."

Mary glared at me. "It's not like you're her best friend, bringing her home after she'd had too much. You're a boy, bringing a girl home drunk. What would you expect them to think?" A long pause. "Well?"

"Uh, that maybe I'd tried something with her?"

"Probably."

"I didn't."

"It doesn't matter. It's what it looks like. Why would her parents believe you? You've only been dating a couple weeks."

"Three."

Mary rolled her eyes.

June 1986 (Senior Year)

After plans for taking a friend to prom fell through, I asked Kayley If she would be my date. "Isaac also got connecting rooms at the Best Western, if you can stay," I added.

"You going to stay?" she asked.

"Planning on it. But if you can't, I can bring you back home after."

"I'll ask my mom but I know we're meeting some of my family the next day so she might want me home early. Jon, uh, are you thinking we're going to have sex after prom?"

That's the plan. "Uh, well, I'd thought about it, but, well, with Hunter, Isaac, Hunter and their dates there, it'll be kind of tough to get any time alone."

"Just so long as you don't expect it."

Shit. "Not expect, no."

"Because I want to wait a while with you," Kayley continued. "I want to be on the pill before we sleep together."

"Oh. You going to do that soon?" *Like tomorrow?*

"As soon as I can. I need someone to go with me because I don't want to go to the doctor alone."

"Won't your mom take you?"

Kayley guffawed. "I'm not going to tell her I'm on the pill. Virginia said a friend of hers did it without her parents finding out."

"You think Virginia will go with you?"

"Probably."

You overestimate her.

#   #   #

Kayley, Hunter, his date and I left my prom after a mere forty-five minutes of atrocious Top 40 music. Hunter and I hauled up the cooler of beer and wine coolers to our hotel room.

Isaac appeared with his date about an hour later with a case of warm beer. "How was the rest of the dance?" I asked.

"Not bad."

"The music get any better?"

"No, not really."

During the next half hour, ten more people found their way to our two adjoining rooms. I pulled Isaac aside. "Did you invite those two Lincoln girls?"

"Yeah. I was talking to them at prom and told them where we were and that you and Hunter were already here."

"Do you talk to either of them?" I asked.

"Not much," he replied. "But they were looking for someplace to go..."

"I think one of their boys wants to get on Kayley," I said. Isaac looked shocked. "No way."

I nodded. "He's been following her from room to room, trying to talk to her since they walked in."

"Serious dick move. They both came with someone else."

"Yeah, but I can't say I blame him," I admitted. "I mean, considering who he came with."

Kayley was in the other room with most of the rest of the people. "But still..."

"Where's everyone sleeping, anyway?" I asked.

Hunter sighed. "Me and Isaac will take the other room."

We get a room to ourselves? Awesome. "What about your date?" I asked.

"I'm taking her and Isaac's chick home in about an hour."

"Wait. I'm the only one whose date is staying all night?" I asked. "What the fuck is wrong with you two?"

"Go to hell," Isaac said.

"Yeah, fuck you," Hunter added.

People from the other room filtered in. Missing were Kayley and the boy pursuing her. The door connecting the rooms had been pulled most of the way closed. *Sure is convenient for Party-Boy.*

Through the crack in the door, I looked for Kayley before entering the other room. She was sitting on the bed closest to the window, Party-Boy standing in front of her. Kayley wasn't looking at him but Party-Boy appeared singularly focused on her.

"What'cha doing Kayley?"

"Talking about school shit. There any more coolers?"

Jesus, I hope not. "We had eight," I replied. "I'll see if there are any more in the other fridge."

I brought Kayley the last wine cooler. "They're watching some kick-ass documentary in the other room. Want to come?"

"Sure," Kayley replied, took my hand and walked with me to the other room. Party-Boy followed.

Hunter returned from dropping off his and Isaac's dates. "Did you pick up any more coolers?" Kayley asked, as soon as the door closed behind him.

"Sorry, Kayley," Hunter replied. "The vending machine was all out."

From the other room, Isaac shrieked, "Aww, fucking A!"

"What's the problem?" I yelled back.

"Someone horked all over the bathroom. Fuck this," he scrambled back to our side. "I'm not sleeping over there, it fucking reeks!"

"Turn the fan on, you pussy," I said. *Was that you, Kayley?*

"I did, but I'm not cleaning up someone else's puke."

"At least close the door," Hunter said.

Six of us remained, including Party-Boy and his date. Isaac and Hunter declared they were sharing one of the beds in the non-stinky room.

We should have the other one.

"I'm going to pull some cushions off the couch and sleep down here," Kayley said.

Hunter grinned. I discreetly flipped him off.

Kayley spread out the cushions between the window and Hunter's bed. Holding my breath, I retrieved pillows and blankets from the other room. Party-Boy, his date passed out on Isaac's bed, was now sitting next to Kayley upon my return, watching TV.

What is your problem? My date, not yours.

Snuggling up to Kayley on the other side, I pulled the blankets over the two of us. Party Boy scooted away.

A couple minutes later, Kayley was breathing deeply. My left hand ran up her leg, past her skirt.

Shit, the nylons are pantyhose.

#   #   #

The sound of the shower woke me. Party-Boy and his date were gone, Kayley still asleep next to me. Isaac bellowed, "Morning, Sunshine."

"Fuck off," I growled. "Hunter taking a shower?"

"Yeah."

"I'm starving. Want to get cheap pizza at Pizza n' Pipes?"

"Shit, yeah," Isaac said. "I still got money from last night."

"Me too." I beat on the bathroom door. "Hurry up, fucker. I got to pee."

"Use the other bathroom," Hunter retorted.

"I am not stepping foot over there again."

"Fuck, Jon," Kayley called. Her head popped up from the far side of the bed. "Be any louder?"

"Sorry. You want to go to Pizza and Pipes with us?"

"Pizza? For breakfast?"

"It's eleven-thirty, Kayley," Isaac said. "We got to be out of here by noon. Hurry up, Hunter!"

"Let me call my mom," Kayley said.

The bathroom door opened. Isaac pushed past me and shut the door.

"Asshole!" I yelled. "I'll just piss in the fridge."

"Don't touch the fridge!" Isaac yelled. "I'll be out in a minute."

"Technically I wouldn't be touching it."

"My mom's going to come get me at one-thirty," Kayley said. "We don't have to be to my cousin's until four."

We covered both beds in empty bottles and cans, then drove three cars across town to Pizza and Pipes, home of the $3.99 large pizza special. Kayley and I made it to the restaurant first, as I'd sped through a yellow light.

Kayley seized my arm in the parking lot. "Did we have sex last night?"

You don't know? "You don't remember?"

"No. I can usually tell when I've had sex, but I'm not sure."

"Well, if it wasn't memorable..." I started toward the front door.

"Tell me," Kayley insisted.

"You honestly can't tell?"

"So we did?"

"I didn't say that. But if you can tell..."

Isaac and Hunter pulled into the parking lot. "Tell me."

"I'm kind of hurt you don't remember." *And kind of frightened.*

Isaac got out of his car, our conversation ended. The four of us went in together, ordered a couple pizzas, and sat at one of the picnic tables covered with a plastic red and white checkered tablecloth.

Kayley sat across the table from me, talking with Hunter and Isaac, while occasionally throwing a nasty look my way.

Finished eating, Kayley and I waited for her mom outside. "Fine, Jon, don't tell me," she spat.

"Did you have your panties on when you woke up?"

"Yeah," she said. "But I could've put them back on."

"Then why do you think we might've screwed?"

"Because I'm not sure and I know you want to."

But you don't want to. "No, Kayley, we didn't. Nothing happened, okay?"

"Really?"

"Yes, really. You fell asleep watching TV."

"You're not lying?"

Fuck you. "No."

She gave me a quick hug before climbing into her mom's car.

Mary interrupted my macaroni and cheese late lunch with, "I'm really happy you guys got a room last night."

You wanted me to have sex? "Why?"

"Well, I didn't want to worry about you kids driving around drunk."

"We didn't drink that much, Mom."

"Oh, I know what happens after prom, Jon," Mary said. "You guys were going to get drunk regardless, so it's better you stayed in one place. How'd everything go?"

"A few of us left early because the music was awful. A bunch of people showed up later. It was all right."

Mary cocked her head to the side. "And did Kayley have a good time?"

"She seemed to." *Drank enough not to remember if we fucked.*

"What about you?"

"Could've had a better time without renting a tux and getting flowers and shit. Some guy who came with another gal was hitting on Kayley at the hotel, then she passed out."

"How are you and Kayley doing, anyway? You getting serious?"

She won't have sex with me, so not too serious.

"You're going to Western in the fall, so you probably shouldn't let things get too involved. Do you think you will stay together once you've gone to college?"

No way. "Probably not."

"Well, you'd be surprised what teenage girls think, Jon," Mary said. "I take it you haven't talked about what you'll do if you're still together when you leave."

"I'd be surprised if we're still together then," I said. "She doesn't seem the kind to take things too seriously." *I'm not.*

"Really, Jon. Before you two let things get too much further, you need to figure out what both of your expectations are."

"I don't even know if we'll be seeing each other this summer. I'm not going to drive out to Spanaway to see her, so I'm not worried about it."

# # #

"How was the doctor's?" on the phone with Kayley, Tuesday the following week. *When can we start fucking?*

"Fine," Kayley replied. "Both Willow and I got prescriptions."

"Was it as scary as you thought?"

"Not at all. The nurse was super nice. We have to go back there to get our refills so our parents don't find out."

"How much are the pills?" *When can we fuck?*

"Free. But only if we go and get them."

"That's worth it then, huh?"

"Yeah," she said. "We can't have sex until after my next period."

What the hell? "When's that?"

"I just finished, so three weeks."

Dammit.

"Before we start having sex there's something I need to know."

"What?"

"Do you see us as a long term thing?"

Not at all. "Well, uh, I'd like us to be but I don't know how well either of us will hold up trying to do this long distance and all."

A long pause. "Are you willing to try and make it work?"

No. "I don't know. Maybe. Why don't we see how things are at the end of summer and figure out what we want to do then?"

"Uh, yeah. That makes sense. I might want to kill you by then."

Or I you.

Kayley went on to tell me everything was finally settled with the moms and she'd move to Virginia's the following weekend. "Maybe you'll stop by more?"

"There's still the Virginia problem."

"If I'm living there, she can't expect you to never come over. Maybe you two can start getting along."

Not going to happen.

July 1986 (Pre-College Freshman)

"We're going downtown tonight," I informed Kayley on the phone. "Hunter got a case of beer and two packs of coolers. You want to come with?"

"Is it okay if Willow comes with us?"

Better than Virginia. "Sure."

Hunter met Isaac, the girls and me in a secluded parking lot across from the new freeway interchange construction area. The five of us, a bottle each, made our way over the cement barricade. Two cranes, a bulldozer, and a dump truck were parked at the far side of the construction area. Nothing small enough for us to liberate remained on the site.

"Has Isaac told you our friend Miranda is back in town from Cleveland?" I asked Kayley.

"He mentioned it, yeah."

"Well, I wanted you to know, we'll probably be spending a good deal of time with her when she gets back from Lake Chelan."

"What does that mean?"

I prefer Miranda to you. "She's only going to be here a week when she gets back, so I'm going to try to spend some time with her before she takes off."

"Oh," Kayley said, face starting to redden. "So you're going to ignore me while she's around?"

Yup. "That's not what I said. I'll have less time to hang out with you that week. Maybe. Depends on what's going on," I tried. "We don't have plans or anything but I'm sure we'll make some."

"Hmph." She opened her second cooler. "I'm going to go talk to Isaac." She left me standing next to a man-size pile of rebar. Willow walked back over to me.

"Is she pissed?" I asked.

"Seems like it," Willow answered. "What'd you say to her?"

"A friend of ours is going to be in town next week and I told her I'd have less time to be with her while she's here. You think she's mad because it's a girl?" *Play stupid. Always play stupid.*

"Oh. Yeah, definitely," Willow said.

"Hmm." I tried to look confused. "I meant to thank you for going with Kayley to the clinic. I'm glad she finally got there."

"How's this for funny? I finished my period, so I'm already on the pill."

"Kayley said you weren't dating anyone."

"I'm not."

Is that a flirty look? "Good to be prepared, then?"

Under her breath, "Yeah."

She IS flirting. "You want to go get more beer out of the car?" I asked.

"Sounds like a good idea."

I yelled to the others, "Getting more beers!" Willow and I headed back to the car.

"I've got to get something out of my purse," she said. I unlocked the door. When she stood back upright, I put a hand on her shoulder, turned her to me and kissed her vigorously. I grabbed her butt, she grabbed mine. My hand struggled down the front of her stonewashed black denim jeans to press a finger inside her. Without pause, Willow kneaded my butt. *Awesome!*

I pulled away and out of her. "We'd better get back."

She gasped, "Yeah, you're right."

Don't smell like pussy. I licked my finger as we headed back. "We probably shouldn't let Kayley know about this," I said.

"I'd be in deeper shit than you."

Doubt it.

Willow handed me the two bottles of Rainier she was carrying, then made a beeline to Kayley. The two of them walked away whispering. The boys came over, taking the beers Willow had set down.

"Come here, Jon. You got to see this," Hunter said. "We can turn the lights on."

We fiddled with the bulldozer for a few minutes. Our bottles empty, Kayley said, "I've got to get home."

Criminy. "It's only ten-thirty," I said.

"I have to be back by eleven."

"Then I guess we're heading out," Isaac said.

After dropping Isaac off, I turned off Proctor toward Virginia's. "Why are you dropping me off first?" Kayley asked.

"Willow's is on my way home from here. It doesn't make any sense for me to drive her home then backtrack to get you to Virginia's." Kayley gave me the stink eye. "Look, it's not like we'd go do something after I drop Willow off," I said. "We're here now anyway…"

"Fine." Kayley got out of the car, then swiftly walked away.

Pulling away from the curb, I asked, "When do you have to be home?"

"Not for another hour," Willow answered.

"You want to go somewhere?"

"Sure."

A half block off Stevens Avenue, I parked. No street lights, no porch lights on, massive oak trees blocked the light from the quarter moon.

In the back seat, Willow and I clung to each other, kissing hungrily. Bumping the front bucket seats of the Tercel, the windows, each other, we got our shirts off. I tried to run my fingers through her hair, but it was too heavy with product.

Willow struggled out of her pants.

My hands slid along her arms. *What do you do? You're firmer than me.*

"Turn around," I told her. *Let me touch you.* Willow turned away from me.

"No, no. Come here." She scooted her butt along the backseat, still facing away.

"Sit on my face." She started turning towards me again. "Leave your head down there and bring your butt up here."

"Oh," she laughed. "I get it."

Four cramped minutes of 69'ing later, I pushed her around on top of me.

My hands caressed her boobs, down her flat stomach, along her toned ass and legs. *Are you a swimmer? A gymnast? You're not on any of the school teams.*

Willow ground into me, her pussy's grip unyielding. She grunted hoarsely with each of her thrusts. *No way Kayley fucks like this.*

Christ, I'm going to come. Too soon. Must. Move. Her. I held the back of her neck, tried to pull her head down. *Kiss me.* Willow continued working my cock. I tugged harder. She didn't budge. *Now, you don't want to kiss me? Dammit.*

A minute later, I was finished. "Oh...God..." I rasped. "Thank...you... That... was... fantastic."

"You bet," she said.

"Kayley doesn't find out, okay?" I asked.

"No, Kayley certainly doesn't find out."

After locating our clothes, I drove the two blocks to her house. "I had a great time tonight," I said, as she opened the passenger door. "Thanks."

"Yeah, me too."

You're lying, aren't you?

# # #

At Hunter's two days later, eleven people from school were strewn around the living room, sharing stories of the summer so far. I went to Kayley, Virginia and Isaac. Virginia got up and sat down across the room, next to Jake. *Bitch.*

On seeing me Kayley said, "We need to talk."

Willow told you? Is she here?

She led me upstairs by the hand. Isaac and I exchanged confused looks on my way up the staircase. She pulled me into the nearest bedroom, Hunter's mother's.

"I thought you'd like to know," she began. "I started the pill yesterday."

"Does that mean we're fucking tonight?"

"That's exactly what it means." Kayley grinned.

Kick ass. I reached out for her hand. "Where do you want to go?"

"We don't have to go anywhere," Kayley replied.

"On Hunter's mom's bed?"

"Why not?"

"Because it's Hunter's mom's bed. And there are people everywhere."

"No one's going to come in here."

The door's not locked. But you want to fuck. Shit. Don't let Hunter walk in.

Kayley stripped and hopped on the bed. Stepping out of my shorts, I followed.

"Oh wait," she said. She got up, reached into her jeans and handed me a condom. "To be safe. The doc said we should take extra precautions the first month."

If I still have to wear a rubber, why the fuck have we been waiting?

Looking at the wrapper in my hand, I stood next to the bed. "We could go back downstairs..." Kayley offered.

If Willow were here, I might.

Still in my briefs, I caressed her boobs. *Not as firm as Willow.* Slid my hand across her stomach, between her legs. *Ask Willow what she does.* I diddled her. *Not as wet as Willow. But wet enough.*

In missionary position, Kayley's breathing grew heavier the entire seven minutes I took to finish. *You came, right?*

Kayley returned downstairs, followed by me a minute later.

"Everything all right?" Isaac asked, in the kitchen.

I grinned. "Seems so."

"You did not," he said. "On Hunter's bed?"

"His mom's."

"Oh, God."

# # #

On the way to my apartment, with Kayley in the Tercel, at ten o'clock the next night. "Did Virginia give you shit about the party?" I asked.

"She's pretty sure we had sex, so she didn't talk to me until this afternoon."

"Why'd she think we fucked?" *Isaac told her?*

"My chest gets flushed after sex. She must've noticed when we came downstairs."

How often she see you after sex? What kind of a slut are you? "So maybe she'll never speak to me again?" *Oh please. Oh please.*

Kayley shook her head. "I don't know why you two can't get along."

Because she's a twat? "She started it."

Four:
July 1986 (College, Freshman Year)

Three days later, I called Kayley. "Wanted to let you know," I began. "Miranda got back today."

"You're ditching me for her?"

Yeah. "We'll be hanging out a lot. I said I'd tell you when she was back, so I'm telling you."

"Thanks." Pause. "Will you still talk to me while she's here?"

Rather not. "Of course I will," I said. "I'm trying to be upfront about what's going on."

"Yeah, that's real decent of you," she replied.

"Okay, I'm going to go. Talk to you tomorrow."

As I put the phone down I heard, "Should I hold my breath?"

"Do whatever you want," I mumbled.

Miranda opened the door to her mom's apartment. Her black hair with blonde roots curled haphazardly, fell to her jaw line over her pale, unblemished face, obscuring her left eye. A svelte five foot eight, full lips, pert B cup breasts and long fingered hands with a couple thick blue veins gracing the tops. *Still stunning.*

"How was Chelan?" I asked, stepping inside.

She shushed me. "Mom's in bed. Not bad," she continued. "My cousin and I got along, but all she wanted to do was lay out and look for boys."

Did you find any? "Isn't that all there is to do in Chelan?"

"I guess, but it's not my thing. Got a lot of reading done, caught up with my aunt and uncle."

"Why'd you go, then?"

"Hadn't been before. Probably won't go back," she added. "What's new with you? How's Kayley?"

Fuck Kayley. "Don't know, been hanging out with Isaac and Hunter a lot. We found a way to get onto the unopened part of the freeway downtown, so we've been there a couple times. Hung out down at Sun Dial Park, bowling, you know…"

Miranda laughed, then grimaced.

"What was that?" I asked.

"Oh, my neck's sore from the bed in Chelan."

"You want me to rub your neck?"

She scowled from across the couch. "I'll be fine."

"You said your shoulders hurt. Let me rub your neck. If it hurts too much, I'll stop." She didn't answer. "Miranda, I promise I won't hurt you."

"Okay." She sat on the floor in front of me. Gently, I guided my fingers along the knotted muscles in her shoulders. She winced but didn't tell me to stop.

Ten minutes later, I told her to get on the couch. She obliged. I lifted her shirt but left her bra alone, massaging the whole of her back. *If she wants to get frisky, she'll unhook her bra.*

Half an hour later, she rolled over. "God, thanks. That was great. I got to get to bed, my sister's picking me up at nine."

Can we get naked?

At the door Miranda said, "I'll call you when I get home tomorrow, okay?"

No kiss? Are we friends now? That'd suck.

#   #   #

A couple days later, Kayley called me before noon. "What'd you end up doing last night?" she asked.

"Went to Denny's for a while," I answered. "Not much."

With a snarky tone, "How's Miranda?"

Cooler than you. "She went out with a friend, so we didn't see her. We're going over to Isaac's tonight, watch 'Love Connection,' catch up." *You're not invited.*

"Oh," she sighed. "Willow's parents are going on vacation, so she said she was going to have a party and wanted to know if you could get her some beer."

"Why doesn't she ask me?" *Love to talk to her. Sneak away again.*

"She knew I'd be talking to you today," Kayley replied.

"When?" *Not this week.*

"The second Saturday in August. You think you can?"

"Maybe. I don't know. It'd be better to ask Hunter, because his cousin's twenty one and buys everything for us. I'd end up asking Hunter, anyway."

"Oh," Kayley said. "I'll let her know."

Later, at Isaac's. "What the hell is up with you and Kayley? She keeps calling me about what we're doing with Miranda and asking why she's not invited."

"Because I don't want to invite her. She'd want to bring Virginia and she'd get all fucking bitchy and ruin a perfectly boring evening." I lowered my voice. "And how am I going to convince Miranda to come home with me if my girlfriend's here?"

"Maybe you couldn't," Isaac said.

"That's no fun."

Back at home, the phone rang at 5.00pm. *C'mon Miranda, not Kayley. Miranda. Miranda. Miranda.*

"Hello?" I answered.

"Hi, Jon," a familiar voice rasped.

"Hi...what're you doing?" *Virginia?*

"I need to talk to you about Kayley," Virginia said.

"Uh, okay. What's up?"

"I don't know exactly what's going on with you two, but Kayley's been pretty upset the past couple days and I think you should talk to her about it." *Don't give a shit what you think.*

"Virginia, I've already talked to her about it," I said. "She knows what's going on. A friend is here from the east coast and I'm spending time with her this week."

"That's what I've heard, but Kayley's annoyed you're not inviting her to meet this Miranda girl."

"Does Kayley want me to bring her by? Would that help?"

"Jesus, Jon, she's pissed because you're sneaking around with some other girl!"

"I'm not sneaking. I told her Miranda and I are hanging out and she didn't have a problem with it. I mean, I'm sorry if she's pissed about it now, but I'm not telling Miranda to fuck off because Kayley suddenly doesn't like us hanging out together."

Virginia's voice mellowed. "Why don't you ask Kayley to come out with you guys next time?"

"I can do that," I said. *Kayley can't stay out that late.* "Is she there now?"

"She went to the corner store for smokes. She doesn't know I'm calling you, so if we could keep this between us?"

No way. "No problem. Have her call me when she gets home, okay?"

"I will. Thanks, Jon."

Kayley called fifteen minutes later. "Where were you earlier?"

"Getting cigarettes. Why?"

"I called to see what you were up to and Virginia said you were out. What are you doing later?"

"My mom was going to take me to dinner after she ran a couple errands."

"Oh," I sighed. "Miranda and I were going to get dinner and visit Isaac at work, and I thought you might want to join us." *Good lie.* "Then head over to Denny's after he's done."

"What time?" Kayley asked.

"He's closing, so we're going to go out around ten and meet up with Hunter at Denny's around eleven thirty or so."

"I've got to be home at eleven."

I know. "That's right. Damn. Well, I'll call you tomorrow when we figure out what's going on, okay? Tell your mom I said hi."

The phone rang at six. "What're you doing tonight?" Miranda asked me.

"Isaac and I were going to hang out at Denny's. Want to come?"

"Sure," she conceded. "I got nothing better to do than hang out at Denny's."

"We'll bowl," I said. "Play some pinball."

"Oooh, bowling."

"There's not much else to do around here, Miranda."

Her voice mellowed. "Suppose not. Why don't I come over around eight?"

"Can you get across the street by yourself?" I joked.

At eight, I opened the front door. Miranda stayed in the entryway.

"Mom, this is Miranda. Miranda, my mother, Mary."

"Nice to finally meet you Miranda," Mary said. "Good to put a face to the name."

"You, too."

"Where you guys heading?" Mary asked.

"You know, Denny's, Tower Lanes with Isaac and Hunter." Miranda rolled her eyes.

"Have fun. Try not to wake me up when you get back, Jon."

"I don't most times, do I?" *Do you know I want to bring Miranda back here?*

"Not usually," my mother said.

"Good night," Miranda waved as I pushed her out the door.

At Isaac's the boys forfeited shotgun to Miranda on the way to Denny's. "Is there anywhere else we could go tonight?" she asked the group.

Hunter said, "Not much is open past ten."

"Everything's open until midnight in Cleveland. Aren't there any clubs?"

"The cool one downtown shut down last spring," Isaac said. "We could go up to Seattle, but by the time we got there, we'd have to come back."

"Yeah," Hunter said. "I've got to be home by midnight."

The four of us split two orders of fries, spending the next two hours laughing about Hunter's girl troubles, Isaac's customers and Miranda's life in Cleveland. Isaac insisted we leave a large tip, as our cups were never empty.

The boys again sat in the backseat on the way to Isaac's without me having to either suggest or demand it. "You got to get back to your mom's, Miranda?" Isaac asked.

"Yeah, she wants me in by midnight too," she replied.

You didn't say that. We could have left earlier. Dammit.

Having dropped off the boys, I drove toward Pearl Avenue. "Why didn't you tell me you had to be back so early?"

"I don't," Miranda replied. "I didn't want Isaac to feel bad."

Why would he feel bad? He knows about us. "Oh. Well, then. What do you want to do?"

"No bowling."

"I don't know why you hate bowling so much. Want to go talk at my place?"

"That'll work."

No talking. Straight to the bedroom to shed our clothes.

"What're you doing during the day tomorrow?" I asked her at her door.

"Watching soaps."

"Why don't you come over instead?"

"And miss my stories?" Miranda asked. "We'll see."

August 1986 (College, Freshman Year)

Miranda and I spent the afternoon in my bed. I went down on her. *You will come.*

Five minutes in she looked down at me. "The only time I've ever gotten off from that was when an older guy tried it."

How much older? Must be forty if you think he's older. You slept with a forty year old? Can't compete with that. "What did he do that was so special?" I asked.

"I don't know," she admitted. "But he's the only one who could do it right."

"Am I doing anything right?"

"It's okay. I don't think it's going to happen for me, though."

We'll see about that.

Ten minutes later I gave up.

Miranda left minutes before Mary got home. I was in the bathroom fussing with my hair when she came in. "What are you doing?" Mary asked from the hallway.

"Getting pretty," I answered.

"You going to see Miranda tonight?"

Leaving the bathroom I replied, "Probably."

"Is she going to come over here?"

Not while you're awake. "I don't think so, why?" *Do you hate her? Oh God, you hate her.*

"I felt underdressed yesterday." She shook her head. "She's such a beautiful girl, I felt uncomfortable when she was here last night."

Uncomfortable? "Uh..."

"I didn't want to take off my make up if she was going to be coming over again."

"Uh, not that I know of."

"So you and Kayley are broken up now?" she asked.

"No." Mary gave me a curious look. "I told her Miranda was going to be in town for a while so I'd be more or less unavailable."

"And you think you two are still seeing each other?"

"Once Miranda goes back to Cleveland, yeah."

Mary snorted. "Let me know how that goes."

#   #   #

Her last night in Tacoma, I arrived at Miranda mother's apartment at ten. "There's something I want to show you," I said.

"Can we talk for a minute before?" she asked.

You done with me? "Why don't we wait until after?"

I drove us up Jackson Avenue, turned onto a residential street, parked beside a twelve foot hedge on the right side of the road. Before us, the entire span of the Tacoma Narrows Bridge could be seen. Seatbelt off, I reclined the driver's seat.

"Jake showed me this spot last year. I love to come here at night and watch the cars go across," I said.

Miranda turned to me. "I want to tell you something and I'm not sure how to do it, so I'm just going to say it."

Not a good start. I looked into her eyes. "You're not pregnant, are you?"

"No," Miranda answered. Her voice softened. "I wanted to tell you I love you."

I love you too. Don't leave. Stay with me.

A moment of silence. "I hadn't thought about it before now, but I love you too."

"I don't know how this all happened," Miranda said. "But you mean a great deal to me. I hate we don't live in the same state."

Wish you were here all the time... "You ever going to move out here?"

"No. I'd kind of like to, but no. My dad isn't cool with me leaving while I'm still in high school even though my mom said it'd be okay."

"Well, what about after?" *We could be together.*

"Maybe. I don't know."

We sat on the hood of my mother's Tercel, watched the silent cars on the bridge float above the water. Our conversation meandered to Isaac, school and when she'd be back in Washington.

Miranda returned to the apartment. Our sex was unhurried, caring, passionate. *Stay.* We fell asleep, our fingers intertwined.

At 4.00am Miranda woke me up. I drove her across the street to her mother's apartment.

Outside her door, "I'm going to miss you," I said.

"You've got Kayley, though."

"That's a shitty thing to say, Miranda."

"Sorry, but it's true."

"If you lived here, she never would've been in the picture." *Never.*

She gave me a peck. I pulled her to me, kissed her gently, then held her tightly. "I really do love you, you know?" I whispered.

"Yeah, I know. I love you, too."

She closed the door.

Will she come back out if I stay here? She can't. She's got a life somewhere else.

Dammit.

Five:
August 1986 (College, Freshman Year)

Isaac and I walked into Willow's, past our friend Beau and a couple gals I didn't know, sitting on the front porch. "Willow and Kayley inside?" I asked Beau.

"Last I saw, yeah. Thought you guys were bringing the beer."

"Really?" I said. "I told Kayley we couldn't get anyone to buy for us."

"Where'd you get that?" Isaac pointed at the beer in Beau's hand.

"I'm a man of many mysteries," he replied.

"And mostly full of shit," I added.

"That too," Beau agreed. "I think there's more a couple more in the fridge."

In the house, Kayley and Willow sat on the couch, coolers in hand. Their conversation stopped abruptly when we moved toward them.

"Ladies. How you doing tonight?" Isaac started.

"Fine," Willow replied.

Kayley, looking at me, "Why don't we talk?" To Willow, "Can we use your room?"

"Sure," Willow replied.

Kayley strode across the living room. Isaac and I exchanged smirks before I followed. Willow's bedroom door shut behind us. "It's good to see you," I attempted.

"Uh huh." Kayley sat down on Willow's bed, a single mattress on the floor in the middle of the room. I sat beside her. "Where's Miranda?"

"Left this afternoon. Won't be back until Christmas." I leaned in to kiss her. She pulled away.

"Did you sleep with her?"

This morning. Putting on my best indignant face. "Why would you ask me something like that?"

"Because you've spent all your time with her this last week." Her face reddened.

"I told you this was going to happen. How do you get from my friend's in town to are you sleeping together?"

"Isaac said you've slept with her before."

Shit. "Last summer," I admitted. *He wouldn't't've told her about this summer. Asked him not to. He'd never give me up, would he?*

"And Christmas," Kayley added.

SHIT! "Oh, that's right," feigning thought. "I guess it was this last Christmas," nodding. I raised my voice, took an accusatory tone, "So what? Did Isaac say Miranda and I had been sleeping together this summer?" *Please no, please.*

Kayley stood up, crossed the room. "No. He said you guys were just friends."

Isaac, my hero.

"But you've slept with her before."

"When I wasn't seeing anyone," I retaliated. "In case you'd forgotten, we are kind of seeing each other." *Kind of.*

"Why didn't you tell me you'd slept with her?"

"Because it wasn't important. And I figured you'd be pissed off about me spending time with her."

"I would've been pissed. I am pissed. How would you like it if I did the same thing to you?"

"Why? Is that something that might happen?"

She stared at me. "It could."

"Oh, you have a friend you'd slept with who comes to town a couple times a year?"

"Not out of town," she said.

What? Wait a minute.

"Beau and I have been friends for a while."

What? Beau? Hold on.

Kayley went to the door, stuck her head out, "Hey, Beau. Can you come here a minute?" To me, "You can go now."

When Beau got to the door, Kayley pulled him into Willow's room. "We'll be out in a while," she said. Beau shrugged, gave me a 'What are you do?' grin before Kayley closed the door in my face.

Bitch!

"What's that about?" Isaac asked.

"Me and Miranda."

"Oh."

While Kayley and I were Willow's room, Virginia had returned empty handed. Virginia came over to me. "Where's Kayley?" she asked.

I nodded toward the bedroom. "With Beau."

"They used to go out," Virginia said.

She's going to fuck him. "When was that?" I asked.

"Last fall. A couple months, on and off. He couldn't handle her bulimia, so they stopped hanging out."

"Her bulimia?" *That's why puking doesn't bother her.*

"She didn't tell you?" Virginia asked. "Haven't you asked her about her fake tooth?"

"What fake tooth?" I asked.

"It's not a big deal. Ask her about it later." Virginia walked away, striking up a conversation with Willow on the other side of the living room.

Why doesn't Willow take me out somewhere while Kayley's fucking Beau?

"You want to take off?" Isaac asked.

"Kind of," I said. "But I don't want to leave Kayley and Beau alone all night either." *If Miranda was still here, I'd've already left. If I could get Willow out of here...*

"Why don't you take me home and come back and get things settled with Kayley?"

She'll think I left. Great idea.

Isaac said good night to Willow, Virginia and the rest of the younger people who were sitting around the living room. "She's probably not sleeping with him," Isaac offered. "Trying make you jealous."

Working. "Maybe," I said.

"Good luck."

I pulled up to Willow's. *Even if they were fucking, they'd be done by now. It's been forty-five minutes for fuck's sake.*

"You came back?" Virginia asked as soon as I walked in the front door.

"Isaac had to get home," I replied.

"Oh. They're still not out yet...you sure you want to stick around?"

"For a little while."

Willow's bedroom door opened. Kayley poked her head out, her hair a mess, her face splotched with red. "I thought you left," she said to me.

"I can leave if you'd like," I replied.

"No. We're done in here." She opened the door. "Thanks," she said to Beau. He walked by me, raised his eyebrows, then rejoined the party in the living room.

"How does it feel?" Kayley asked.

"We even now?" I replied.

"Miranda was here for a week..."

Won't put up with this for a week. "Virginia said I should ask you about a fake tooth."

"Oh, this?" She reached into her mouth and pulled out a retainer with a single tooth attached to the front. "Why'd she bring this up?" A dark space remained where front left tooth should've been.

I stared at Kayley's mouth. *You look retarded.* "Uh, she mentioned bulimia." *Put your tooth back in.*

"Oh, that," she replied. "I've been dealing with it for a while." *You are? Nasty.*

"Uh, er, how you doing these days?"

"Not too bad, for the most part. It's tough when I gain a couple pounds, but I'm all right most of the time."

A couple pounds? You're skin and bones. No wonder you're so damn thin. Put your retainer back in!

"I need to talk to Willow for a minute," she said. "Can you go get her?"

Beau came over to me when Willow went to join Kayley. "Sorry about that, man," he said. "We didn't sleep together. That'd be seriously uncool."

"Thanks, Beau," I said. "I know it was all Kayley. We're good." *Dick.* Beau resumed the conversation he'd left.

Kayley returned. "Willow said she'd take Virginia home, so can we get out of here?"

"Uh, sure," I answered.

In the Tercel. "I don't have to be back to Virginia's for another hour because we're at Willow's. Can you think of anywhere to go?"

"To do what?"

"Be alone a while," she said. *You want to fuck after all that?*

"We could go back to my place, but we'd have to be quiet."

"Can we park somewhere?"

A couple blocks that way? Did Willow tell you about us fucking? "Like where?" I asked.

"Not too far away. Somewhere dark." *She did tell you.*

"There's nothing this way," Kayley said, after a couple blocks. "What about over by the cliff?"

At the same locale Willow and I christened two weeks earlier, I parked the Tercel.

# # #

I called Kayley before I'd unpacked from my stint as a counselor and then a camper at two different Methodist youth camps. "What'cha doing?"

"Waiting to see if you'd call," she said.

"I'm calling." Silence. "You mind if I come over?"

"If that's what you want to do."

Good Lord. What's your fucking problem now?

When I hung up the phone Mary asked, "How are things with you and Kayley anyway?"

"Who knows? She insisted we take a break while I was at camp so now I'm going to go see."

"A break, huh? How'd that go?"

"Doesn't sound like it went very well. I'm heading over there now."

Mary turned back to her book. "Have the car back before I have to go to work."

"Don't I always?"

On Virginia's front porch, Kayley, cigarette in one hand, phone in the other. "Hey," I said from the bottom of the stars.

"Hey yourself," she responded.

Fuck you. I'll leave now. "If you don't want me to be here, I'll go," I said, continuing to look at her.

Her glare softened. "Took you long enough to call."

"I called as soon as I got home."

"I thought you got home last night. That's what Isaac said anyway."

Silly Isaac. "Nope. Got back about an hour ago." I remained at the bottom of the steps. "Maybe we should go for a walk?"

"Yeah. Virginia's home."

Isn't she always?

"How was camp?" she asked, walking past me.

"Not bad. Counseling was interesting. I've got a couple stories, but I'd rather discuss the guy you've been seeing."

Looking away. "Oh, you heard?"

Isaac tells me everything. "I did," I said. "And?"

"I want to talk to you first. Did you get together with anyone the past two weeks?"

"Nope. What's your story?" *Slut.*

"Nothing," she mumbled. "I met this guy at a party. We talked on the phone, I met him at the mall, we went to the movies. He's a nice guy." *Nicer than me?*

"And?"

"I mean, he's okay. He wants to keep seeing me, but I told him you were coming back and I'd call him if things didn't work out."

Real gracious. "You want to stay together, then?" I asked.

"Yeah. I know we only have a month, but I'd rather have a month than not."

The nicest thing you've ever said to me. "Me too." *Almost a real relationship.*

"Oh, I meant to tell you, Virginia got a job."

"No way, doing what?"

"Working at a little boutique over on Twenty-sixth, near Proctor."

"Great...I guess."

"I've got the house to myself most afternoons now."

"When does Virginia work again?"

"Tuesday, I think. I'll let you know," Kayley said. "I should get back for dinner."

#   #   #

"I hear you and Kayley got back together," Hunter said.

"Uh, did Kayley tell you?"

"Naw, Isaac."

How much does he talk to Virginia? I whispered, "Is he fucking Virginia?"

Hunter leaned forward. "God, I hope not."

"Gobble gobble, fuckers!" Isaac yelled at us, having bowled his third strike in a row. He strutted back toward Hunter and me, a huge grin on his face. "Next time, we bowl for money."

"What money?" asked Hunter.

"You're the one with a job," I added.

"Fine then. Loser picks up two games of pinball for the other two."

"Shit, we'll be here all night," Hunter said, picking up his ball.

"Where you got to be?" I asked him.

"Nowhere." He bowled a strike. "Looks like you're buying, Jon."

"Damn you both." I stood up. "Isaac? What's up with you and Virginia?"

"I don't know. She calls every night and talks about you and Kayley."

"That's kind of psychotic," Hunter said.

"Kind of," Isaac agreed. I threw, leaving the 10 pin.

"You guys talk about anything else?" I asked.

"Oh yeah," Isaac answered. "But you two always come up. Has Kayley told you about Miss Charlotte?"

"Who?" I asked.

"Kayley named one of her boobs."

Hunter and I looked at Isaac. "What? Why?"

"Virginia said one of them's bigger than the other one so she named it Miss Charlotte."

"Well..." Hunter said, looking at me.

"I don't think so. They look like boobs."

"It must be fucked up or why would she have named it?" Hunter said. "You're going to have to pay more attention, Jon."

"They're the same. Why would Virginia tell you that, Isaac?"

"We were talking about you naming your dick Sir Galahad," Isaac answered.

Hunter started laughing. "How did Jon's dick come up in conversation?"

"She asked if I'd named mine. I said no but that you and Jake had, back in junior high."

"Fuck," I said. "Thanks, Isaac."

"Aw, who cares? She probably won't remember anyway. She knew it was a joke."

"Kind of how you forgot about Miss Charlotte?" I said.

#   #   #

Kayley and I spent the next week of afternoons at Virginia's house by ourselves, fucking as soon as I got there in case Virginia or her mom came home unexpectedly. Each time we took off our clothes, I looked closely at Kayley's chest and compared her boobs. *Cute. Perky. The same.*

#   #   #

On Wednesday the following week. "Do you have a nickname for one of your boobs?"

"Oh, you mean Miss Charlotte?" She cupped her right breast. "Virginia and I named her a couple years ago. She used to be a lot bigger. I was pretty lop-sided."

"I can't tell," I admitted. "Let me see."

She took off her shirt and her bra. "They're the same."

"Miss Charlotte's fuller," Kayley said.

"If you say so." I pulled her onto her bed, she sat on top of me.

"Watch." She bounced up and down a bit. With all the sunlight coming into her room, her right boob jiggled slightly less than her left.

"Okay, now I see it." I led my cock into her. She continued bouncing. I felt my dick leave her on her up and move back in on her way down.

That's not right. Kayley stopped. My hands, on her ass, touched. *I'm in her butt.*

"You all right?" I asked.

"Yeah. Surprised." She paused another second. "Keep going. I'm all right."

This feels fantastic. We should to do this more often. Why didn't we think of this before?

"Okay," she said. "I'm done with that now."

So soon? I pulled out.

Kayley continued, "No, no, we're done back there. Come here." She sat back down, guiding me back into her pussy.

The front door opened an hour later. Kayley beat me downstairs, where I found her and Virginia talking about a customer at the boutique.

"I should get home," I said. "See you guys later."

"Later, Galahad," Virginia said, after Kayley kissed me goodbye.

Bitch.

September 1986 (College, Freshman Year)

Kayley ended up with a bladder infection as a result of us going back to front, so our afternoon trysts were put on hold for a week while she recuperated. I spent time with Isaac and Hunter bowling and on a couple of occasions bringing one of Isaac's girlfriends back to my place for an extended make-out session.

Kayley and I resumed our naked afternoon sessions once her antibiotic/cranberry juice regimen was completed, both of us careful to avoid any anal contact.

# # #

The day before Mary was to drive me to Bellingham to start school, I started to pack.

"I don't understand why you left this until the last minute," Mary said. "You knew when we were going up there."

"It's not going to take that long. Besides, I can always come home and grab anything I forget. It's not like you're across the country or anything."

"Have you and Kayley figured things out?"

"I guess," I said, throwing all my underwear into a suitcase. "We've talked about it. I'm leaving, she's staying here. She doesn't drive, I won't have a car and probably won't be back until Thanksgiving. We're letting it go once I'm gone."

"Hmm."

Twenty minutes later, I took my overstuffed suitcase to the living room. "Can I take the car?"

"Don't stay out too late," Mary replied. "We're leaving at ten and still need to load up the car."

Kayley and I ended up back at Virginia's. "I thought they were going out," Kayley said, both Virginia and her mother's cars in the driveway. "Oh well."

Down the block from Virginia's house, a waist-high fence jutted out perpendicular to a ten foot hedge, over a vast gulley which dropped eight hundred feet, ending at Commencement Bay. The sun fell quickly behind us. Arms around each other, Kayley and I watched Vashon Island.

Looking into my eyes, she said, "I can't believe you're leaving tomorrow."

"I know. I'll be a big college guy," I joked. "It's been fun most of the time, hasn't it?"

"When it was fun, it was real fun. But I've wanted to beat the shit out of you a lot, too."

A cough. "Me too."

"I didn't expect to fall in love with you because I knew we were only a summer thing. But I did anyway."

No way. You tell me you love me the day before I leave. "I know what you mean." *I'm going to miss you. But I'll never tell you.* "Even though we've both been shitty at times, yeah, I love you too."

I caressed her face. "Can we go somewhere?"

"Any place in particular?" she asked.

"I know a quiet spot over by the cliff..."

Six:
September 1988 (College, Junior Year)

The second night back in the dorms, Sofia, one of several female friends in my large group of friends, sat down between my neighbors in Mathes Hall, Neal and Ezra.

"You see that table over there?" Sofia pointed at a round table with seven gals, forty feet away. "I'm friends with the blonde. Anyway, last night, I was having dinner with them and the gal there in the pink sweater, looks over to the table you guys were at and says, 'I can't stand those guys. They're so loud and obnoxious. They're just creeps.' Obviously she didn't know I was friends with you all."

The eight guys seated around the table exchanged looks. Ezra to me, "You creep."

"You are such a creep." I said to Neal.

"I feel so totally creepy."

"Oh God," Sofia shook her head. "I shouldn't've said anything."

On our way out, all ten of us detoured past the gal in the pink sweater, muttering, "You've always been kind of creepy."

"Just let me creep past here..."

After dinner, in Ezra and Neal's room on the sixth floor of Mathes Hall, two doors down from my room, the three of us were shooting the shit. I'd invited my new roommate, Hunter, a friend from high school, to join us, but he wanted to get completely unpacked.

"What's the latest?" Neal asked me.

"Remember that whore I fucked a couple times last spring?" I started.

Neal's expression turned to shock. "You fucked a whore?" he asked.

"Not a real live whore, no," I answered. "Ezra's girlfriend's slutty friend. I think she gave me genital warts."

They cringed; Ezra crossing his legs, Neal covering his crotch.

"Holy shit," Ezra said. "Seriously?"

"Oh yeah," I stated. "Been going to the dermatologist for a month now. And now I get to tell the gals I slept with last year to go get checked out."

"Sounds fun," Neal said.

"Real fun," I agreed. "Have you seen that slutty girl since last year, Ezra?"

"No," he said. "Not since all of us were hanging out together."

Neal spoke up. "Do they treat genital warts the same as regular warts?"

"I don't know, I've never had real warts. Do they burn off real warts with liquid nitrogen?"

"Oooh!" They cringed again.

"Yeah, sometimes," Neal answered.

"How often do you have to go to the doctor?" Ezra asked.

"Every two weeks."

"Do you get numbed up or anything?" Neal asked.

"I could," I said. "If I wanted shots in my pecker."

Another collective moan.

"Jesus, that's got to hurt," Ezra said.

"Best part is, the whole time my doctor is trying to push a big Q-tip through my dick, he's just humming along, happy as a clam."

#   #   #

A gal, who lived on the first floor of Mathes Hall, Tiana, showed up at the gym Sunday for open volleyball. She waved at me then rotated in with the team I was playing against. "Hey Tiana. How're classes?" I asked.

"Not too bad. You?"

"Eh. Working on a book through Fairhaven. A seven credit independent study."

"Lucky."

The next time we were in the front row opposite each other, "You play every Sunday?" she asked.

"Try to. I'm on the men's club team. We've talked about using Sundays to scrimmage but there's only a couple guys here today."

Afterward, Tiana and I walked back to Mathes together. She was from a town in southwest Washington and played volleyball in high school but didn't try out for the Western team. Straight, golden hair to the middle of her back, light eyebrows above glistening green eyes, a kind smile. Five foot six, thin with C cup breasts. Her black spandex shorts clung invitingly to her tight, little butt.

"You going to come out next Sunday?" I asked her once we'd entered the dorm.

"Probably."

Invite me down to your room.

"See you."

"Bye."

Dammit.

# # #

Tuesday night after volleyball practice started, Tiana and her roommate, Danielle, sat down on the bleachers on the far side of the gym.

Didn't tell her we were practicing.

Next to each other, on the opposite side of the court from me, Tiana looked toward my side, I smiled at her. She smiled back.

Tiana looked my way again. I smiled. Tiana didn't but Danielle did. A couple minutes later, Danielle smiled again.

Not you. Tiana.

The next time Tiana looked over, I winked. Danielle winked back.

If I'm friendly to her, will that be an in with Tiana?

Finished with practice, I approached the girls. "Howdy, ladies. What brings you here?"

"Thought we'd see if you guys were any good." Tiana stood up, walking toward one of the other guys on the team.

Tiana several steps away, Danielle inquired, "Were you winking at me?"

Not you. Tiana. "Oh, you noticed."

"Good," Danielle sighed. "I wasn't sure and didn't want to seem like an idiot if you had something in your eye."

"Nope. What do you think of practice? Not all that entertaining if you're not playing."

"You guys aren't bad. It was fun to watch, even though we didn't watch much."

"I noticed you two giggling a lot over here," I said.

"Well, Tiana's got a crush on whatshisface but his roommate keeps calling her and asking her out."

"And how's that going?"

"She doesn't like the roommate at all, but whatshisface doesn't seem to notice her."

I've still got to chance?

Tiana was laughing it up with whatshisface twelve yards away.

Shit. "Well, I'll see you around Mathes, I imagine."

#   #   #

"Who's that?" Ezra asked me, noticing Danielle smiling at me from across the dining hall.

"Danielle," I said. "Lives on the first floor."

"You going to ask her to join us?"

"Naw. I'm trying to get friendly with her roommate, the little blonde a couple seats to her left."

"Mmm. Good luck with that," Ezra said.

"Yeah, no shit."

Neal looked at both girls. "Why don't you go after Danielle? She keeps looking over here."

"I'd be off-limits to Tiana."

"Only if she finds out about it..." Ezra offered.

"True..."

Danielle headed back to the food service area. I came up behind her at the salad bar. "Hey, Danielle," I said. "How you doing?" *Damn, she's as tall as me. Almost as skinny as Kayley.*

She turned, "Oh, hey Jon. Good, thanks." Thin lips, light brown eyebrows over dim blue eyes. Her hair full, brown, a weak curl down to her shoulders. She brightened, "What're you up to?"

"Need to fill up before work," I replied.

"Where do you work?" she asked.

"Over in the Nash Hall computer lab."

"How's that?"

"Uneventful for the most part. Setting appointments and making sure there's paper in the printers. Gives me an opportunity to work on my book, though."

"A book? What's it about?"

"A collection of short stories, different relationships between guys and gals."

"Can I read it some time?" Danielle asked.

"Yeah, sure," I said. "If you come over to the lab tonight there's a couple stories I could show you."

"Maybe I'll swing by," she stated.

Danielle walked into Nash's computer lab an hour later. There were three students working among the eight stations around the circular room on Nash's top floor.

"Can I sit here and read some of it?" Danielle asked.

"Sure," I said.

She sat at one of the empty stations. Watching her, I noted every smile, each breath of escaped laughter. "How many of these are you writing?" she asked, handing both stories, all eight pages, back to me.

"Fifteen. What'd you think?" *Please like them.*

"Funny," she said.

Thank God.

"True stories?" she asked.

"Kind of, sort of. Based on true, for the most part." I described how I was attempting to link all the stories together but keep them separate, the male character was the same in each though no one else was, trying to use as few words as possible.

"When do you think you'll finish?" she asked.

"End of the quarter, maybe. Hopefully." Looking at the clock, "Oh shit," I whispered. "I got to close up."

Danielle walked back to Mathes with me after I'd locked up. "What're you doing now?" I asked her.

"Nothing."

"You think Tiana's around?"

"Probably. What about your roommate?"

"He stays at the library until it closes ever since school started, so he's probably still there."

"Let's go to your room then."

But Tiana's in your room.

Hunter wasn't there. Danielle looked through my music collection, making comments about bands she recognized. She picked up a Human League album, turned it over. "The only song I know of theirs is 'Don't You Want Me'? You've got like ten albums."

"Mostly singles," I said. Danielle sidled up to me, I kissed her. The lock on the door clicked then opened. Danielle started, quickly stepping away.

Hunter stood in the doorway, eyes wide. "Oh, sorry, Jon."

"No worries," I said. " Your room too."

"You want me to come back later?" he asked.

"No," Danielle said. "I should get going. I'll see you tomorrow, Jon. I'm Danielle, by the way."

"Sorry," I said. "This is Hunter. Lunch tomorrow? Noon?"

"Yeah. I'll see you there." She squeezed by Hunter on her way out.

"Man, I'm really sorry," Hunter said. "She didn't have to leave."

"No problem. I'd rather bag her roommate so it's better if nothing happens with Danielle anyway."

Hunter sighed, shaking his head.

# # #

I introduced Danielle to Ezra and Neal at lunch. She was from Vancouver, Washington, came to Western for the education program, had two sisters, one sixteen, the other five. "Doesn't Hunter eat lunch with you?" she asked.

"Not yet," I replied. "You know, I don't know where he eats. I'll have to ask."

Ezra and the rest of our group drifted away to class. Done for the day, Danielle and I ended up back in my room.

Against the desk, I lifted her shirt, her bra. My hands roamed her back, around her midriff, up to her breasts, brushing her nipples. Danielle caressed my back, then tugged at my shorts.

Shit, shit, shit. "Uh, hold on a sec," I said. "Well, uh, you need to know, I'm being treated for genital warts."

"Oh, uh, okay," she said.

We're done then?

Danielle looked into my eyes. "You got rubbers?"

"Yeah, but they're not a hundred percent. There's still a chance you could get them."

"But if we're careful, I won't, right?"

You're not giving me the finger? "More than likely, yeah."

"No need to stop then," she said, her jeans fell to the floor.

Delicious. Pert, perfectly shaped breasts, thin hips, smooth, alabaster skin, a scant thatch of light brown pubic hair. *Stunning. Tiana look this good naked?*

Condom in hand, I guided Danielle against the dresser, kissing her passionately. She put her left foot on one of the drawer's handles and bent her right knee. We ground into each other, Danielle's foot slipped once. Then again.

"You want to move to the bed?" I asked.

"Only if you do," she gasped.

Want to stay inside you. "I'm good."

Danielle hurriedly found her clothes when I'd finished. "Where you going?" I asked.

"I've got to get some reading done before class tomorrow, so I should split."

You can stay. "See you at dinner."

October 1988 (College, Junior Year)

"Oh, shit! Is it three-fifteen?" I squealed.

"That's maybe a couple minutes fast," Neal replied, nodding at the clock on the television.

Jumping down from Neal's bunk, "I'm going to be late."

"For what?" Ezra asked.

"My burning."

Ezra called, "Say hi to Doc Smiley for me!"

Ezra and Neal were in the hall trying to sink putts into a red plastic cup from thirty yards when I returned to Mathes. "How'd it go?" Ezra asked.

"Doc Smiley hummed the entire time," I responded. "I think he likes musicals."

Neal sniffed the air. "Is that you?"

"What?"

"Smells like pickles?"

"Oh, shit. Yeah. They use vinegar to find them," I said. "I don't even notice any more."

I approached my room in the middle of their green. "Seriously though, you should shower before dinner," Ezra added.

"I like pickles," I retorted.

I showered anyway.

\#   \#   \#

In the hall outside my room Danielle said, "I got to paper due tomorrow in English." She kissed me. "If I finish before it gets too late, I'll come back up."

"I'll probably be in Neal and Ezra's room," I said.

In their room I yanked their Magic 8 Ball off the top of the mini-fridge. "Will I ever fuck Tiana?" I shook it.

<u>Don't count on it.</u>

Ezra and Neal laughed. "Aw, fuck."

"Are you bullshitting me?" I asked.

<u>No.</u>

"Why can't this thing ever fucking lie?" *Once would be nice.*

I tossed the 8 Ball to Neal. He shook it, "Will all three of us get laid by Halloween?"

<u>It is decidedly so</u>.

"Hot damn," I said. "But not Tiana."

"At least you'll get some this month," Neal added. "Be happy about that."

"A given with Danielle and all," I admitted. "But still..."

# # #

"It's the twenty-fifth, guys," I observed at lunch on Sunday. "You still need to get laid?"

"I'm good," Neal declared.

"That brunette you left the party with last night?" Ezra asked.

"Yup," Neal replied.

"You going to see her again?" I asked.

"Maybe," he shrugged. "I told her I'd stop by this afternoon so we'll see how it goes."

"Ezra?"

"Nothing yet." *How? You're the best looking guy I know.*

# # #

The next day Ezra stopped me in the hall. "I asked the 8 Ball if you and Danielle could substitute for me if I don't get laid by the thirty-first. It said it was all right."

"Substitute? How's that work?"

"Have sex for me. Fuck and say it was for me. I don't need to be there or anything."

"Oh, no problem."

Danielle didn't respond when I told her about the possibility of having to step up for Ezra. "Danielle, it'd wouldn't be the three of us or anything," I said. "We'd just have to say it was for him."

"Yeah, I get that," she said. "But it seems kind of weird."

"It's only if he doesn't get some before Halloween."

"I don't know." Danielle sighed. "Don't like the sound of it."

"There's nothing to it. We screw and say it was for Ezra. Easy."

"I don't know."

"We've got 'til Halloween, okay?" I took off her shirt.

At dinner I let Ezra know Danielle wasn't keen on taking one for the team. "I don't have a problem with it," I said. "But you should to take care of this yourself."

"I'm working on it, but I'm not having any luck," he said.

You can't be trying too hard. Every girl around here would fuck you in a heartbeat.

"Dude, go to a party and get on some drunk girl."

"Hasn't panned out yet."

# # #

Halloween, nine-thirty. "Ezra, there's a party over in Higginson Hall. Go over there, find some cute girl and finish this up," I said.

"I've been trying, Jon. I'll go over there, but I don't think I'll have any luck."

"Neal, go with him and make sure he's trying," I said.

Neal and Ezra left the sixth floor. Forty-five minutes later they returned, Ezra shaking his head.

"Did he even try?" I asked Neal.

"Really Jon, there weren't any good options."

"It doesn't need to be a good option," I said.

"It's up to you now," Ezra said, patting me on the shoulder. "You've got to say it's for me."

"I know."

In my room, Danielle was reading at my desk. "Did Ezra finally get some?" she asked.

"No, it's up to us now." I reached for her hand.

She didn't move. "I don't want to do this."

"Why not? It's just sex."

"All the guys are in the hall and they know what we're doing."

Yeah. So? "But they're not in here...come here."

I bent over and kissed her, she kissed me back. I pulled her upright. *We only need to fuck. What's the problem? We do it all the time anyway.* The sounds of the boys in the hall dropped off.

I helped Danielle out of her clothes while I groped on her. *Half an hour to get this done. Can't start with sex, she'll stop. Get her off first.*

Up from between her legs, donning a condom. We kissed as I entered her.

As I came, I bellowed, "For Ezra!"

Cheers from outside in the hall.

Danielle twisted out from underneath me, scooching under the covers. In shorts and a t-shirt, I walked two doors down.

"There. It's done," I said, inside Ezra's room. "Don't think Danielle's all that happy about it, though."

"What are you doing here then?" Ezra asked. "You should go make sure she's all right."

"Yeah, but I wanted to make sure you knew it was done before midnight."

"Thanks," Ezra said.

On the way back to my room, three fellow sixth floor guys high-fived me. Danielle, dressed, was gathering her books when I opened the door. "You're not staying?" I asked.

"No, I'm not. I can't believe you did that when I told you I didn't want to."

"Danielle, Jesus, it was just sex. It's not like we weren't going to fuck anyway. The Magic 8 Ball doesn't lie." *And I'm not going to be the one who lets it.*

"Whatever," she said, closing the door behind her.

November 1988 (College, Junior Year)

"I'm sorry about last night," I said to Danielle at lunch the next day. "If you didn't want to have sex with me, you should've let me know."

"I wanted to have sex with you, not the entire sixth floor," she said.

"They were outside."

"But they all knew what we were doing and then you yelled to them. They were all congratulating me when I left your room. It was humiliating."

"But you were helping out. They appreciated it. You shouldn't feel embarrassed by it."

"But I did. I do." She took her tray, leaving me with the creeps.

# # #

The next day I went to Danielle's room before dinner, "You want to join me for dinner?" I asked her.

"Up at SAGA?"

"Uh, yeah." *You want to go out?*

"You're asking me to dinner at SAGA?" She scoffed.

"We could order pizza if you want."

"SAGA's fine, I guess," she said. "You could take me somewhere sometime."

"Where do you want to go?" I asked. "You heard of anywhere that's any good?" *And isn't expensive?*

"No, not really," she said, closing the door. "It'd be nice to go somewhere else some time."

We've already paid for the food here.

Someone mentioned Halloween at the table. I lowered my eyes, unobtrusively shaking my head. The topic dissolved.

After dinner Danielle joined me on the sixth floor. She looked up from her reading an hour later. "When's Hunter coming back?" she asked.

"Tomorrow night," I said.

"So I could stay here tonight?"

Like every other night? "Yeah. Why?"

"Tiana said a guy might stop by tonight, so if I could make myself scarce, she'd appreciate it."

You've forgiven me? "What were you going to do if he was here?" I asked.

"I don't know, stay here anyway?"

# # #

After Thanksgiving dinner, at my mother's new apartment south of Tacoma, overlooking Lake Louise, I explained Danielle's offer to have me stay with her for a few days over winter break to Mary.

"Do you want to?" she asked.

"I think so. Her parents seemed pretty cool when they came up a couple weeks ago and I think it'd be fun to hang out with Danielle away from school."

"Are you and Danielle getting serious?"

"I don't know about serious, but we spend a lot of time together."

"How do you feel about Danielle and your relationship?"

"Things seem to be going well," I admitted. "We spend most nights together and don't fight much. Only one time, I can remember." *About fucking.*

"What does she say about you coming down to stay with her?"

"She wants me to," I said. "She keeps bringing it up; Christmas shopping, playing games with the family, cooking dinner and such."

Mary thought a second. "Well, how serious are you two?"

"How serious?" *There are levels of serious?* "What are my options?"

"Staying with someone's family is a big step, Jon. You two have been dating for what, two months? Have you talked about where you're going with this?"

"Uh, no," I stammered. "I mean, we're not seeing other people or anything."

"How would you feel having her stay here so early in your relationship?"

"I don't know. I probably wouldn't've thought to ask." *Now that you put it that way...*

Mary continued, "If you want to go there, you should. We're not doing anything before the twenty second, so if you can get down there, you have my permission."

"Well, thanks. Do you think Danielle wants to get married?"

"You'd have to ask her," Mary said. "But I wouldn't be surprised if she's thought about it."

Marriage? After two months? That's psychotic.

#   #   #

Sunday afternoon, back at Mathes Hall, Danielle found me in my room, "Well? What did your mom say?"

You don't want to know. "She said it was all right so long as your family is okay with me being there."

"My parents wouldn't've asked you if it was an issue," she said.

"I know, but still..." *Is it a good idea?*

"My sisters are looking forward to meeting you." Danielle looked at Hunter's empty bunk, sitting atop the dressers on the left side of the room, nearer the window than the door. "Is Hunter back yet?"

"Haven't seen him, but that doesn't mean much. I barely see him these days."

She reached over and locked the door, then pulled up her shirt.

With Danielle asleep next to me, Hunter on his bed, I watched the digital clock's green numbers change until 1:41.

Do you want to marry her? Is she the one? Could we slow things down? But if I go stay with her family, is that saying I'm in it for the long haul? Am I? Does she know I'm the guy she wants to marry? How can she know already? Doesn't it take a couple years to figure it out? She's only a freshman, how can she know? Is this what I want?

#   #   #

Thursday of Dead Week, during lunch with the creeps, I relayed the fact that Hunter was moving to one of the Ridgeway dorms. "Because I'm always there?" Danielle asked.

"He said that wasn't it," I said. "Said he was spending most of his time up there anyway so why keep trekking back to Mathes."

Back at my room, Danielle asked, "What if we move the two beds together in the center of the room?"

"I don't know if I'm going to have a roommate or not next quarter, Danielle."

"Yeah, I know. But if you don't..."

"Actually, I've been wanting to talk to you." I closed the door to my room.

"About what?"

"Us."

Her energetic glances around the room stopped. "I think things are great but I'm starting to get freaked out about us getting so close so quickly. I mean, we're spending every night together, I'm coming down to stay with your family and we're talking about stuff like this." I pointed around the room. "We're moving pretty fast, don't cha think? Maybe we should slow down and see what happens."

"Really?" Her eyes welled up. "What does slow down mean? Are you still going to come down?"

No. "I don't know if it's a good idea." A single tear lingered on her cheek. "Maybe we should spend some time away from each other for a while."

"We're breaking up?"

Yes. "Taking a break," I said.

"You want me to leave now?"

Don't you want to? "Is there more to talk about?"

"No," she said. "I guess not." Danielle went to my closet, gathered her toothbrush and other toiletries she'd been keeping in my room.

"Are you going to talk to me anymore?"

"Danielle," I tried to sound comforting. "We're taking a break. We're still friends. I hope you don't stop talking to me."

"Okay." The door clicked closed behind her.

That sucked.

December 1988 (College, Junior Year)

A friend of Danielle's had introduced me to me to a young lady, Britney, at a party in Mathes Hall the previous evening. Hastening my pace to catch up with her as she left the dining hall after lunch, "Hey, Britney."

She turned. "Oh hi, Jon."

"How was your final this morning?"

"Oh, uh, fine," she said.

"You do all right?"

"Think so."

"Where you heading now?"

"To study more. I've got another final at eight tomorrow."

"That sucks. I heard there's still beer in the keg and they'll be tapping it again tonight. Should I expect to see you there?"

Britney, "Maybe."

"Cool, then."

Later that night, I was shooting the shit with Ezra in the hallway, Britney came around the corner, alone.

"What's your final in the morning?" I asked.

"Sociology."

Ezra casually slipped away.

"Multiple choice?"

"Yeah. It shouldn't be too tough."

"Maybe you can stay out a little later tonight?" I asked.

A little grin. "Maybe."

"Good. Nothing happened after you left last night. Isaac and I ended up going to bed about half an hour later."

Britney and I entered the party room together, talking the better part of an hour to the exclusion of the other ten people in the room.

"Can we go somewhere else? Somewhere quieter?" I asked her. She nodded. "My roommate moved out so we could hang out there," I suggested.

"I can't stay too long," Britney replied, as my door shut behind her. "I want to get some sleep tonight."

"Not going to keep you against your will." My hand tangled into her shoulder length, tightly curled, brunette hair. In the entryway, between the two closets, her right hand skimmed across my jaw line to grasp the back of my neck.

She's touching me!

Delicately, Britney kissed me. "I really want to get some sleep tonight," she whispered.

"It's still early," I replied, after kissing her again. "How much sleep do you need?"

"I'd like eight hours," she sighed, pressing against me.

"Well, even if you leave now, you won't get that." My lips momentarily left hers as I lifted her shirt. I nuzzled down her neck, her ashen shoulders, her chest, drawing her jeans down the entire time. Britney stood motionless before me. I nibbled her taut belly while caressing her slender, toned legs, her firm ass, her silky smooth back.

Goddamn, she is astounding. Britney held my head, her fingers grasping my hair. I looked up; her eyes were closed.

Gorgeous. Her left breast in my mouth, she pulled my shirt over my head.

"Do you have to go?" *Please don't go.*

"Not yet."

Kneeling on the bed, between her legs, I removed her panties. My hands held her butt up, off the bed.

You going to let me eat you? Awesome. A thin line of hair above her pussy.

Do you shave? No stubble. Goddamn, amazing. Perfect little body and a hairless pussy. Spectacular. Licking, nibbling. *She wants to leave. Can I get a rubber without putting her down? She's going to leave once she sees I'm getting a rubber. Going to say it's late and leave. Go quick.*

I hustled to the dresser, watching her. She smiled at me from the bed.

She's going to stay?

Britney opened to me. *Going to come right now. Wait. Wait. Slow down.* Hands drifted across her chest. Mouth bit her neck. *Going to come. She feels so incredible. Wait. Wait!*

Three minutes in and done. *Dammit. She's going to leave.*

I draped a leg over her.

"Ever since I saw you in the computer room," she whispered, caressing my face, "I've wanted to get to know you better."

No way. "This is better?" I joked.

"Definitely," she said. "I should go though. I've got that final and I really should get some sleep."

"Could you stay a little longer?" I asked. *Don't go.*

The clock displayed 12:31. "Okay, but I'm definitely leaving at one."

"Absolutely. You need your sleep."

We talked about nothing and everything. 12:49 my hand adjusted between her legs. *If she's going to leave, she'll stop me.* We had sex again. Tender. Intimate.

"Jon, I need to go," she said, as the clock changed to 2:04. "I want to stay, really. I want to, but I've got to get some sleep."

"I'll let you sleep." *No, I won't.*

"No, you won't."

"Stay anyway." I took her hand as she got out of bed.

"I can't. I'll be a mess if I don't sleep and I have to do well on this final. I'm sorry." *Me, too.*

"I'm having a New Year's Eve party at my mom's in Tacoma, if you're interested," I said. "People are spending the night, so no one has to drive. You should come."

"Sounds like fun," she said. "But what about you and Danielle?"

You know about Danielle and slept with me anyway? You're the coolest. "We're taking some time off and seeing other people. She's not in the picture right now." *Only you.*

She wrote her phone number down and put it on the dresser. Dressed, Britney kissed me. Still naked, I tried to pull her back to the bed.

"Stop that. I'll see you tomorrow."

#　#　#

Each time someone entered the dining hall at lunch the next day, I looked up. After nearly an hour and a half of watching the entryway, around one o'clock, Britney came in with her friend, Hillary, and sat at another table. *Thank God. Don't want to talk to Hillary.*

Hillary ate quickly and left, leaving Britney gathering her things. I waited for her near the exit.

74

"When are you heading home?" I asked as we got outside. *Spend the night with me.*

"About four."

Dammit.

"You?" she asked.

"Friday. I usually stick around until I have to leave," I said. "I'll give you a call so we can figure out New Year's."

"You better," continuing to walk toward her room in Nash Hall.

"Oh, I will," breaking off from her, continuing to Mathes.

A knock on my door at 4:30. *Britney found another ride?*

Danielle stood in front of me, sullen faced, a couple of wrapped presents in her hands.

"Oh, Danielle. What's going on?" *Are those for me?*

"I had a couple presents for you and I wanted you to have them," she said. She held the gifts out to me, neither bigger than a paperback.

Taking them, "Thanks. I haven't gotten you anything yet." *Not planning on it.*

"That's okay," she said. "I found these over Thanksgiving and well, they're for you, so…" She stopped. "I was hoping we could talk for a couple minutes."

You going to cry at me? "Sure. C'mon in."

The bed wasn't made. *No crusties.* Danielle sat on one of the uncomfortable, barely padded desk chairs. I straightened the bed before I sat, facing her.

"I've been thinking about what you said," she began. "About how things are moving too fast and I think you're right."

I'm right?

Danielle continued, "I'd like to see how things go if we go slower."

"What do you mean when you say slower?" I asked.

"Well, I've know I've talked of us moving in together and what would happen with us later and who knows?"

Scares the shit out of me.

"I keep trying to figure things like that out and I'm going to try to stop," she said. "I want to focus more on what's going on with us now and let whatever happens happen."

That'd be perfect.

"Besides, I've really missed you."

"I've missed you too," I said. "Slow sounds good, Danielle."

"My parents are going to be here in an hour and I've still got some packing to do. Want to come down and say hi?"

No. Wait. Why weren't you Britney? "All right."

Her mom greeted me warmly from the passenger's seat. Her step-father, Walter, nodded. Her sisters, Madeleine and Opal, snickered in the backseat.

Did she tell them we were taking a break? They don't act like anything's wrong.

Danielle hugged me tightly after I lifted her suitcase into the trunk. "I'll call you," she whispered.

What about Britney?

# # #

Danielle greeted me at the door of her house in Vancouver on Tuesday the following week. "You got anything else in your car?" Walter, Danielle's step-father, asked.

"Nope, that's it," I said, setting my bag next to the door.

"Well, let's make sure," he said, walking outside.

Walter took on a serious expression. "I know you and Danielle have been having a difficult time and I understand these things happen."

She told you?

"I hope you can keep any disagreements private."

"That won't be a problem," I said. "We don't fight, we just..."

"I don't need to know," Walter interrupted. "Also, while I'm sure you two are intimate, it's not okay for you to sleep in Danielle's room while you're here. There's her sisters to consider. I know you'll understand better when you're a father."

"Honestly, Walter, I don't need to be a father to know where you're coming from. I'm fine wherever." *Except for the morning wood issue.*

"Good. I'm glad we're on the same page," he stated. "Let's get back inside before the girls think I'm clubbing you with a tire iron."

# # #

Poking my head out of the bathroom with a towel around me, "Danielle? You got any gel I can borrow?"

From downstairs, "Should be some in the other bathroom!"

"Can you grab it for me?" I called. "I left my clothes in my bag."

"No one else's here," she replied. "Go ahead."

Why'd they leave us alone? Gel in hand, "Where'd they go?"

"I didn't want to go shopping with them," Danielle said, traversing the stairs. "Wanted to spend some time with you."

"Oh. You taking a shower?"

"In a minute," she said. "You said you wanted to see my senior yearbook?"

"I do."

After flipping through her yearbook, our make out session fell from her bed to the floor. She scooted out of her pajama bottoms, stuffing them under her butt. "Did you bring any condoms?"

"Ten," I replied. "Better too many than not enough, right?"

"Did you think we'd have that much time alone?"

"I had no idea." *Stop now and you can still have Britney. Danielle looks so righteous naked. And she's here. Her family's awesome. And they like me. Britney was great. Want to see her again. But Danielle's here and she shaved her pussy.*

My tongue ran up the side of her left labia.

Britney's smoother. Must be natural.

# # #

Back in Tacoma, I waited a day to call Britney. I explained I'd spent a few days at Danielle's house and we were getting back together. "I kind of expected that," Britney said.

How could you? "Really?"

"You two didn't seem done."

You saw us? When did you see us?

"Will it still be okay to come to your New Year's Eve party? Hillary and I already made plans to come down."

"Absolutely. I'm not taking back an invitation. That'd be seriously uncool."

"Won't Danielle be pissed I'm there?"

"I haven't told her about us," I said. *Don't plan on telling her.* "Can we keep this to ourselves?"

"Yeah, yeah. I don't want to get you in trouble."

That's sweet. "Trouble? Danielle and I weren't together. But anyway..."

"She'd still be pissed," Britney said. "A friend of mine told me about a club in Seattle she thought I'd like. I was going to invite you to come with me..."

"Invite me then."

# # #

Danielle called Christmas Day, eventually asking if I'd like her to come to Tacoma for three days.

Hadn't considered it. "Hold on, I need to ask my mom about it."

Mary gave me an inquisitive look. I whispered, "It'd give you a chance to get to know each other." Into the phone, "Why don't you come up a couple days before the party and stay a couple days after?"

"I was thinking about coming up on the twenty seventh and leaving New Year's Day."

Not the twenty seventh. "I've got plans on the twenty seventh."

"What're you doing?"

Be vague. Maybe she won't ask. "Meeting up with some people in Seattle," I tried.

"Ezra?"

"No, some other friends."

"Oh. Who?"

Dammit. "Hillary's friend, Britney," I said, as dismissively as I could. "We've been hanging out the past couple weeks and we're meeting up to go dancing on the twenty seventh." Silence. "Britney and Hillary are going to be here for New Year's Eve, too." *See, friends. Friends.*

"I'll see if I can work with those dates and I'll call you tomorrow," Danielle said.

Mary looked over at me. "What's the plan?"

I explained the situation with Britney and Danielle. Mary rolled her eyes.

# # #

Danielle arrived late afternoon on the twenty-eighth. I recounted the story of getting lost in Bothell with Britney the night before. "Didn't have any idea where she lived," I spat. "Couldn't fucking believe it." *Friends. See, friends.*

"Hmm," was the extent of Danielle's comment on the subject. "Where should I put my bag?" she asked.

"My room's fine," I said. "My mom doesn't care if we sleep in the same bed."

78

"You're not going to join us tonight?" Danielle asked, filling a bowl with tortilla chips.

"No," Mary answered. "I'm sleeping at my friend's upstairs. I'll probably be in bed by ten. You guys aren't planning on burning down the apartment or anything?"

"Not planning on it," I said. "But you never know, do you? You'll be upstairs, you'll probably smell the smoke first."

Britney and Hillary knocked on the door. *Why are you here first?* "C'mon in."

"Hi, Jon," Hillary grunted. *Britney told you about us? Shit.*

"Should we bring our stuff in now?" Britney asked.

"Probably," I replied. "You can claim the extra room if you put your stuff in there first. Everyone else will have to take the living room floor. You need any help?"

"No," Britney said. "It's not that much."

Danielle assailed me with icy eyes when I stepped back in the kitchen.

I introduced the girls to my mother. "Can we help with anything?" Britney offered.

"Thanks, I think we're good," Mary said.

Been naked with all three of these girls in the last couple weeks. This was a bad idea.

Britney and Hillary took their bags to the extra room. "Not very social," Danielle muttered.

A knock on the door. *Thank God.*

Ezra, Neal and another creep, Flynn, burst in. "Where's the beer?" Flynn cried. He saw my mom standing in the kitchen. "Just kidding, Mrs. Sims."

Smiling, Mary said, "Beer's in the fridge, boys."

"I got dibs on Jon's bed," Ezra declared.

"I don't think so," Danielle said.

Neal went to the fridge and doled out beers to all. I asked Flynn, "I thought you were bringing a couple people."

"Yeah, well, Skip and the others went out last night and couldn't get out of bed before Neal came and got me."

"Skip?" I asked.

"My buddy, Vance," Flynn replied. "When we started skateboarding back in grade school, he would kind of hop instead of jump. Looked like he was skipping."

Mary pulled me aside. "Don't get too stupid." She then looked to the rest of the group. "And no one drives if they've been drinking."

Nods of agreement from all. "We shouldn't need to go out for anything," I said.

"You kids have a good night." My mom picked up her travel case, leaving to a chorus of good nights and thank you's from the group.

Several more creeps arrived, along with more food and alcohol.

After midnight, my supply of grocery store parking lot fireworks exhausted, Neal, Danielle and I sat on the couch, bullshitting. Britney stumbled over to us. "Can I sit here?"

Danielle, sitting next to Neal on the far side of the couch, got up. "Go ahead." As Britney fell into her spot, Danielle went to the kitchen.

"You okay?" Neal asked Britney.

Her head weaved, eyes at half-mast, Britney slurred, "Yeah, good."

"Maybe you don't need that beer," I suggested.

She pulled the bottle closer. "I like beer."

A creep who'd been watching Britney the entire night, made his way to the couch. "Scoot over," he said. The creep pushed his ass between Neal and Britney, a space of five inches or so.

"There's not room," Neal insisted.

"Sure there is," the creep replied, shoving Neal away from Britney.

Don't touch her.

Standing up, "Where'd Danielle head off to?" I asked no one in particular.

As Hillary exited the bathroom, "Can you keep an eye on Britney?" I asked. "I don't think she can fend off any unwanted advances."

"What?" Hillary replied. She looked over to the couch, the creep had his arm around a bobble-headed Britney. "Probably not," she said.

"You okay to do that?" I asked.

"Absolutely," she responded, straightening her posture.

Don't let the creep sleep with her tonight.

# # #

Morning, Ezra confronted me in the living room. "I've been through every cupboard. What kind of house doesn't have coffee?"

"My mom's," I replied. "Forgot to pick some up. Sorry."

"You sir, are a piece of shit," Ezra said. "Okay boys," he announced, turning to the rest of the creeps assembled on the deck, "we're off to get coffee."

Britney followed the boys, returning inside. "Thanks for having us over," she said. "Sorry I wasn't more social."

Did the creep get all over you? "As long as you had a good time," I said. "Thanks for coming. See you in a couple days."

While Britney retrieved her stuff, Hillary approached me. "Britney crashed hard last night," she said. "I tried to get her to the bedroom but she wasn't moving so we both slept out here. Nothing happened."

How would you know if you were asleep? "Thanks Hillary," I said. "I didn't want anyone taking advantage of the drunk girl."

January 1989 (College, Junior Year)

A week into the new quarter, still without a roommate, I pushed the two beds together in the middle of the room. "You're not getting anyone?" Danielle asked, returning to my room after class.

"It's been a week. I got to figure this quarter's good," I replied.

"I'm going to grab some stuff," she said, and left.

Moments after, Flynn strolled in. "What was Danielle all smiles about?" He noticed the new configuration of my room. "Never mind," he said. "I'm meeting Neal and Skip for some Ping Pong. We need a fourth, you coming?"

"Shit yeah," I answered. I wrote a quick note to Danielle, left the room unlocked and went to the Viking Union with Flynn.

"What's with you and that Gail girl?" Vance asked Flynn during a heated Ping Pong battle.

"Not much, any more," Flynn answered. "We hung out the beginning of the year but she kept staying in our room and wouldn't leave even after my roommate went to bed."

"She wanted you," I said.

"Of course she does," Flynn said. "But a man's got to sleep."

"A pussy of a man," I joked.

# # #

"My girlfriend's gynecologist started using Podophyllin on her," I said, unwrapping my dick from the vinegar soaked gauze. "Can we try that?"

Doc Smiley set the steaming thermos of liquid nitrogen on the rolling metal table. "I've found it to be too lightweight for guys.

"Another study suggested the surrounding area also contains the virus. So I'm going to be a little more generous with the nitrogen today."

Crap. "It's been six months now. We any closer to getting rid of these things?" I asked. "Not that I don't enjoy coming here."

Doc Smiley chuckled. "They're staying small," he said. "That's promising. We're starting to think the virus might never go away. Some people might be carriers who never show any symptoms, but pass the virus along anyway."

Maybe it wasn't the whore?

He marked three spots and brought out the cotton swab.

I interrupted his humming of an indecipherable show tune. "So I may never be rid of them?"

"Honestly don't know," he answered. "We could clear you up but you might end up being able to infect others." *Don't want to wear rubbers forever.*

"Go ahead and pull up. Oh, that's right, you want to wash up."

# # #

Tiana opened Danielle's door. *Almost forgotten about you. Still scrumptious.*

"Hey, Jon," Tiana said. "Danielle just woke up. C'mon in."

"How've you been?" I asked her. "Haven't seen you since we got back from break."

"Good. Same ol' really."

Danielle was on her bed, which had been set on the top of the dressers. "Can you rub my neck before we go to dinner?" she asked. "I slept on it funny." I climbed up, perched myself on Danielle's butt.

Grabbing a towel and toiletries, Tiana said, "I've got to get a shower before dinner."

You look delicious. The door closed, unlocked, behind her.

After a couple minutes, "How's that?" I asked Danielle.

"Better, thanks."

82

"We got a couple minutes, yeah?"

"Probably," Danielle answered.

Yanking Danielle's sweatpants to her knees, I entered her. *Tiana's naked. In the bathroom. Twenty feet away. Soap all over her wet body. Her tits, her ass. Running her hands across her body. Going to walk back in here, drop her towel, climb up here, join us.*

I came.

Wiped myself on my underwear, pulled up Danielle's pants, lifted her shirt, pressed my hands into her lower back. She fussed with her pants, staying on the bed.

Tiana returned. "I thought you guys would already be gone."

Still kind of hard. "Since I was already rubbing her shoulders, she figured I should do the rest of her back," I said. "You want to join us for dinner?"

"I'm going over to a friend's down on High Street for dinner tonight, but thanks."

"I'm starving," Danielle said.

"Can I be done now?" I asked.

April 1989 (College, Junior Year)

A knock on the door. "There's a seminar in the main lounge in a couple minutes," Neal said. "You guys want to come?"

Standing in the doorway, "Seminar?" I asked. "About what?"

"I don't know," Neal admitted. "Our RA told me she'd like it if some of us showed up because no one's been coming to them. It's only forty minutes long, so I told her I'd try to get some of the creeps to come down."

"We're not doing anything," Danielle said from behind me. Neal smirked.

"Crap."

By the time we got to the main lounge, there were no seats left. Neal and I pulled over a couch which had been repositioned to the side to create additional room around the presentation area.

Never would've missed us.

A dark haired gal put a large sign on the easel. I whispered to Neal, "Isn't our RA doing the seminar?"

"Guess not."

The sign read, "Date Rape."

This'll be fun.

The presenter began by giving the definition of rape. Continuing, "Let's look at the story of freshman, Chelsea. Chelsea was asked out by a guy in one of her classes. He was cute and during dinner he was nice and funny and a perfect gentleman at the end of the evening. The next time they went out, they went to the movies and held hands and when he dropped her off, they kissed good-night and that was it. On their third date, they went to a party where Chelsea had too much to drink and her date took her home and had sex with her. Because Chelsea was too intoxicated to give her consent for sex, this was rape.

"Date rape isn't limited to being unable to give consent, it is any time a person says no. If two people are in the middle of things getting hot and heavy and the woman says no, then it is the man's responsibility to stop." This statement caused hands to shoot up from the crowd.

"Before I answer any questions," the presenter said, "Let me say this; no always means no. It doesn't matter when it's said." All the hands went down. "I know a lot of guys have heard no sometimes means yes, but it doesn't.

"Also, simply because a woman does something once, doesn't mean she is giving permission for every time in the future."

Wait, what?

"A woman has the right to say no even if she's slept with the man before. Remember, she can say no at any point and if the man goes further, it is date rape."

What?!? Any point? Like before anything starts?

My hand lifted from my leg. *Don't ask.* My hand fell back down. Danielle looked straight ahead.

Does she think I raped her?

The presenter closed. A small group from the audience surrounded her but the majority walked away silently.

"I think we're going to hang out," I said to Neal when Danielle hadn't moved.

Almost alone in the main lounge now, I got down on one knee next to Danielle. "Well, what did you think about all that?" I asked. *You never said no after we started.*

"I...uh...I don't know..." tears welling up in her eyes.

"Danielle, I'm sorry."

Her tears came. "I never thought of it like that," she whispered.

"What are we going to do?" *Tell me to fuck off. Call the police, have me arrested.*

"I'm going to go," she said, standing up.

I'm going to jail. Should I let Mary know? Shit, I'm going to jail. Maybe we'll just break up. If we break up, she'll going to press charges. Convince her not to break up.

After dinner, I went to Danielle's room. Her expression blank as she stood in the doorway. "I've been thinking," she said.

"Kind of figured," I responded.

"I don't know what I want to do."

Leave the police out of it?

"I can't stand the thought of breaking up with you but I can't see you for a while," she said.

"All right," I said. "You know where I am." She closed the door.

#   #   #

The next afternoon I answered the knock on my door. Danielle stood there. *This can't be good.* "You want to come in?" I asked.

"I thought about it all night," she began, following me inside.

You can't stand the sight of me.

"And I decided I'm happier with you than without you, and I'd rather be happy."

I'd rather not go to jail. "So, um, how do you want to go about things?" I asked.

"I thought about that too," she said. "I want to take it easy for a while."

"I totally understand."

"I'm going to sleep in my room for a while. You know, until I get okay with everything again."

"Okay," I nodded. *Whatever you want.*

We stood, motionless, looking at each other. A second passed. Then two. She hugged me. "You already had lunch?" she asked.

"Yeah."

"I'm going to head up there before they close," she said.

#   #   #

After shooting the shit the next night in Ezra's room, Danielle walked down the hallway with me to my door. I put my key in the lock. "G'night Danielle." I gave her a quick peck.

"You could invite me in," she said. *What happened to sleeping in your own room?*

"You're always welcome here," I replied. She shut the door behind us.

May 1989 (College, Junior Year)

"You figured out your living situation for next year?" I asked Danielle. *Talked to those friends of yours I've never met?*

"Not yet," she answered. "One gal isn't sure she's going to be coming back next year. The others got a house together and don't have room for another."

"What's your plan?" *Back to the dorm? With who?*

"I was going to wait and see a while longer."

"We could get a place," I offered. Danielle looked at me curiously. "Doesn't make much sense paying rent in two apartments when we spend most of our time together."

"Guess not," she agreed. "I didn't bring it up because I thought you wanted to go slow." *You've been living in my room for the past three months.*

"That was then," I said.

"I don't know if my parents will let me." *Won't let you? Can't you make your own choices?*

"Why not?"

"They might think I'm too young to move in with my boyfriend."

"Couldn't you do it without their permission?"

"Not if I want them to keep paying for school."

"Why don't you ask and see what they say?"

#   #   #

Danielle and I signed a year lease for an apartment on Forest Street, a block off campus, at the bottom of the hill below Nash Hall.

The two bedroom's front door opened onto a walkway which would overlook Bellingham Bay had it been on the third floor instead of the second. The carpet was a short cut, patterned green wall to wall, years of stains scattered on it. The appliances matched the carpet and while not new, appeared in good shape. Hook ups for a washer and drier plus large bedroom closets.

On the way back up the hill back to Mathes, Danielle said, "I hope my parents will put up the extra money for the deposit. Don't think they were expecting to pay rent in June, either."

"I might be able to cover it," I offered.

June 1989 (College, Junior Year)

After Danielle's parents and my mother had dropped off kitchen stuff, towels, sheets and other beginning household necessities our first weekend in the new apartment, Danielle laid next to me in bed. "They want me to get a job for the summer since they were expecting me at home this summer."

"Got anything in mind?" I asked.

"Not really," she admitted. "Dairy Queen would probably hire me if I can't find anything else."

So would Burger King. "Most jobs on campus are probably already gone but SAGA always has something. I could talk to my manager," I offered.

"I'm not working at SAGA," she declared.

You disappointed I do? "You wouldn't need a car. No insurance, no gas." *We could work together.* "Free food. If you worked dinners, we could work together. C'mon, serving food to college kids has got to be better than dealing with the public."

"I'd rather work at Dairy Queen. They pay better and I could work full time there."

"You don't know that."

"I'll have to, in order to afford rent and everything else. I'd never be able to get enough hours at SAGA unless I worked every shift and I'm not doing that."

#   #   #

"There's a new treatment I've been reading about," Doc Smiley began. "Seems to be working well in the trials but hasn't been approved as a standard treatment so your insurance might not cover it."

You cut my dick off?

"Interferon injections twice a week until you're cleared up."

More injections? Christ.

"Why don't you check with your insurance and see if we can give it a try? It's pricey so we won't want to try it if they're not going to cover it."

"Injections, huh?"

"After all this," he pointed out, "a couple needle pricks shouldn't phase you."

"Probably not."

"Is your girlfriend still clear?"

"Far as we can tell," I said.

# # #

"I got you a present," I told Danielle while grocery shopping at Fred Meyer's.

"What?"

"I'll give it to you when we get home."

"Tell me," she whined.

"It's a surprise."

Before we started putting the groceries away, "What is it?"

"I didn't wrap it or anything, so close your eyes." I retrieved the black bag from the bedroom and handed it to her. "Open your eyes."

She pulled out the hard plastic phallus. "A vibrator?"

"Yeah. I thought it'd be fun to try out. And when you're here in the afternoons, it'll give you something to do."

"I'm looking for a job," she said.

"I know you are," I assured her. "Want to go try it out?" *Want to see you come.*

She hesitated. "Uh, maybe later."

That's no.

# # #

The next morning, Sunday, Danielle let me run the vibrator over her. "Oh God! It tickles!" I took it away. "No, here. Hold it here."

"You want me to move it around at all?" I asked, the white plastic above her clit.

"Maybe a little to the sides. Slowly. Yeah, like that."

Five minutes later, she came.

"What's it like?" I asked, after I'd finished off inside her.

"Pretty cool. Don't know how to describe it."

"You'll use it again?"

"Yeah, probably."

"By yourself?"

"Maybe. I told you, I don't think about sex when I'm alone."

How can you not?

"Oh, my family's going to Sun River the third week in August and Walter wants you to join us."

Why? "Where's Sun River?"

"Down in Oregon. Takes about four hours to get there from Vancouver. There's all sorts of bike trails, tennis, swimming. We always have a good time."

"I'll pass on the swimming."

"But you'll come to the pool with me, won't you?"

To see the hotties in bikinis. "I guess."

August 1989 (College, Senior Year 1)

Ezra and I had brought a soccer ball with us to Forest Street Park, two blocks away from my apartment. "Danielle closing tonight?" Ezra asked me, as I laced up my cleats.

"Off at seven," I answered.

"You've been in a funk, Jon. What's going on?"

"Shit," I shrugged. "I guess I hoped that being on vacation with Danielle would kind of mellow things between us. Sixteen hours in the car together and we barely talked."

"Why do you think that is?" he asked. "You guys act all right when I stop by."

"When people are around, everything's dandy but when we're alone, it's like there's nothing to talk about. Or have sex about. Didn't fuck once at Sun River. Aren't you supposed to screw on vacations?"

He passed the ball back to me. "Were her parents in the way?"

"She was always near them," I said. "Or her sisters. The only time we were alone was in bed. And we just slept."

"Besides that, how's the sex?"

"Barely there. We had sex two weeks ago. And a couple weeks before that. Once."

"You asked her about it?"

"What? Like, why don't you fuck me anymore?"

"Essentially, yeah," Ezra replied. "Nothing's going to change if you don't say anything."

Don't want to talk about it. "But I'll be the horny asshole boyfriend who wants to fuck all the time." *And she thinks I raped her.*

"Well, do you?"

"The shots don't fuck up my dick so I'm pretty much good to go all the time and once every couple weeks ain't cutting it."

"Ask her if she's happy with your sex life and see what she says," he suggested. "When she asks if you are, tell her you'd like to..."

"Fuck like crazed weasels?"

"Yeah."

When I walked into our apartment, Danielle stood over the stove. "How's Ezra?"

"Good," I replied. I began to fill a pot with water.

"Really? Mac and cheese, again?"

"Food of the Gods," I replied. *Ask her.* "Danielle? You okay with our sex life these days?"

She regarded me for a few seconds. "Yeah, aren't you?"

Not at all. "Well, I'd be all right if we had sex more often." *Like every day.*

"Aren't the shots hurting you?"

"Not like the liquid nitrogen. I've been fine later in the day."

"Oh," she turned back to the stove. "I thought you didn't want to do anything because you were sore. You haven't seemed that interested."

"I'm plenty interested," I said.

Danielle took her plate into the living room then turned on the television.

After dinner, Danielle kissed me. "I've got to get up early to do laundry, so I'm going to bed."

You want me to join you? Say you do. "Good night." *Guess not.*

A couple hours later I cuddled next to her, running my hand down her back to her butt. She didn't move. *Can't consent if she's asleep.* I flipped to my other side.

September 1989 (College, Senior Year 1)

"What're you going to do in the fall?" Hunter asked.

"Pick up shifts at SAGA, I guess," I moaned. "I got to quit working there."

"But you're so good at it," Hunter joked.

Once Ezra stopped sputtering his beer, "You should talk to Seth about getting on with the sound guys at the Viking Union."

"That'd kick ass," I said. *Love to be a sound guy.*

Hunter's girlfriend along with a couple gals came into the living room. "We're going to the library, so you guys can continue being as loud as you want."

"We could keep it down," Hunter said.

"That's okay," she replied. "We've got to find a few things before we can do anything else."

At the apartment, Seth's number in hand, I asked Danielle, "You going to stay at Dairy Queen after classes start?"

"Hell no," she said. "My parents hadn't budgeted for me to pay rent year round." *Lucky.* "You going to call Seth?"

The clock read 8.45. "It's late. I'll call him from work tomorrow." *You want to get naked? Give me a signal. A kiss? Anything? It's early.*

"Can you clean the bathroom?" Danielle asked. "I got to start some laundry and finish the dishes but the toilet's nasting me out."

#   #   #

The apartment was empty when I returned after lunch the first day of classes. *She's finished at one. Where's Danielle? Her car's still here, must still be on campus.*

Light from the television shone through the curtains of our apartment when I returned later that evening. *Where've you been?*

"Where've you been?" Danielle asked, while I took off my shoes.

"Tech crew meeting," I said. "I was home this afternoon, was going to let you know then."

"I ran into Flynn and Vance on my way back from class. We went over to the music listening room for a while."

Four hours?

"You could have left a note."

"Sorry," I said. "I figured I'd run into you on my way to class. You got homework?"

"I finished it up in the VU," she answered. "Can you tell me when you're going to be late like this? I was going to cook dinner for us, but when you weren't home at six thirty, I made myself a sandwich."

"I will. You remember I've got that five o'clock English class Mondays and Wednesdays, right?"

"That's right. I forgot."

#   #   #

Late Saturday afternoon, "What're you going to do tonight?" I asked Danielle. *Sit and home and wait for me? Be naked on the couch with the vibrator when I walk in?*

"I'm going up to Gail's for a while."

Gail? "Which Gail?"

"Flynn's old girlfriend," Danielle replied.

"What're you guys doing?"

"Maybe go over to a party in Kappa."

You're going to a party without me? "When would you head over?" I asked.

"Not sure. We'll leave a note on Gail's door where it is, so you can find us. She's in nine-oh-one Mathes."

"I can't get in without a key," I pointed out.

"Someone will let you in," Danielle said.

After working my first volleyball match as a sound guy, I stood outside the main doors of Mathes Hall for five minutes until a gal walking through the main lounge let me in. At room 901, the white board on the door was blank. *Doesn't help.* I knocked. No answer. Again. Nothing. *Seriously uncool, Danielle.*

Laughter in the stairwell, then Vance, Gail and Danielle giggling onto the ninth floor, all smiles. "Hey Jon," Vance said. "What's new?"

"Spinning tunes at a volleyball game. About it."

"How'd it go?" Danielle asked, as the four of us entered Gail's room.

"Got a compliment from one of the officials, so not too bad. You guys heading up to Kappa now?"

Gail snorted. "Naw, we were just up there, it's dead."

"What're you going to do now?" I asked.

"Looks like nothing," Gail replied.

Danielle shrugged, looked at me, "Let's go home."

"Stop by and have lunch with me after my shift tomorrow," I suggested to Danielle, as we walked down the hill to our apartment.

"I told Flynn and Vance I'd meet them over in the gallery after my one o'clock."

"They won't care if you skip out."

"Eh," she hesitated. "I told them I'd show up. Besides, you know I hate SAGA food."

October 1989 (College, Senior Year 1)

Every corner of Hunter's living room was filled with people so Ezra and I made our way downstairs to a rec room where Hunter and his roommate had also put a couch, a television and extra beer. "Danielle went to the show without you?" Ezra asked me.

"I came here without her," I said. "Same thing."

Kirstie, a friend of Hunter's, walked in. "Hey you two," Kirstie started. "Why aren't you upstairs having fun?"

"Just got here," I said. Kirstie stumbled, plopped down on the couch, then burst into laughter.

"Is she okay?" Ezra whispered to Hunter, who'd followed her downstairs.

"Started early," he replied.

"What're you watching?" Kirstie asked, too loudly.

"Drag racing," Ezra answered.

Hunter, "Come out to the garage. I put up a heavy bag yesterday."

"Is your girlfriend here tonight? I so want to meet her," Kirstie asked me. "Why doesn't she ever come over here?"

Ezra got up from the couch. "Let's see it. You coming, Jon?"

"Go ahead."

Hunter and Ezra exited through a door at the back of the room.

"She doesn't hate Hunter, does she? Who could hate Hunter? He's such a sweetie. Didn't you guys go to high school together?"

Kirstie jumped onto my lap, kissing me frantically, sloppily. *You taste like blue.* I kissed her back. Our tongues pressed into each other's mouths.

"I've got to tell Hunter something," she declared. Kirstie pushed herself up.

Should I wait here? That was an okay kiss. She'll come back. Should I kiss her again? I don't want to kiss her again. She kissed me. Wouldn't be happening if Danielle would've come with me.

I waited ten minutes. *She's not coming back. Shouldn't kiss her again. Danielle's going to be pissed if she finds out. How could she find out? She's never met Kirstie. Ezra wouldn't say anything. Hunter might, but probably not. Not going to say anything to anyone.*

Where's Kirstie?

Upstairs, twenty minutes later I casually asked a friend of Kirstie's if she'd gone home. "She was in the bathroom throwing up, last I saw her."

She's that drunk?

*What if Kirstie calls tomorrow and Danielle answers?
Maybe if I tell Danielle someone kissed me, she'd get jealous and
want to spend more time with me. Or she could tell me to fuck off.
Don't want to be with Kirstie.*

# # #

When Danielle closed the bathroom door the next morning,
I got Kirstie's number from Hunter. The shower still running, I
called Kirstie. "Hi, Kirstie, it's Jon." Pause. "Hunter's friend."

"Oh, hi, Jon. Sorry, just woke up. What's new?"

"Wondering how you were doing today. You were kind of
goofy last night. Thought I'd check and see how you were holding
up." *And if you're going to start calling me.*

"You were there last night?" she said. "Really? I don't
remember seeing you there at all."

You don't? "Yeah, you'd had a few by the time I got there,"
I said. "But you got home okay, apparently."

"Hunter's girlfriend brought me home," she said. "I
remember that. You were there? Did we talk? Did I say something
stupid?"

"No," I lied. "You were silly. I laughed at you a couple
times, and until you fell asleep on the couch, you were the life of
the party."

"Oh God, I fell asleep on the couch? I'm going to have to
call Hunter and apologize. It must've been the shots we were
doing."

As long as you don't remember mounting me.

The shower stopped.

"Well, glad to hear you're all right. I should get to studying.
See you soon, I'm sure."

"Yeah. And thanks for calling. That was sweet of you."

Not really. "Bye." I hung up, turned the television on and
sat on the couch.

Danielle opened the door of the bathroom. "Who was on
the phone?"

"Nobody," I said. "I wasn't on the phone."

"I heard you talking to someone."

"I wasn't on the phone."

"Yes, you were. You were saying goodbye to someone."

How could you tell what I was saying? "I couldn't have
been," I protested. "Did you hear the phone ring?"

"No," Danielle, stone-faced.

"Well, I didn't call anyone," I tried.

"Tell me who you were talking to."

"No one."

She sighed, went to the bedroom and finished getting dressed. She asked me about the phone call again. I continued to deny it, suggesting she heard the television. "It wasn't the TV," she said. "Why won't you tell me who you were talking to?"

"Because I wasn't talking to anyone."

"Fine. If you're not going to tell me…" and didn't finish her thought.

# # #

Danielle was in bed, already asleep when I lumbered in after finishing up a lengthy show at the Viking Union. Naked, I climbed in next to her. She rolled to face me when I pulled the blanket up and whispered, "Are you my Skippy?"

Am I Skippy? You mean Vance, Skip? What the fuck? "What did you say?" I asked.

"Are you my Skippy?" she repeated, running her hand across my face.

"No, I'm not your Skippy," I insisted. "I don't like that nickname at all."

She mumbled, "I like it."

"Uh-huh." *Vance? Naw, he's so, odd.*

# # #

"What's with the whole Skippy thing last night?" I asked, when we met in the bathroom in the morning.

"The what?" she asked, continuing to the kitchen.

"You asked me if I was your Skippy when I came to bed last night."

"Really?" she asked, opening the refrigerator. "I don't remember saying that."

"Where'd it come from?"

"I don't know. Maybe the neighbor kid from Family Ties," she answered. "We used to watch it all the time."

"Oh." *Bullshit.*

Stumbling back to the table at Denny's Saturday morning, I fought off my severe hangover nausea as Ezra, Danielle, Vance and Flynn finished breakfast.

Only an hour and half to Seattle. Can do that. Never play quarters with rum and Coke again. Only an hour and a half. There's no way.

"I can't make it, Danielle," I said, on the way to the parking lot. "You're going to have to take me home."

"What? You aren't coming?" she asked.

"No. There's no way I'll last that long in a car. And I don't want to feel like this once I'm there."

"Fuck Jon, you made it here," Danielle hissed.

"Barely."

"We're right next to the freeway," she continued. "I can't believe you want me to take you back across town."

"Danielle, I feel like shit, I want to suffer at home." I turned to Ezra. "Will you please take me home?"

As Ezra opened his mouth, "But I'm following Ezra to Neal's," Danielle said.

"I know, but if you won't take me..."

"Fine." Vance got in Ezra's car.

Danielle didn't say a word on the drive home, except, "Hope you feel better," when I unfastened my seatbelt.

"Thanks. Have a good time."

Why won't you stay here with me?

On the couch dozing to TV, under a blanket, cycling between nausea and hunger. *She's probably fucking Vance right now. That's why she went without me. Went outside and hid somewhere.*

Danielle opened the front door at 2:06am. Still on the couch, I started awake. "Wasn't expecting you back so early."

"Things wound down around midnight. We got there early, so I was ready to go," she said.

"And you had a good time?"

"Oh, yeah." She went on to describe the costumes and a couple of other people's activities.

What did you and Vance do? Where were you two holed up all night?

96

November 1989 (College, Senior Year 1)

Thursday afternoon, Danielle standing at the dryer folding clothes. "Wasn't expecting to see you here in the middle of the day," I said.

"I was hoping to catch you before you went off to work," she started.

Don't like the sound of this.

"You got a minute?"

"I'm free the rest of the evening," I replied.

"We've been having a tough time," she began. "I know I haven't been helping by staying on campus so much, but I've been trying to figure out what to do about what's going on with you and me."

Nothing's been going on between you and me. Unless Gail convinced you to press charges.

"I think we got into things too fast," she continued. "I mean, I thought I was ready to live with someone, but I'm not."

What're you saying?

"Gail isn't going to have a roommate next quarter, so I'm going to move in with her," Danielle declared. "Until then I'm going to sleep in the extra bedroom."

You're breaking up with me?

She continued folding clothes.

"Why don't you move in with her now?" I asked. *You're breaking up with me?*

"They won't let me move in until the new quarter, plus it'll give you time to find someone to take over my half of the lease. I'm going to take some stuff up to Gail's so I can stay up there if it gets too late or anything."

"But you're going to pay your half of December rent and stuff, right?"

"I hope you're going to find someone to move in by then," she answered.

"How the fuck am I going to find someone to move in during Finals?" *You've lost your fucking mind.*

She paused. "Yeah, I guess you're right."

Yeah, I'm right.

"My parents will probably cover stuff here in December. I haven't asked them about it."

You've already talked to Gail and your parents but not me? You made this decision without talking to me about it, at all? Don't want to try to work things out? Talk to me? Anything?

Danielle took the laundry basket to our bedroom. I followed. Her suitcase was open on the floor, already full.

"Is this because of Vance?" *You're fucking him, aren't you?*

"It's about us, Jon," she said. "Vance and I are friends."

Sure you are. Why did you call me his name when you were asleep? "Then why are you doing this? We haven't talked about any of this."

She put clothes from the laundry basket into the suitcase. "That's part of the problem," she said.

"And what's the rest?" *Vance?*

She looked up from the suitcase. "You don't show me you love me."

Don't show you? What are you talking about?

She zipped the suitcase. "I'm going to stay at Gail's tonight," she said.

"So this is it, then?" I asked.

"I don't know, Jon," she said. "I don't know what I want right now. I do know I'm not happy the way things are with us so I'm doing something about it. I think it's best."

Why did you move in with me? This was what you wanted, isn't it? What am I supposed to do now?

Alone in the apartment, I called Mary. "I don't get the show her part," I admitted, after describing our conversation. "I tell her I love her, I'm here for her. She wants more than that?"

Mary didn't hesitate. "Women like men to do things for them so they know you're thinking about them. Making dinner, backrubs, something you see at the store you know she'd like. Not only on Valentine's Day, birthdays, Christmas."

"She wants more presents?"

"That's not what I'm saying," Mary said. "Anything showing her you're thinking of her. What about something you know she likes and surprise her with it?"

"Should I even bother, though? She's already moving out."

"But she hasn't yet," my mother said. "If she's still spends time at the apartment when you're there, she could change her mind."

I can fix this?

After I got off the phone, I went to the grocery store. *What does Danielle like? Chocolate.*

I bought Danielle a Hershey's bar.

# # #

Late Saturday evening when I got back from a gig, the door to the spare bedroom was closed. A faint knock. No answer. Cautiously, I opened the door to find Danielle still asleep.

I took the Hershey's bar from the kitchen and left it on the bathroom counter.

# # #

When I went to the bathroom late the next morning, the Hershey's bar was gone and there was a note taped to the mirror,

Thanks for the chocolate.

That didn't help.

# # #

Thursday night I went to see Danielle at Gail's room but she wasn't there. Gail invited me in. "She was going to the library," Gail said. "Sometimes she goes up to the Ridge to study afterward. One of the girls in her biology class lives right there."

Gail and I talked for half an hour.

Where's Danielle? "I think it's good Danielle's moving in with you," I said. "We kind of rushed into moving in together. I keep forgetting Danielle's still young and finding herself and what she wants to do."

On her bed, Gail sat silent.

I continued, "After she's had some time on her own, we'll probably get another place."

With her eyes on the floor, Gail said, "I don't know how to tell you this Jon, but well, I don't think Danielle's looking to get back together."

We were moving too fast. "Uh, okay." I said. "She's said there's still a chance..."

"Well, I don't know anything for sure, but most of the nights she's been here, Vance has spent the night too."

My mouth opened but nothing came out.

"I don't know what they've been doing, but it sure sounded like they were having sex," Gail said.

They couldn't've been having sex. She said they were friends. "I've asked her more than once. She said they weren't fucking."

"I'm sure they were, Jon. I was here." She climbed down from her bunk. "They've been sleeping together for about a month or so."

"A month..." I whispered. "Bitch."

"I'm going to run to the bathroom real quick," she said. "You okay 'til I get back?"

She must see the tears in my eyes.

"Yeah, I'm good."

When the door closed, I found a mix tape I'd made Danielle the prior spring, pulled it out, broke it, then wound it back into the cassette. *Tape deck ate it.*

# # #

Seth, my boss with the Tech Crew, strode into the dining area at the Viking Union, pizza and pop in hand. He sat down next to Porter at a round table near the center of the room. "Where you been?" I asked him.

A smirk. "Christening the equipment closet."

"Eww," Porter, the building manager for the student union, exclaimed.

"Which one?" I asked.

"Next to the main lounge," Seth replied.

"You didn't leave used rubbers everywhere, did you?"

"I have to work in there too," Seth answered. "Something about the risk of getting caught makes an orgasm better."

"Yeah," I said. "But I don't think there's such a thing as a bad orgasm." Seth and Porter allowed me to continue. "I mean, really. On a scale of one to ten, the worst orgasm you've ever had is still at least a five. Even by yourself."

"If the worst orgasm is a five," Porter began, "then what's a ten? Coming with someone you love?"

"Uh," I paused. "No. Because I can have an earth-shattering orgasm with someone I don't know, much less love."

Seth, "I think we're looking strictly at the physical response. Leave emotions out of it."

"Okay," Porter said. "Based on that then, is it amount of jism or distance or what?"

"If the scale works for both genders, then it can't include come," I said. "Simply how your body responds. Like, you ever get the trembly legs after you come?" They both nodded. "But not every time, right?"

"No," Seth said. "Hasn't happened in a while."

"There was one time I couldn't move after I came," Porter said. "I tried but I couldn't. That had to be a ten."

I want one of those. "How long did it take you to recover?"

"Thirty seconds. Maybe a minute."

"You think you could have a better orgasm than that one?" I asked.

Porter said, "Maybe."

"How about a ten is unable to move for five minutes after? Physically incapable of moving."

"And five is like, 'Yeah, I came,'" Seth suggested.

"Like the Richter Scale," Porter said. "The difference in numbers is a factor of ten. Not being able to move would translate into what? A nine point five or so?"

"Something like that."

#   #   #

Gail answered when I called her room Saturday morning at nine. "Sorry, Jon, she didn't stay here last night. She's probably down in Vance's room."

I ran up the hill to Mathes Hall to Vance's room at the end of the hall on the second floor. I knocked. A couple times. A couple times more, each stronger than the last. I pressed my ear to the door.

Is that a girl's voice? I kept listening. The sound of wood.

Across the hallway, six feet from Vance's door, I stretched out on the large windowsill, the morning sun pouring over me.

Why did you lie? A month? Why Vance? Weren't you the one talking about marriage? I'll do better.

My stomach growled.

Go home and eat. Call Danielle later and ask her. Maybe Gail was wrong. Go home. Leave. What if she isn't here and Vance comes out? What am I going to say to him?

I closed my eyes. *Leave.*

I opened my eyes and got down from the window. A door opened. Two doors down, a gal walked into the hall.

I've got to know. I'll stay here all fucking day. If she's in his room, I'll kill her. Not kill, slap. Not slap, punch. In the mouth. Fucking Vance?

She has to come out some time. What if she left while I was coming up the hill? She'll deny she was here. She could've fallen asleep up on the Ridge with that girl from her biology class.

Returning to Vance's door, no music. No shuffling of feet. No groans of ecstasy. Nothing.

No one's here. Vance's going to walk down the hall, see me sitting here and laugh. Tell him I stopped by to borrow some music and figured I'd wait until he got back from breakfast. The sun's warm. Why go back down the hill since I'm already here. This is stupid, leave. No one here. Get up, go home and eat. I'm starving. Do I have enough milk for cereal? What cereal do I have? Cereal's going to taste good.

The click of a door. Danielle backed into the hallway from Vance's room, finishing a conversation. She turned, closing the door behind her.

"Danielle," I said. She spun to me, mouth agape. "Why did you lie to me?" My voice cracked, "Why did I find out like this?"

"Jon, I..."

"What?" I yelled. "You what?!? I fucking asked, you said you were friends!"

"We were, it just got to be more."

"I see that!" I stormed through the fire escape door. "Fuck off!"

Danielle called at 1:43. "Jon. Hey, look, I'm sorry about everything."

Fuck you. "When are you going to come get the rest of your shit?"

"I can come down tomorrow. Is there a time that works for you?"

"I don't plan on being here," I said.

"Yeah, I understand. Does one work for you?"

"Sure," trying not to yell.

"I really want to tal..."

You don't get to. "Got to go." And I hung up.

I called Isaac, filling him in on what had happened since I'd written last. "Damn Jon, that sucks. Sorry," he said.

"Thanks, man."

"You think she's trying to get you back for Britney?"

That was forever ago. "I don't think so, but maybe...if she found out, I could see where she'd be pissed about that. Or maybe the bullshit with Kirstie?"

"The phone call wasn't your best idea."

"I know that now."

"Are you guys done for sure?"

"Sure feels like it," I said. "But I'd be okay getting back together with her. We're even on the sleeping around now, so we could start again, square."

# # #

The next afternoon, Danielle's stuff was gone. I looked through the kitchen and the bedroom. *Like she was never here.* The spare bedroom's dresser held nylons, two bras, socks. *Why would she leave this?*

I called her. "When are you getting the rest of your stuff?"

"I was hoping you would let me keep it there until Walter can make it up."

"When's that going to be?"

"After finals?" she asked.

"I guess." *If she's leaving stuff here, she must want to see me again.*

"Oh, did I leave a bunch of nylons in that dresser?" she asked.

"Yeah, I wondered about those."

"Could I come by Saturday morning sometime and grab them?"

"You still have a key," I said.

"But I should ask."

December 1989 (College, Senior Year 1)

The front door squeaked open at 9:08am, Saturday.

Danielle? Shit. Miranda's in bed with me. She won't believe nothing happened. We'll never get back together. She's going in the spare bedroom. She wouldn't come in here. Why would she?

Another door opened. *Spare bedroom? She won't come in here.* I watched the bedroom door. It opened. I closed my eyes.

Shit. Shit. Shit. No, this is good. She'll realize how jealous she is with me fucking someone else and want to get back together. Perfect.

The bedroom door closed.

Danielle, make a scene. Start crying. Beg me to forgive you. Take you back.

The front door opened and closed. *She's going to come running back to me.*

"Thanks for coming up guys," I said, hugging Isaac at the front door at 11:34am. "That was a great time."

"Yeah, man," Isaac replied. "You get another kick ass foggy night like that again, let me know so we can bring Miranda a big fluffy coat."

"Go to hell, Isaac," Miranda said. "Good to see you, Jon. See you in a couple weeks, yeah?"

"Absolutely."

#   #   #

Danielle called the next day. "Hey, why didn't you stop by yesterday?" I asked, unable to suppress a grin.

"I did," she said. "Who was in bed with you?"

"Oh, Isaac and Miranda came up to play in the fog. Why didn't you say anything while you were here?"

"I got upset when I saw you in bed with someone else."

Sweet. I swallowed a laugh.

"I just left," she continued. "I didn't think it would upset me, but it did."

Good. Hope you cried all night. "Sorry."

"Did you sleep with her?"

Lie. Make her suffer. "No," I admitted. "Our bed's bigger so she crashed in here. You need to come by and grab those nylons?"

"No, I saw Isaac in the spare room and was going to wake you and tell you I stopped by but...no, I got them."

You did? You don't have to come back? "Okay."

"Well, I got to go. Bye."

She's going to realize how much she misses me and doesn't want me to be with other people. And since I didn't sleep with Miranda, she can't hold anything over my head.

#   #   #

"Ran into Parker at a club last night," Isaac said a couple minutes into our call. "She asked about you. Said you should call her."

Parker? The uber-hot ballerina from high school asked about me? "What's she up to?" I asked. "Been over a year since I've seen her. When we were at that club downtown. You get her number?"

"Don't I always have your back?"

# # #

The next day I called her. "Parker? Hey. It's Jon."

"About time you called me," Parker replied. "You said you'd write back and you never did, schmuck."

"Yeah, but I told you I'm not too good about writing."

"Isaac says you write him these huge ten page letters and come down and see him. You don't come down to see me."

I would. "Yeah, well," I stumbled. "I, uh..."

"Kidding, Jon," Parker said. "But you could come down and see me. It'd be good to catch up."

"You could come up here. I got nothing going on next week. Could show you around my little corner of Washington."

"I don't know if my car could make the trip," she said. "But if you've got all this free time, you should swing by."

# # #

Parker's door opened from the community hallway on the tenth floor of a downtown Seattle high-rise into a tiled, four by five space with the kitchen immediately to the left and the living area straight ahead.

Is there a bedroom here somewhere? Does the couch pull out? "Tenth floor," I said. "Swanky. Got a view?"

"The express lanes," she replied. Parker was still svelte, her straight black hair framing her heart-shaped face. "Not very exciting. It's not much, but it's next to everything and rent's not bad.

"Isaac told me about breaking up with your girlfriend." Parker sat next to me on the couch. "How're you doing?"

"Honestly, I've been a mess," I said. "We'd talked about getting married and now she's moved out, been sleeping with some other guy and lied to me about doing it. Eh, fuck her."

"Sounds like she's a bitch," Parker said.

Don't call her that. "I'm sure I had plenty to do with the whole mess."

"Like what?" Parker asked. "Were you sleeping around?"

"Not recently."

"What does that mean?"

"We broke up for a while last December and I slept with someone else then."

"But you were broken up," she said. "That doesn't count. You tell her about it?"

"No."

"Did you ever hit her or anything?"

"Hell no," I said. "I wanted her to get some friends of her own. So she did, then fucked one of them."

The next half hour, we covered a variety of topics ranging from her job to Isaac's problems with girls. Both of us were mid-laugh when Parker declared, "There's something I've been wanting to tell you for a while."

"Should I be scared?"

"It's not a big deal," she replied. "I wanted you to know, you were my first."

First what? Your first? No longer laughing, I stared at her. "You were a virgin?" *You lied to me?*

"Yeah, but you said you didn't sleep with virgins, so I didn't tell you." She smiled, continuing, "I wanted us to have sex, so I didn't say anything."

"What the fuck, Parker?"

Her smile fell. "It was years ago, Jon. I wanted to do it."

"But I wouldn't've if I would've known," I said, getting up from the couch. "Fuck, Parker, I thought we were friends."

"We are. We were then, too."

"But you left that little detail out?"

"I'm sorry, Jon." She looked up at me. "It was almost five years ago. I didn't think you'd care anymore."

"The one fucking thing you know I won't do, and you tricked me into doing it?"

"I'm sorry. What else can I say? It wasn't the right thing to do, but I wanted to get it out of the way." *Why?* "That's why I didn't say anything."

I stood, silent, looking at her. *She didn't think you'd care, stop being a dick.*

Sitting back on the couch, "I wish you would've told me back then. But you got to admit, it was kind of a shitty thing to do."

"Yeah, but if I told you..."

"Maybe, but who knows? It was my decision to make, right. You still might've been able to convince me to, anyway." She flushed. "Why did you want me to be your first?"

"I liked you, a lot," she said. "And you gave me the green M&M's, and those notes. I still have them, you know?"

"The M&M's?"

"The notes." She pushed me. "No one had done anything like that for me before."

Hard to believe.

"It meant a lot to me you took the time to do that."

My fingers ran through her hair, pulling her onto my lap. *Should I be doing this?* Hands went under her shirt, up and down her back. Palms pressed into her thighs, then around to her butt. *This is exquisite. Would she fuck me like this? We've never fucked like this.*

Dick straining uncomfortably against my jeans, I stretched my left leg. *Didn't help. I do not have to pee. Dammit.*

"Hold on, I got to go to the bathroom," I said. Parker sat back on the couch. I got up, trying to hide my erection.

Staring at myself in Parker's bathroom mirror. *If you sleep with her, Danielle will never take you back. She's so hot. Do I want Danielle back? Parker lives in Seattle. We can't be a couple. She's so hot. Danielle'll never know if you don't tell her. Never take you back.*

Parker was standing outside the bathroom door when I opened it.

"Got to go too." She closed the bathroom door behind her.

Nothing's happened, leave now. I didn't move. *Be at the door when Parker comes out. Leave now. She's so hot. Always wanted to be with her. Could we make it work?*

The bathroom door opened. I captured her, forcing her against the wall. Yanked off her shirt, wrenched off her pants. Unhooked her bra, pushed the straps off her shoulders. Kissing her neck, I slid her underwear over her ass then kissed down her body. *Superb.*

My hands drew from her calves to her thighs, across her pubic hair to her erect nipples as I stood to kiss her again. I lifted her leg, pressing my hips into her. *Never take you back.* I pushed against her, raised her hands above her head. *Still be a carrier. What if Parker gets them? Don't do that to her. Don't put her at risk. Never take you back. Don't do this to her.*

I stepped back. "I'm sorry Parker. I've got...I can't do this."

"Did I do something?"

Never take you back. "No, no, of course not," I said. "It's me. I've got something. I can't. I need to go."

Her voice broke. "You don't have to go."

Don't go. Don't infect her. You will, if you stay. "I do, I'm sorry." I went to the door. Parker put her shirt on, following me.

"Why do you have to go?" tears in her eyes.

"I just do." I kissed her. "I'll call you, okay?" closing the door.

Jesus, she was crying. How could you do that to her? It's better this way. She's better off.

# # #

The morning of the 27th, I asked Mary what she thought about Danielle wanting to stop by later that afternoon. "What do you think that means?"

"Hard to tell," my mom replied. "Do you still want to get back together?"

"Yeah, I think so."

"You think you can overlook the past couple months?"

Maybe. "Probably. I mean, she'll be in the dorms until the end of the year, so things would be different with us not living together. I think it would help us to become friends again."

"It's hard to move backward in a relationship," Mary said.

"But it's forward from where we are now."

Every commercial break, I looked at the clock on the stove. *Her family talked some sense into her. She'll say she's sorry, she'll ask to stay here tonight. Will Mary let her? Does Vance have a bigger dick? Is that why she dumped me?*

At one-thirty, I leapt from the couch at the sound of a knock on Mary's door. "Hi, Danielle," I said. "C'mon in."

"Thanks," she said and went to the living room. "Hi, Mary."

Not looking up from her book, "Danielle. How are you?"

"Good, thanks," Danielle said. To me, "I've got something for you in my car."

"Okay," I said.

"How've you been?" she asked. "We don't talk much anymore."

"No, we don't, do we?"

"I want us to be friends still. You've been such a big part of my life. I miss talking to you."

"Yeah, that's been tough," I said. *Not my fault.*

She opened her trunk. "I got you a Christmas present a while ago, so here."

"Thank you," I said. *I fucked this up again?* "I didn't get you anything, sorry."

"That's okay."

"Do you want me to open it now?"

"Doesn't matter, whenever."

"Thanks." I leaned in for a kiss.

"Uh," she pulled back. "How 'bout just friends?"

Dammit. Quick, save face. "Well, yeah, that's what you said. I can give you a friendly kiss still, then?"

"Well..."

A peck on the cheek. "Friends, right?"

"Yeah, okay. Mom's having a party tonight and she needs help with the house. I told her I'd be there by four, so I got to get going."

"Oh, okay." I gave her a hug. "I've missed you."

"Call me when we're back at school."

"Okay, I will." *I will.*

I stood in the parking lot of my mom's complex, watching her. She didn't look back as she drove away.

"That was a quick visit. How'd it go?" Mary asked.

"She gave me a Christmas present and had to get back home."

"Oh." Mary put down her book.

"She says she misses talking to me and still wants to be friends."

Mary frowned. "Can I make an observation?"

"Please do."

"She's telling you that to make herself feel better," Mary said. "You being hurt and distant reminds her of what she did and how she's been treating you."

"Uh...all right."

Mary continued, "I'm sure she thinks she means what she's telling you but underneath she's trying to not be the bad guy in all this."

Not the bad guy? "How can she not be the bad guy?" I asked. "She's the one who lied and cheated?"

"Yes, that may be. But she justifies it because she felt she was missing something in your relationship. Then it was okay for her to see someone else."

"Uh-huh." *If that's true, why would I want to be her friend?*

A picture her youngest sister drew for me was in one package. "An apron?" I asked aloud, unfolding it. "Why the hell would I need one for mac and cheese."

Not one thing to make her feel better. Not now, not ever.

Seven:
February 1992 (College, Senior Year 2)

Tate, a fellow SAGA employee and current roommate, and I were sitting at a table after our lunch shifts with a couple other creeps. "I'm a virgin," I declared. Scattered chuckles around the table.

"How do you figure?" Tate asked.

"You know when a car hits a hundred thousand miles, the counter goes back to zero. Well, I've finally rolled over."

Someone muttered, "You are so full of shit."

Tate bit. "You've had sex with a hundred thousand people?"

"God, no. Every sexual encounter has a point value attached to it," I explained. "And I've finally rolled over."

Silence.

"I'm going to save this virginity for someone special," I stated. "I'm going to wait until I'm married."

"Bullshit!"

Our apartment on Wilson Street was a newer, thin, two-story duplex with a bathroom on each floor, all three bedrooms on the second. The entryway led straight up the stairs to the second floor, the living room to the left and a two-person kitchen at the back. Tate came into the living room with a pot of chili. "How does your rolling over thing work?"

"Simple," I said. "Uh, well, each time you have sex you get points."

"Each time is worth one point?"

"No, that wouldn't work." I pondered. "Depending on how the sex is, who it's with, where it is, changes the point value. And different positions add points."

"Then like doggie would be worth more?" Tate asked.

"Right."

"What's one point then?"

"Um, sex with someone you know. No, someone you're having a relationship with, so not a one-nighter or anything, a real relationship, on a bed, missionary, with the lights off. That's one point. And every variation to that increases in point value."

"Okay, then, what's the highest point value?" he asked.

"It'd have to be practically impossible." A moment's consideration. "A nun."

Tate exclaimed, "You have to rape a nun!?!"

"Can't be rape," I replied. "Rape has no point value, has to be consensual. Fucking a nun, in the ass, on the altar, while she's on the rag, fifty thousand points."

"During a service?"

"Yes," I said. "But you wouldn't have to be seen by the congregation for it to count. Beneath the altar works."

"What about skullfucking some girl you just met in the back of your car?" *Skullfucking? Is that a blowjob? Cool expression.*

"I haven't gotten that far yet, Tate. Several points, I imagine."

With a mouth full of chili, "There any other ways to get your virginity back?"

"Oh sure," I said. "If you don't have sex for a long time, your body will revert to its natural state. That of virgin."

Tate put his spoon down. "What's a long time?"

"I don't know. A year?"

"Fuck me," he said.

"You a virgin again?"

"Not yet," he said. "But I will be in a couple months."

#   #   #

Sitting in my room, the other two roommates gone, I picked up the phone. "Hi, Mallory, this is Jon. We met last fall, downtown, with..."

"Oh, hi," she interrupted.

Was that a good hi? "How're you doing?"

"Good, you?"

"Quite well, thank you. I hope it's okay that I'm calling, I got your number from Sasha...she's in a class with you..."

"Oh, yeah," she said. "No, it's fine."

"Well, I'm kind of skittish about calling someone who hasn't given me their number. But there is a reason for the call...uh, well, I was hoping you'd join me for coffee sometime."

Say yes, say yes. "Oh, sure. When were you thinking?"

"Well, I'm busy tomorrow and well, the next day isn't good, so what about Saturday the fifteenth? I'd say let's do Valentine's Day, but that's way too much to put on a first date."

"Oh yeah, Saturday's much better. But what about dinner instead?"

Dinner? Like a real date? "Dinner's good," I said. "What about Stanello's?"

"I've never been there, but I've heard it's good."

"Six-thirty, then?"

# # #

Mallory answered the door in a black knee-length, form-fitting dress. Her straight, thick, black hair was styled in wavy curls and her blood-red lipstick was a stark contrast to her Washington pale. Admiring her trim five foot four figure, "You look terrific," I said. "Should I go home and put on something else?"

"No," she said. "I like dressing up sometimes."

During dinner we covered the essentials, where we grew up, our majors, our plans post-graduation. "You really want to be a DJ?" she asked.

"Yeah," I admitted. *Small hands, but beautiful nails.*

"Do you have a lot of music?"

"Some. Probably three hundred CDs or so, four hundred albums."

"Can I see your collection?" she asked.

"Yeah, you want to stop by on the way back to your place?"

"Okay."

Mallory had met Tate up on campus at a party or two. They joked about mutual acquaintances. Gina, our other roommate, came downstairs.

"Mallory, this is Gina. Gina, Mallory."

Gina grunted a hello at Mallory on her way to the kitchen. Tate and I exchanged glances. A glass of water in hand, Gina returned upstairs.

"Sorry about Gina," I said. *Rude bitch.*

"We kind of know each other already."

"Oh, really? Do tell."

"Later," Mallory whispered. "You going to show me your CDs or what?"

She methodically flipped through my music in my room. By the time she'd reached the end, she'd amassed fifteen discs in her borrow pile. "You sure it's okay if I take all these?" she asked.

"I already said I didn't mind."

"Yeah, but so many?"

"Well, you know what it means?" I asked.

"No, what?"

"You'll have to see me again."

"Well, yeah, I figured that."

Great. "We should get you home, yeah?"

"Uh, sure."

In the car, Mallory asked, "How long have you known Gina?"

"Porter found her when he balked on our apartment with me and Tate. We didn't meet her until she moved in."

"You guys friends?"

"Far from it. She barely talks to us. Mostly stays in her room. What's the deal?"

Mallory told a tale of friends of friends sleeping with this person and that and somehow Gina had contracted some venereal disease from one of Mallory's friends.

"And that's why she won't talk to you? Because someone else gave her the clap?"

"For the most part." *That's not the whole story.*

At her apartment, Mallory opened the passenger door. *Invite me in.* "Do you mind if I call you in the next couple days?" I asked.

"No, please do."

"Well, I'm going to need to get those back, so I'll be calling..."

Back home, I tried to explain the issue between Mallory and Gina to Tate. "Must've given her Raging Bitch herpes," Tate said.

#   #   #

"I had a great time Saturday even with Gina being Gina," I said to Mallory on the phone, Monday night. "Hope it wasn't too uncomfortable for you."

"Not at all," she said. "I'm sure she was more uncomfortable than I was."

"What are you doing now?"

"Got a bunch of studying to do tonight."

"Maybe you could bring your books and we could study here?" I asked.

"Why don't you come over here?"

"Well, I guess I could," I replied. "Is there a problem with my place? Besides Gina?"

"No, I like Tate, Gina's pretty much it. I don't want to upset her by being around."

"Oh, it's okay. We'd love you to annoy Gina."

"Well, why don't you come over here tonight and I'll come hang out there soon."

Soon is good. "Be right there."

Mallory was in the middle of cooking dinner, chicken cacciatore. "Would you like some?"

The smell from the kitchen was superb. "Well, okay, if you have extra."

On her couch, we watched bad TV, eating good food. "This is excellent, Mallory. Give me the recipe?"

"Sure, but I could cook it for you sometime."

You want to see me again?

After putting the dishes in the kitchen, I sat next to her on the couch. "How often do you have your hair cut?" I asked, purposefully running my fingers through her hair. "I mean, it's so thick, it must grow like crazy."

She relaxed into my hand. "Every three or four weeks during the summer, to thin it out, or it gets too damn hot. Less often in the winter."

Withdrawing my hand from her thick brunette mane, a coo escaped her. I kissed her passionately. After reclining, then getting uncomfortable, she led me to her bedroom.

Mallory never turned on the light, simply closed the door behind us. Our clothes discarded, I kissed down her body.

Not as firm as Felecia's.

I took my time licking and nibbling her. Mallory uttered approving noises but nothing resembling an orgasm. Ten minutes in, she pulled me up, spun me on my back, and squirmed between my legs.

Skullfucking Felecia yesterday was better. This'll never get me off.

I guided her up as she'd done to me. She lifted a condom out of the nightstand.

Modern girl.

"God, I'm sorry that wasn't longer," I apologized after my four minute run.

"It's fine," she said. "I should already be asleep. I've got an eight o'clock." She kissed me. "You can stay, if you want to."

"I'm going to let you sleep," I replied, getting out of bed.

\# \# \#

After dinner of homemade Fettuccini Alfredo later that week, Mallory and I retired to her bedroom. Naked and groping, she opened the drawer next to her bed. "Dammit," she muttered. "Did you bring any condoms with you?"

"No," I said. "I thought you still had some."

"I thought so too. My roommate must've borrowed them."

"Hmm, well, uh…" *Your blowjobs haven't done it so far.* "You been tested for HIV lately?"

"About a year ago," she answered. "What about you?"

"Maybe six months now. We should probably do that, you think?"

"Yes, we should. It's ten bucks at the Health Center, isn't it?" She paused. "We're getting tested this week, all right?"

"Planning on it," I said. "Should I run to the store?"

"Don't worry about it then." She pulled me onto her.

I kissed her at her front door. "See you tomorrow," I said.

"My roommate and a couple other gals are going down to Speedy's tomorrow night, so I'll catch up with you on Saturday, okay?"

Why can't I come? Invite me.

\# \# \#

Sunday morning, I stopped by Mallory's apartment. "You feeling better?" I asked.

"Yeah," she said. "I didn't realize I'd had that much. Sorry I didn't want to talk yesterday."

"How much did you drink?"

"Well, I started with a Kamikaze and then kind of lost track. We got a couple pitchers and I've got no idea how many beers I had."

Kind of scary.

"Hmph," I responded. "Who all ended up there?"

"A couple of my friends from the dorms and my roommate. A few guys from school I knew were there."

"Anything interesting happen? How was the DJ?"

"Okay," Mallory said. "We danced, shot the shit, nothing spectacular. I'm heading up to the library, so I should get going."

#   #   #

My main responsibility during my lunch shift at SAGA was sitting next to the exit doors to ensure students didn't leave with food. And keep the cereal bins full. My friend Sasha walked toward me. Several creeps had pushed together two tables so I could be included in the conversation without leaving my post.

Sasha introduced the friend who sat with her. "Everyone, this is Paula. Paula, everyone."

She's cute but looks twelve. The top of Paula's head reached Sasha's shoulders, getting her close to the five foot mark. Her figure straight, boobless and hipless.

"Where do you live, Paula?" one of the creeps asked her.

"Edens," she replied.

You don't look spooky.

Her straight, brown hair hung to her shoulders where it curled up around her heart shaped face and dazzling hazel eyes.

Scooting toward the table, I asked, "Edens? How is that?"

"Not quite what I expected," Paula answered. "I thought it would be different."

"How do you mean?" Sasha asked.

"Well, I knew it was the quiet dorm before I signed up to live there, but I'm the only freshman I've met in Edens. And everyone is so uptight."

"Hey," I interjected. "Can I come over and see what it's like? I've never been inside."

"I don't know," Paula said, her petite, thin-lipped mouth shrinking further. "My roommate's never had anyone over and she might freak out if someone stopped by. And you'd have to get past the RA's. They're hardcore about keeping out people who don't live there."

That's stupid. "Even if I was stopping by to study?" I asked.

"Doesn't matter," Paula said.

"But if I was being quiet and going to study, why would they care?"

"They don't think anyone who doesn't live there can be quiet," she said.

"Fuck them then," I added. *I must get in there.*

March 1992 (College, Senior Year 2)

Friday, at Mallory's apartment, enjoying another home-cooked dinner together. "Want to go to a movie tomorrow?" I asked her.

"I've got to finish up a paper for Sociology," she replied. "Maybe next weekend?"

I looked at her, puzzled. "What about Sunday?"

"As long as I finish the paper I won't have anything to do on Sunday."

"Right..."

"I told you I was going to Speedy's tomorrow night."

What does that have to do with anything? "I remember."

"I won't have to get out of bed on Sunday."

"You're going to spend the day in bed?" I asked. *Without me?*

"Hope not, but I might have to," she stated.

You plan your hangovers?

#   #   #

Monday after my shift at SAGA, Paula was walking across the street, toward Edens. "Hey, Paula, you heading back to your room?"

"Yeah." Her miniscule mouth shrank. "Why?"

I crossed the street to her. "Let me see your room."

"It's just a room, Jon."

"Yeah, yeah, but I've never been in there. I want to see it."

She looked at her watch. "Well, my roommate shouldn't be back until three." *Sweet.* "But you can't go being a shit and get me in trouble. Once we're inside, no talking."

No talking? "Seriously? No talking?"

"You're kind of loud," Paula said. "Follow me. Quietly. And if one of the RA's stops us, you'll have to go."

That's stupid.

We walked to her dorm. "Do the RA's hang out in the halls looking for strangers?" I asked.

"Sometimes," she said.

We walked up the large staircase to the majestic main doors. "Not a word," Paula warned me.

Edens' lobby floor looked marble. A huge, imposing desk sat to the left of the main doors. Directly ahead, a spectacular staircase. Three plush cream couches formed a U-shape around a grand fireplace.

Why do the dorks get to live here?

I followed Paula up the stairway, past the elevator on the second floor to her room halfway down the eerily quiet, deserted hall.

"This place is astounding," I whispered. "Too bad it's wasted on people who study all the time." Two beds separated by four feet, two desks against the opposite wall and space to move about in the center of the room.

Twice as big as Mathes rooms, at least. "How much do you hang out here?" I asked.

"Some," she said. "Usually the afternoons. It's better than the library because I have all my stuff here. I was here one Saturday night back in the fall and it was the same as it is now."

"I couldn't do it," I said. "I mean it'd be all right for the week, but all the time? I'd go fucking nuts."

Paula went to her desk, picked up a notebook. "My sister sent me this," she said. I looked over her shoulder at the drawings in the notebook. She whirled around and kissed me.

Excellent. Wasn't expecting this.

Pushing her to her bed, I nibbled her neck and lifted her shirt. "We've only got a couple minutes before my roommate's done with class," she protested.

"Then give me a couple minutes," I said. She laid back down. I pushed her bra aside. Her boobs were tiny, cute.

Adorable. I suckled and nibbled on them. Her nipples didn't respond. *Odd.*

"You need to go," she said.

"Only if we can get together again soon," I insisted. *Mallory gets drunk every weekend. Got plenty of free time.*

"Sure," she said. "But now you need to go." She straightened her shirt, got up and walked me out.

"Do you have a phone in your room?" I asked her, once we got outside.

"No," she said. "I don't think anyone on our floor does. I have to use the phone downstairs to call my parents."

"I'll see you around SAGA then?"

"Oh, you'll see me."

#   #   #

After spring break, Mallory stopped by SAGA and asked if I wanted to join her at Speedy's Friday.

"You go ahead," I said. *Don't need to eat you for an hour again because you're too drunk to come.* "Tate and I already have plans to drink beer and play Nintendo."

Later that shift, Paula sat with the creeps. When she'd finished eating, I casually followed her to the tray drop-off. "What are you doing Friday night?" I asked.

"Uh, nothing. Why?"

"You want to come over?"

"And do what?" she smirked.

#   #   #

"Where's Tate?" Paula asked, looking around the apartment early Friday evening.

"Some party, trying to lose his newfound virginity again."

"Still? That boy has the worst luck. Don't you guys live with some girl, too?"

"Gina. Yeah," I said. "She's never here on the weekends. We're nowhere near cool enough to hang out with. You want to play something?"

"We can skip the Nintendo, thanks," she replied.

She stood there, naked, in my bedroom, allowing my hands to explore her. Delicately caressing her boobs, her nipples again didn't respond.

Still clothed, I kissed down her neck to her boobies. *You will get stiff.* I licked, sucked, finally able to coerce both nipples to spring up. *There.* I continued down her body. She giggled as my tongue passed her belly button.

"I'm kind of ticklish," she said.

"Sorry." I continued down, nibbling the entire time. My tongue ran the length of her. And again, continuing for five minutes until she pushed away from me.

"You're done now?" I asked.

"Why do you still have your clothes on?"

"I was busy."

"Take those off," Paula insisted. I obeyed, fetching a condom.

"Oh, you think we're going to fuck now?" she asked. *We're not?*

"Kind of presumptuous of you, don't cha think?"

"Uh," I stammered. "I, uh..."

"Kidding," she snickered. I unrolled the rubber onto my dick and made an attempt to get into Paula. *She's plenty wet. Why can't I get in?* I jockeyed about. Paula reached down and guided me inside.

The phone rang. *No chance, not now.* The answering machine picked up after the fourth ring. I could make out a female voice over the music. *Not Mallory. Is she coming over? Why would she come over? She's out drinking. She never stops drinking.*

I stopped. *What if she's on her way over?*

"I should see what that's about," I told Paula.

Pulling on a pair of shorts, I went downstairs and pressed play. Music, muffled voices then Mallory yelling, "Are you there? Where'd you go?" *I'm not here. Don't come here.* "My friend told me they're picking up tickets for The Cure tomorrow morning and wanted to know if we wanted to go. Where are you? Should she pick you up a ticket too? If we don't let her know by the end of the night, she's not getting tickets for us." A long pause filled with music, more muffled voices. "Fine." The message ended.

"Was that Mallory?" Paula asked, when I returned.

How do you know about Mallory? We're done now, aren't we? "Yeah," I admitted. "She wanted to know if I wanted to go to The Cure."

"Did you call her back?"

"No, I'm here with you. That would've been rude." I took off my shorts, got on another condom and we continued fucking.

Finished, I looked at the clock. "Why don't you crash here tonight?" *Stay. I'll dump Mallory.*

"I can't," Paula replied. "This whole thing with you and Mallory is too damn weird. I think I should go."

She's a drunk.

# # #

"Where were you last night?" Mallory asked, immediately after I entered her apartment.

"Playing Nintendo with Tate," I lied.

"Didn't you get my message?"

"What message?"

"I called you last night to see if you wanted to go to The Cure."

"Really?" I feigned surprise. "We had to go get more beer," I started. "I didn't look at the machine when we got back. Sorry. Did you end up getting tickets, anyway?"

"Yes," she said. "But I thought it'd be cool if we could go together."

"The Cure's okay, but I can miss them," I said.

Mallory marched out to the kitchen. "My roommate also mentioned last night she's getting tired of hearing us fuck all the time."

"Uh...okay."

Scowling, "It's not like I haven't heard her and her boyfriend fucking plenty of times."

"I guess I missed that," I said. "What does that mean?"

"You can only stay here maybe one or two nights a week."

You'll have to stay at my place. "Does that mean you're going to come over?"

"You know I don't like being around Gina."

"I thought..."

"She's a cunt and I don't want to be around her."

You're cutting me off because of my bitch roommate? "Should I take off now?"

"No," she mellowed. "Stay here tonight and we'll figure stuff out later."

April 1992 (College, Senior Year 2)

Paula and I spent Saturday afternoon listening to music, naked, in my room. "What's the story with you and Mallory anyway?" she asked.

She's a drunk. "She's more of a party girl than I appreciate."

"But she's still your girlfriend?"

"I don't know what we are," I said. "I enjoy spending time with you."

"Yeah, me too," Paula said.

Then why don't you call me?

"We might have to just be friends though."

No. "That'd suck. Does that have to start right now?"

"Tomorrow." We fucked again.

# # #

"What're your plans after you graduate in June?" Mallory asked me as we walked from campus to her apartment.

"Shit, I don't know," I said. "Keep working at SAGA until something better comes up? Talked to a couple bands, see if they need a sound guy, but it wouldn't pay much." *You're moving home for the summer, so we're breaking up, right?*

"But you'll be up here this summer?"

"Undoubtedly," I replied. "You staying at your mom's?"

"There's a class I want to take but I'd need to find a way to pay for it. Don't think my parents would spring so I'll need to find something. Part-time, anyway."

If you're here, we can stay together. Long distance is not happening. "Where are you going to live?"

"A couple of my friends got a house out by Lake Whatcom so I was going to see if they have room."

All you'll do is drink and hang out with your friends. I'll never see you. And then it will be my fault when we break up. "Why don't you move in with me?" I suggested. "We could get a couple other roommates and split rent four ways."

"Isn't Tate living with you next year?" Mallory asked.

"No, he's moving in with another friend of his. They needed a fourth at this other guy's house in the fall. He'll be getting a real size room."

Mallory considered a few moments. "I'll think about it."

"I mean the amount of time we spend together, we might as well."

"Yeah," she mumbled. "But I don't know, Jon. That's a big step."

"It's not like we're getting married," I reasoned. "Financially, it makes sense."

# # #

Holding Paula's left leg up on the washing machine, I thrust into her. "Shhh," I whispered, "Gina's home."

We finished, she pulled her pants back on. "You staying in the dorms next fall?"

"God, no," Paula said. "Unless I moved up to the Ridge."

Live with me. "We're going to have an extra room or two," I said. "You should move in here."

She looked at me curiously. "I don't think my parents would be okay with me living with a guy."

"There'll be other people here too. Isn't Sasha looking for a place?"

"I think so." She finished getting dressed. "Let me talk to my parents about it."

# # #

Mallory sat next to me in my 1974 orange Super Beetle on the way to Teddy Bear Cove for a bonfire on the beach.

"My friend's already got someone to take their extra room this summer so can I move in once school's finished?" Mallory asked.

"Shouldn't be a problem. Gina talked about moving out before finals but I wasn't paying much attention to her. Now we need one more for fall."

"Thought we needed two," Mallory said.

"Oh, Paula's taking one of the rooms," I said. "She told me yesterday as long as she wasn't living with all guys, it'd be okay with her folks."

Her face hardened. "Why didn't you talk to me about it before inviting her to live here?"

Because it's my apartment. "Well, I asked Paula before you'd made up your mind," I reasoned. "It's not cool to ask her then say, 'Oh, hold on, I changed my mind.' Paula said Sasha was looking for a place. Is Sasha cool enough?"

"Sasha, of Crazy Hank and Sasha?"

"Yeah," I said. "I was going to talk to her at lunch Monday."

"No, Sasha's cool."

"Is it okay if I ask her?"

Mallory turned to the window. "I guess."

"Did you have someone else in mind?"

"Yeah, I was going to ask this one friend of mine if she'd found a place already."

"Well, you should and I'll wait to talk to Sasha. When are you going to see her?"

"Monday in class."

August 1992 (Real World, Year 1)

Isaac called me. "Guess what?"

"You're pregnant?" I tried.

"I am. It's yours."

"I wore a condom," I protested.

"About time," he said. "Actually, I was hoping you could do me a favor. I'm going to be moving up to Bellingham next month." *No way!* "And I was hoping you could send me a couple newspapers so Holly and I can try and find someplace. I'm going to try to get into Western once I finish up a couple things so we figured we might as well head up there now and get settled."

"Holy shit! That's kick ass. Whatever you need, Isaac."

"How about a job?"

"I don't know if Haggen is hiring, but I can find out for you. When are you planning on getting up here?"

"As soon as we can find some place that takes pets and I find a job. No later than end of September, though. I got to get some credits from Whatcom CC. How's things?"

"Not too bad," I said. "Putting my degree to good use. Being a cashier at Haggen is pretty mindless, but being on my feet for eight hours a day is tough. Never thought I'd miss SAGA but sitting on my ass making sure people didn't take food was definitely cush."

"You're just figuring that out? You and Mallory still together?"

"Yeah, living together since June," I said. "Going to see Paula next weekend down in Edmonds. Work is having me help out with a new store opening."

"You two still fucking?"

"Last time I saw her, we did. Mallory and I aren't much, so with any luck..."

"What about when she moves in?"

"I'll worry about that later," I said.

#   #   #

After my first shift at the Top Foods in Edmonds, I checked into the hotel. *A bed and a television. What more do I need?*

Paula knocked an hour later. "Sorry I'm late," she apologized. "Traffic was horrendous."

"At least you made it," I said, offering her a seat on the bed. "How's summer going?"

"Not too much happening. I'm working but all of my friends from high school are busy so I don't go out much."

124

I leaned in to kiss her. She pulled back. "I had a Colposcopy yesterday. They biopsied my cervix, so nothing's happening tonight."

Why'd you come over then? "Why'd they do that?"

"Abnormal pap."

"Danielle had to have one and she said it hurt like hell," I said. "How are you feeling?"

"Not too bad, I didn't feel anything. But I've been spotting all day."

"Could you use a backrub?" I offered. *I'll rub your ass then you can blow me.*

"I'd love one," she replied.

She stretched out on the bed, I sat on her butt and began at her shoulders. "I had a three-way last week," she said.

Why are you fucking other people? "You did? Was it with another girl or two boys?"

"Two boys."

You're kind of a slut. "Who were they?"

"A guy I used to date in high school and a friend of his."

"Was it any fun?" *Be fun, then you can try out me and Mallory.*

"It was okay," she replied. "One of the boys couldn't keep it up so it ended up being a lot more work for me than I would've liked. He kept trying but it didn't work out."

"More like fucking one guy with a limp dick kind of hanging around?" I asked.

"Essentially."

"Did Limpboy ever finish?"

"I can't remember," she admitted. "I don't think so."

"Were they ever hard at the same time?" *Could I be hard with another guy fucking the same girl?*

"A couple times for about a minute at a time."

"That's kind of disappointing." *You should try again with me and Mallory.*

"Yeah, I'm not sure I'll try it again."

"Well, it would probably be better if both guys could keep it up. Maybe you need to find other guys?"

"Maybe."

I lifted her shirt off, undid her bra, "Have you talked to Sasha at all?"

"A few weeks ago."

"Either of you bringing any furniture with you in September?"

"I don't think either of us have much of anything."

I tugged her shorts off. Working the small of her back, on to her butt. A loud crinkle. A pronounced bulge in her panties.
World's biggest maxi pad.

Paula twisted back to look at me. "Jon, this isn't going to happen tonight."

You could still suck my dick. "Okay then," I said, moving back to her shoulders.

"I should probably get going. We both have to work in the morning," Paula said.

You're not even going to stay? Why did you come over? "You coming up to Bellingham before you move up?"

"Probably not," sliding her shirt over her head. "I'm working most days and the family's going on vacation for a couple weeks in September."

"Well, give me a call if you find yourself on your way up before then."

"For sure. I'll let you know when we figure out what day we'll be moving me up."

She hugged me at the door but didn't offer a kiss.
Guess we're friends now. Solves the Mallory problem.

September 1992 (Real World, Year 1)

"Did that new porn store downtown hire Isaac?" Mallory asked me, throwing her blouse in the hamper in the closet.

"Yeah," I replied, already in bed. "Worked out well. My buddy who was working there started at the parks department the day after Isaac got hired so everybody's happy. Isaac said they'll probably be giving him more hours in a month or two. And it's three blocks from the apartment he and Holly found."

"Is Hank still here?" she whispered.

"I think so. I didn't see him leave. Do you care?"

She climbed into bed. "I don't want him being crazy first thing in the morning. He's psycho."

"He's funny, Mal," I said. "Overly energetic but still it's nice to have more testosterone around here. I can already feel my boobs getting bigger."

"He's not energetic, he's fucking obnoxious."

Mallory turned off the light, then went silent.

"Want to fuck?" I asked after two minutes of nothing.

"I got to get up early and go to the bookstore. Rain check?"
If you'd ever let me cash it.

October 1992 (Real World, Year 1)

Paula sat on the couch of our apartment reading a magazine. *Is that Penthouse?*

"It was in the mail today," she said. "You don't mind, do you? I love reading Forum," Paula said. "They're always such bullshit."

"Yeah, that's what makes them fun," I said. "Have you noticed all the names and addresses are withheld? I think it's one guy who writes them all."

"Really? You think so?"

"Oh, yeah. This shit doesn't happen in the really real."

Hank came downstairs from Sasha's room. "Oh, man I love Penthouse. Let me see it."

Paula handed it to him and he started reading the first letter to Forum to us.

Sasha came out of her room ten minutes later. "What's so funny?"

"Reading the latest Forum," Hank replied.

"You guys," Sasha scoffed.

"Have a seat Miss Prissy Pants," Hank said. "This shit is genius. Let me start over, you should know what's going on." He cleared his throat, "I never thought anything like this would ever happen to me but..."

By the second story we were guessing how big the writer's dick was, which slang terms he'd use to describe the girl's boobs and pussy and how many orgasms he would provide the girl.

"She'll have a vice grip snatch," I declared.

"God, I hate that word," Sasha said. "I even like cunt better."

"The c-word is the worst," Paula added. "I'd rather be called a snatch."

"If you're calling someone a cunt, that's worse," Sasha said. "But to describe a vagina, snatch is the worst. Reminds me of a Venus Fly Trap. Icky."

"Mallory hates pussy," I said. "Insists I use snatch instead."

"Pussy's so cute though," Paula said.

"Yeah," Sasha agreed. "No one says snatch. It's vulgar."

November 1992 (Real World, Year 1)

"Where's Mallory?" Paula asked me Sunday morning.

"Still in bed," I replied. "Don't imagine you'll be seeing her today."

"Weren't you going to take her out for her birthday?" Sasha asked.

"She got pissed I had to work last night when she was going out with her friends, so she got shitfaced," I whispered to them. "Won't have to pay for a movie and dinner at the Cliff House now." We giggled. "Either of you want to go to the movies with me?"

"Got to study," Sasha said.

"Me too."

"Well, screw you both."

Upstairs, I cracked the door to our bedroom. "Mallory," I whispered. No response.

When I got back to the apartment two hours later, Mallory was upright on the couch. "Where'd you go?" she asked.

"Get food," I said. "You were pretty out when I left."

"Aren't we going to do something for my birthday?" she asked.

"You up to it?"

"I'm all right now," she said. "Needed some more sleep."

"It's your birthday, what would you like to do?"

"Dinner at le Chat," she replied.

Not there. "We going to need reservations?" I asked.

"We can sit in the bar."

And you can drink more.

Later, Mallory and I made our way to le Chat Noir, sat in the bar and ate Caesar salad. Mallory polished off two glasses of white wine while I nursed a whiskey sour and a glass of water. I gave her a book she'd been wanting and a scarf she'd pointed out.

In the car, "You want to do anything else," I asked.

"I've got to finish a paper tonight, so we better get back. Thanks for dinner."

"My pleasure," I said. "Maybe a backrub later?" *And some sex?*

"Maybe."

In the bedroom, I took off my clothes and waited for Mallory to finish brushing her teeth. She closed the door behind her. "Candles, huh?"

"Backrub?"

"Sure, but I'm not sure if I'll be able to stay awake through it."

"Then fall asleep," I said. "Still your birthday, right?"

"It is. Thanks for everything."
Ten minutes in, Mallory was asleep.

December 1992 (Real World, Year 1)

Christmas Day with Mary in Tacoma after Christmas Eve dinner. The hullabaloo of opening presents over, the turkey remains still on the table, Mary asked, "Are you and Mallory going to get married?"

Where'd that come from? "We've talked about it," I said. "But not for a while. Once we both have real jobs and get settled."

Mary's expression didn't change. "All right," she said. "How's her drinking?"

"Mellowed," I said. "At the party we had last week, she always had a drink in her hand but she never got loopy or anything. Didn't spend the next day hung-over, which was a first."

"Are you happy?" Mary asked, watching my expression.

I hesitated. *We don't fuck much anymore. We don't do much together. She complains about Paula and Sasha a lot.* "I'm not unhappy. I mean, work sucks. I can't stand being on my feet for eight hours at a time but Mallory and I don't fight."

"There's a huge difference between not fighting and being happy in a relationship." Mary said. "What do you want out of a partner anyway?"

Another long pause.

Smart, funny, loves to fuck. A redhead? Has to be more. "We have to be sexually compatible," I started.

Energetic? Spontaneous? "I want someone like those 7-Up commercials. You know, where the people are doing all the crazy shit and laughing all the time? Yup, that's what I want I'm looking for. Spontaneous and silly at times and able to carry on a decent conversation the rest. Oh, and likes to cook and fucks like a banshee."

"I don't think I've seen it," she said.

"I'll point it out the next time it's on."

"Is Mallory those things?" Mary asked.

No. She is smart. Not spontaneous or particularly energetic. "Not everything," I admitted. *But she likes me.* "She's a great cook. She's smart and can be funny. We have good conversations." *Not that often. But she likes me.*

"Okay," Mary said. "You know I worry about you. I only want you to be happy."

"I know." *Does Mallory make me happy?*

"What about your other roommate, Petunia?"

"Paula," I said. "We haven't slept together since Mallory moved in."

"That's something," Mary said. "Your choice or hers?"

"Hers. But it's probably better we're not trying to sneak around."

# # #

New Year's Eve, a handful of customers meandered through Haggen. Around one, a supervisor asked me to start facing items in view of the front entrance. *Maybe Mallory will stop by after her friend's party.* She didn't.

Maybe she left a note on my car of what she was going to do to me when I get home. She didn't.

A light was on in the living room of the apartment when I arrived. *She wants to have a romantic, candle-lit fuckfest.*

The living room empty when I opened the front door. Paula tiptoed down the staircase and whispered, "Happy New Year."

"You too."

"How was work?" she asked, sitting on the couch.

"Slow as shit. Where's Mallory?"

"She went to bed about an hour ago."

Bitch. "Glad she waited up for me," I said. "Well, thanks for waiting up."

"Thought it'd be lame if no one was up to wish you Happy New Year when you got home," Paula said.

"Yeah, it would've been. Thanks."

"How are you and Mallory?" Paula asked. "Things seem tense."

"That's a good way to put it," I said. "My mom and I talked about whether or not Mallory and I were going to get married and I'm not sure we are."

"Really? I kind of thought you guys would."

"I don't think so, there's too many little things. Stuff I'm not sure either of us can work through. Or maybe I'm being a dick," I offered. "Who are you seeing these days, by the way?"

"Oh, I've been hanging out with a couple guys..."

"The pizza guy?"

"No, a couple guys from work."

"Oh, that's too bad. I liked the pizza guy." I put my hand on Paula's leg.

"You think this is a good idea?" she asked.

"I'm quiet," I replied, helping her out of her pants. My finger circled her clit, she held back a moan. *Wonderful little pussy.*

Paula convulsed on my hand. "Thanks," she whispered. "First time you've done that to me."

"My pleasure." As I unhitched my pants, a noise upstairs.

"You think that was Mallory?"

"Could be," I replied.

Paula scooped up her clothes from the floor, fleeing around the corner to the downstairs bathroom.

A minute later, when no one had appeared on the stairs, Paula returned to the living room. "I'm going to go to bed," she said.

Where's mine?

January 1993 (Real World, Year 1)

The next morning I asked Mallory, "How was the party last night? You were home pretty early," I said.

"Yeah, we left about one. There wasn't anything going on after the hootin' and hollerin' at midnight."

"Why didn't you wait up for me?" I asked, pulling on a pair of shorts, heading toward the bedroom door.

"Because I was tired."

#   #   #

"You actually eating that for lunch?" I asked Caprice and Glynne as they came through my line at Haggen, both of them in their all-white Haggen bakery uniforms.

Glynne, the blonde with full lips and bright green eyes, asked, "What's wrong with it?"

"He's screwing with you, Glynne," Caprice smirked. "Maybe we shouldn't invite him, if he's going to be like that."

"Invite me to what?" I inquired, scanning their bottles of water.

"Nothing." Caprice raised her nose in the air.

"That's not cool," I said.

Handing me cash, Glynne said, "I'll tell you later." *If you're going to be there, I'll come.*

"I don't think he deserves to know," Caprice added, taking her lunch off the check stand. Glynne shrugged before heading to the break room.

On a break, I went back to the bakery. Caprice was at the counter putting pastries away. "What's the big secret?" I asked her.

"We're watching movies in my room tonight," Caprice replied. "Glynne thought we should ask you if you wanted to join us."

She thought that? As long as it's Glynne wanting me there. "What time?"

"Around eight. Can you make it?"

"I think so," I replied. Caprice gave me her room number in the Upper Highland dorm.

When I got back to my apartment after six, no one else was there. Out of my tan slacks, white button-up shirt and muted tie. The front door opened while I was brushing my teeth. *Please don't be Mallory.*

Hank and Sasha came upstairs. "Hey guys," I called. "Can you let Mallory know I went to watch movies with some people from work."

"No problem," Sasha said. "What time you going to be home? She'll probably ask."

"Don't know," I replied. "Late."

After eating a leisurely meal at Arby's, I made my way to Western's campus and Caprice's room. Glynne was sitting on one of the beds when Caprice let me in. Instead of the ponytail she wore at work, Glynne's straight hair fell around her face a couple inches down her chest. She had on a plain white t-shirt.

Little boobs? Nice. Damn Haggen aprons. "You guys haven't started yet, have you?" I asked.

"Nope," Caprice replied. I sat across the room from Glynne. Caprice went into the shared bathroom area between her room and her suitemate's.

A minute later, "I can't believe she's doing this," Caprice mumbled, slamming the door behind her.

"What's up?" Glynne asked her.

"My suitemate is studying for a test tomorrow and won't let me borrow the TV. She won't go to the library. You know where we could watch a movie?"

"My three roommates wouldn't be too cool on it, being a weeknight and all," I answered. "Can we go to your place, Glynne?"

"I still live with my parents," she admitted.

Your parents? How old are you?

"Did you know Glynne was on the Sehome swim team that took state last year?" Caprice asked. "My yearbook's around here somewhere."

A freshman? Crap.

The three of us flipped through Caprice's yearbook. Glynne was taking a year off school and wanted to travel Europe over the summer, working full time at Haggen to pay for it. After touching on swimming, movies, Caprice's classes and revisiting the work topics, the conversation slowed around midnight.

"I should probably get going," I said. "I got an early one tomorrow."

"We'll have movies soon, really," Caprice said.

"Let me know. Night, ladies."

The apartment was dark when I returned. I got into bed. "You awake," I whispered.

"Yes."

Crap. "Didn't wake you up, did I?"

"No," Mallory answered. "Where've you been?"

"Didn't Sasha tell you?"

"She said you were watching movies with people from work."

"Up at Western," I said. "You ever been in Upper Highland? Kind of like Higginson. I could never live in one of those rooms again. Not with someone else. Jesus, they are so small."

"Uh huh."

"When do you work tomorrow?"

"Noon," Mallory replied.

"I got to be in at ten. Good night." Onto my side, facing the wall.

# # #

Hank was reading my latest *Penthouse* Forum to Sasha and me, when Mallory came through the front door. "Shit," I said, getting off the couch. "Is it really that late? I'm meeting Porter over at the Quarterback." Mallory stared at me. "You want to come?" I asked her.

"I can't. I open tomorrow." *I know.*

"Oh, sorry," I said. "I'll tell him you said hi."

At the Quarterback Pub and Eatery, Porter and I caught up on life after graduation. He'd moved out of the house he'd been in and was now in a little apartment, by himself, downtown. "You still seeing that gal?" I asked him.

"Naw," he said, throwing a dart. "She got an internship down in Seattle, then got hired on so we kind of gave up."

"Sorry man," I said.

"Thanks. It was time anyway. How are you and Mallory doing?"

"I'm here alone, aren't I?"

"That bad?" he asked.

"Naw, but we haven't been talking much. Hung out with this cute gal from work yesterday and shit, I don't know, if she would've tried something, I probably would've."

"Probably?" Porter raised an eyebrow.

I rolled my eyes. "No, not probably."

#   #   #

The next night, I watched from the bed as Mallory picked out clothes for work. *We're both here. It's early. We should fuck.*

Mallory turned to me, "What's going on with us?"

"How do you mean?" I asked.

"You know damn good and well what I mean," she said.

"Well, it doesn't seem very good these days, does it?" I replied.

"Do you want to end things?"

"We probably should, don't cha think?" I reasoned.

"I'm not happy with you or us, so yeah."

Why aren't you happy with me? This is all you. "So, then, what are we going to do about the lease here?" I asked.

"I'll move out," she said. "I could probably stay with my old roommate until I find a place."

"You want me to sleep on the couch tonight?"

"It's your bed, so I can't really kick you out of it," she said. "You want me to sleep on the couch?"

"No." *We should fuck.*

"Can you keep your hands to yourself?" she asked.

"I imagine."

Dammit.

#   #   #

Mallory's car was in the driveway when I got home from Haggen the next evening.

She's still here? "Did you talk to your friend?" I asked Mallory.

"Yeah," she said. "She doesn't have space for me right now, but my other friend is looking to move out so I'm going to see what we can find. Is it going to be all right if I'm here until then?"

No. We're not fucking. Leave. Don't be mean. "Suppose," I said. "Should we change the sleeping arrangements?"

"I'm okay if you're okay."

You still might fuck me?

Mallory went to bed at eleven. Half an hour later, I went upstairs. She didn't say anything when I got under the covers, but I didn't hear sleep breathing.

Maybe she's awake. If she fucks me, we could probably work all this out. Why doesn't she want to sleep with me? I jostled her leg with mine. No reaction.

Waited too long to come upstairs. Earlier tomorrow.

# # #

On her way to Haggen's bakery department, Caprice stopped by my check stand. "We're having pizza and movies tonight."

"Sure you are," I sighed.

"We are. I made my suitemate promise."

"What's the movie?" I asked.

"Don't know yet," Caprice said. "Glynne's coming. You know she has a crush on you?"

A crush? People still have those? "I didn't," I said.

"You should come."

Caprice's suitemate and roommate couldn't agree on what to get on the pizza. A forty minute debate ensued for the five of us to agree on toppings.

Midway through the second movie, which everyone in the group had already seen, Glynne announced, "I've got to get going. I got the early shift tomorrow."

"Okay," Caprice said. "I'll get my coat."

"Where do you live, Glynne?" I asked.

"Up on Yew Street Hill," she answered.

"I can take you home," I said. "I should get going too."

Caprice looked over. "As long as it's not out of your way."

"Naw," I lied. "No problem."

"Since you live with your parents, do you have to be home at a certain time?" I asked Glynne once we were in the car.

"No," she said. "They don't care now that I've graduated."

"Could I keep you out a while longer then?" I asked.

"Sure. What did you want to do?"

"Get to know you better."

I stopped in a dark lot overlooking the water at Lake Padden Park. Turning to face her, "Glynne, I would love to ask you out, but I'm living with my girlfriend still and it wouldn't be cool for me to go all two-timing."

"Yeah, you're right. I'm attracted to you to but I don't want to create problems with Mallory."

You know her name? Shit. "We've been having a rough time and we'll be broken up pretty quick here. Technically, we're broken up, even though we're still living together. She's moving out in a week or so."

After a few silent moments, Glynne asked, "Why is she still living with you?"

"Uh, she's trying to get a place with a friend of hers and it hasn't quite panned out. It's not like we hate each other or anything."

"That's good, I guess."

Our conversation continued a while longer. During a pause, "I'd really like to kiss you. Would that be okay?"

Facing the windshield, she replied, "Yeah."

A few soft kisses later, "I should be getting you home. You've got to get up early."

#   #   #

At eight-forty Mallory stood in the middle of the bedroom, arms crossed, "Where were you last night?"

"Out with some friends from work," I croaked, pushing the comforter down.

"Until after three?"

"Apparently," I said. "I don't have to work today."

She stared at me, silent. *We're broken up, remember? Not another word.* Naked, I walked past her, to the bathroom.

Mallory was no longer in the bedroom after I peed.

Don't be a dick. Make up something.

I yelled downstairs. No reply. Not in the kitchen, the other bathroom. Her car was gone.

Porter and I met up at the Quarterback again after he got off work at seven-thirty. I told him of my adventure with Glynne the prior evening and Mallory's reaction this morning. "Did she come back?" he asked.

"Not while I was there," I replied. "What should I tell her when I get home?"

He laughed. "I don't think the truth is a great idea."

"Wasn't planning on it," I said. "Maybe went over to someone's house after the bars closed and shot the shit a while?"

"Better than nothing," he agreed.

Sasha and Paula were on the couch, the TV on, when I walked into the apartment. "What did you do?" Sasha asked.

"Came home late last night," I admitted. "Why?"

"Mallory packed up a bag and stormed out of here about an hour ago," Paula said. "She said she was staying at her old roommate's but not to call her."

Wasn't going to. "I get the bed to myself tonight? Rock n' roll."

"You're a dick," Sasha said.

"She broke up with me then stayed here, sleeping in the same bed. How am I the dick?"

"You didn't have to stay out all night like that," Sasha said.

"It got her to leave though."

Paula said, "Thanks for that. But I don't want to pay more rent."

"How's this, I'll cover the increase in rent, if you guys are okay with splitting the bills three ways?"

Sasha spoke up, "Can you afford that?"

"As long as my hours are the same, I'm good."

# # #

"What's up with you and Glynne now that Mallory's gone?" Isaac asked me when the remaining customer left the video store.

"She came over last night after work. Sasha and Paula were gone, so we spent some quality time in the bedroom," I said. Lowering my voice, "Do you still expect girls to stop you from like, touching their boobs and stuff?"

"Hell, yeah," he said. "I was so nervous the first time Holly and I starting making out, she had to put my hand up her shirt. Did Glynne slap you?"

"No, not at all," I said. "But I kept expecting her to. I mean, she graduated last year so I figured she wasn't terribly experienced or anything."

"People do fuck in high school, Jon."

I laughed. "Yeah, yeah. But Glynne's so quiet most of the time. I was ready for another 'I don't want to burn in hell,' when I put my hand on her ass, but..."

"Shit, did you two fuck last night?"

"Yeah. That's what I'm saying. I wasn't expecting to, but every time I tried something, she went along with it, so I kept going."

"And?" he asked.

"Nothing spectacular," I said. "She didn't seem real into it or anything." *And her pussy felt strange.*

"You already said she was young."

"Yeah, but I guess I expected her to be more, what, perky? I did all the work."

"But she let you do her," Isaac said.

"And that's plenty."

February 1993 (Real World, Year 1)

Glynne told me she was done Saturday at five and as I had the day off, I stopped by the store to grab dinner. Glynne was at the time clock when I saw her. "What are you doing now?" I asked.

"Nothing," she said. "Going to go home, change, then who knows?"

"Could I get you to skip going home and come over instead?"

Grinning, "I think so."

Glynne followed me back to the apartment. We sat on the couch, eating lunch. "Where are the roommates?" she asked.

"Sasha went home for the weekend and Paula is working until eight so the place is mine, all mine! Bwah ha ha!"

When we'd finished eating, we retired to my room. *Why did your pussy feel so odd last time?*

"Turn around," I said.

She did, setting her butt square onto my face. She spun my dick around in her mouth. *That's not going to do much. Still can't see your pussy.* I pushed her butt up.

Wow! Both Glynne's inner labia hung down an inch and a half from her. *Those are huge!* I ran my tongue between them, pushing her up every so often to see her snatch. *Is it bigger than normal? Looks monstrous.*

"Come here," I said. She brought her face to mine, staying on top of me. *Doesn't feel big.* Glynne ground into me but didn't look close to orgasm, so I came without her. When she settled beside me, hand plunged between her legs.

"I should probably get going," she said, standing up.

Want to play with you more. "I didn't think you had anything going on," I said, still on the bed.

"I don't, but my parents might get freaked out if I don't show up pretty soon."

"Thought you could stay out as late as you wanted."

She scowled. "Last week they got all pissed and told me as long as I was living there I had to be home by midnight."

"That my fault?"

"Well..."

"Sorry."

"I've been staying out with Caprice lately, so it's not just you," Glynne said.

# # #

Sasha already at class, I went upstairs when the shower stopped. At the top of the staircase, Paula stood in her room, naked, one foot on her desk, spreading lotion down her leg.

"Uh, Paula? Do you think maybe you should close the curtains so you don't give the people across the street a show?"

Not moving, she replied, "I don't think they're home now."

"But wouldn't it be considerate of you to close the curtains. Just in case?"

"Probably." She pulled the curtains closed.

Walking into her room, "Let me see what you did yesterday." *Did you shave off all your pubic hair?*

Still naked, she sat down on her futon. "Lean back, I want to see the whole thing." She did, then opened her legs, a good sized triangle of hair above her vagina. "It doesn't look like you did much."

"I couldn't bring myself to shave it all."

Tugging at her hair, measuring the length, "With all you left in the tub, I was sure you were bald now."

"Kind of looked like it, didn't it?"

Peculiar. Paula's inner labia were thin, ridgeless swaths of pink skin, which didn't protrude from her outers. *Nothing like Glynne's. Or Mallory's.* Both blended into the walls of her vagina, leaving a smooth, angled slope into the bottom of her pussy. *Tiny, like her.*

Leaning forward, I ran my tongue across her exposed clit.

"What're you doing down there?" she asked.

"Since I'm here..." I licked her again.

"Since you're there..."

Paula came ten minutes later.

Me now?

"I need to get to class," she said, rising from the bed.

Shit.

#   #   #

"Why'd Mallory call you?" Porter asked, handing me the darts at the Quarterback Pub.

"Not sure," I replied. "Rub it in that she's living in Hawaii, working for her stepmom, having a good time and I'm working at a grocery store that's annihilating my feet."

"Wuss," Porter teased.

"You get cortisone injected into the bottom of your feet and see how you feel," I countered. "At least Mallory's living with her dad. I've got my own place. Well, kind of."

"Does Paula know about Glynne?"

"Don't think so," I said. "Who knows? Glynne hasn't been over when the roommates have been there. Last night, Glynne and I ended up fucking in the front seat of my car at the rest stop south of Lake Samish because we had nowhere else to go."

Porter laughed, almost spilling his beer. "You could tell Paula. Then you could fuck at home, like a normal person."

"Paula finds out I'm screwing someone else, she'll pull the plug."

"Which one you like hanging out with more?"

"Shit, I can't hang out with either of them," I said. "Neither one's twenty-one. And neither talk all that much when we're together."

#   #   #

Mallory called again the following week. She talked about her job and life in Hawaii. I kvetched about my increasingly harrowing visits to the podiatrist.

Is that guilt? "There's something I need to tell you," I began.

"Oh, what's that?"

"Well, we've been getting along, and I kind of want to tell you but don't know that I should."

"Why not?"

"Well, since we're all broken up, there's no need to get into it."

"Now I'm curious, so you'd better tell me," she demanded.

"Uh, well, Paula and I kind of had a thing before you moved in here."

"Fuck, I knew it."

No way. Why did you let her move in, then? "You knew?"

"No, but something never felt right about you and her. How long?"

"Well, right up until you moved in."

"Were you two fucking while I was living there?"

"No, not while you were here." *Jerkin' her off doesn't count.*

"That's really fucked up."

"Yeah, I'm sorry."

"So the whole time I was living there, you two had this secret. God, Paula always acted superior. No wonder. Christ, I feel like such an idiot."

"Mallory, I'm sorry. I thought you should know. I don't feel like lying to you anymore." *About Paula last spring.*

"Well, thanks for telling me," she said. "I'm going to go. I'll call you if I can talk about this more."

March 1993 (Real World, Year 1)

Mallory called after ten. "I've been thinking about the Paula thing…"

I'm a dick and you hope I die?

"And while I feel kind of stupid all living with her and all," she said. "It doesn't bother me that much."

"Really?" *You're lying. You should be furious.* "Well, I'm sorry about lying about it for so long. It was one of those things I found myself in the middle of and I didn't know how to deal with it all so I kind of kept…" Silence from the other end of the phone. "Oh shit, I'll stop talking now."

"Good idea," she said.

"Yeah. What are we doing with all this talking, you and I?" I asked. "I mean, we're talking more now that you're in Hawaii than we have in last couple months."

"I know, I like it. I'd like us to keep it up."

"Yeah, I'd like that too."

Another hour on the phone before I went to bed. *Could Mallory be the One? What if she's my soul mate and I let her move to Hawaii? Paula and Glynne don't talk to me the way she does. Barely get five words out of Glynne. Paula wants to go out with every cute guy she sees but she'll play with me when there's no one better around. But Glynne likes to fuck. And Paula's cute as hell. And Mallory's in Hawaii.*

# # #

Again, Paula was rubbing lotion on her leg, one propped on her desk, naked, with her bedroom door open. "Can I help you with that?"

"Sure," she replied, squirting some lotion on my hands.

"You ever going to close your curtains while you're prancing around here naked?"

"I don't think about it."

My hands sliding over her butt, she turned around to face me. "Get on the bed," I said. She did.

Kneeling on the floor, I ate her. A short while later she came.

How many times can I get you to come? I continued. She came again.

"I don't think I can..." she said, her breathing interrupting her. I kept licking. She came again. "I'm good, really. You can stop now."

My nose on her clit, "I can keep going," I said, continuing. She came again.

She pushed my head away. "Stop. Stop! Can't...breathe... can't breathe."

"You sure? I can still move my tongue."

"No, no. I'm done. Seriously."

"I'm willing to stay here," I said.

"That's okay," she said. "Get off the floor already."

Paula scooched off the bed, my shorts in her hands. "I don't usually give blowjobs," she admitted. "I've got TMJ so it hurts when I do it for too long."

"What's too long," I asked.

"A minute or two."

Not much of a blowjob. "Try using your hands when your jaw starts to bug you."

She ran her closed hand along my shaft. "Like this?"

"Exactly like that."

She alternated having my cock in her mouth and her hand. After fifteen minutes, she was primarily using her hand. *Got to*

142

come in her mouth. Get close, get close. She put me back in her mouth, I came quickly, quietly. She resumed stroking me.

I started to get soft. "Thanks for that," I said.

"What, did you come?"

"Oh yeah." I replied.

Wide-eyed, "So I swallowed?"

"Well, yeah, you did." *You didn't notice? Must not have come that much.*

"I've never swallowed before."

"Well, you have now," I said. "Congratulations."

"Cool. That wasn't bad at all."

"Good to hear. You did a great job with your hands."

"Thanks," she said, handing me my shorts. "I'll use my hands from now on."

# # #

"A friend of Mallory's stepmom knows one of the concert promoters in Honolulu and he has an opening in his office. I'd love to get back into it," I told Mary after another lengthy discussion with Mallory.

"But in Hawaii? Isn't there something around here?"

"Sure, but I don't have any contacts here. The ones I have from last year are in California and even those aren't all that great. I'm going there for an interview and see what I think. I've got to find another job," I continued. "My feet are destroyed from standing all day. I can't go back to the podiatrist again. I tried to claw my way through the damn wall when he was injecting cortisone into my heels."

"What about you and Mallory?" Mary asked.

"We've been talking a lot since she moved there," I replied. "I don't know if we'd be getting back together or anything."

"Uh huh," she said.

"I don't. That's not my plan anyway. I'm going over there to see about a job and if Mallory and I end up back together, well, all the better then."

"How do her parents feel about you staying with them for a week?"

I hesitated. "Not real keen on it, but I'll be on the couch. I'm going to try and stay out of the way."

"And when are you going over?"

"In a week," I said. "Coming back on Saturday morning. Uh, could I get a ride to the airport on Sunday."

"I was wondering when you were going to get to that. What time?"

"Eleven. And maybe could you pick me up when I get back?"

"Probably."

# # #

It took twenty-five minutes from Mallory's parent's place, a two story unit, set into the hillside, toward the back of Manoa Valley to get downtown to my interview. Forty minutes after Mallory dropped me off at the promoter's, "He offered me a job," I said to her. "I told him I'd call him when I moved here in three weeks."

She hugged me. "I'm so happy for you. Much better than Haggen, huh?"

"Wouldn't take much," I admitted. "I actually have a job in promotion. Awesome."

"Did he tell you what you'd be doing?"

"Some of this, some of that. Sounded exactly like the stuff I did at Western last year. An assistant position but working with bigger acts."

"What're you starting at?" she asked.

"Ten an hour," I said. "It's a foot in the door. Any weeks with gigs, I'll probably get more than forty hours."

We got back to Anthony and Cleo's before noon. "I'm going to lay out."

"You want lunch?" I asked.

"Not yet."

"Finally feeling hungry." I pulled out some grapes and sandwich fixings. Mallory left her room and went out to the deck.

That's a nice bikini.

On Mallory's bed, I finished eating then went out on the deck. "How long you going to be out here?" I asked.

"You got somewhere to be?"

"Not this second."

"I'm getting hungry," she said, getting up. "Can you grab my water for me?"

She walked inside ahead of me. I flicked water at her back. "Stop!" she squealed, running toward the bathroom. I followed her and threw more water at her.

Mallory tried to shut the bathroom door before I caught up to her but I pressed my way inside. "Enough with the water."

"Once more," another handful at her stomach. She jumped away.

"All right, I'm changing now."

"Go right ahead," I said. "I won't stop you."

She looked at me, we kissed. I lifted her onto the counter and pushed her bikini to the side. "Not here," she whispered. She took my hand and led me to her bedroom.

But the bedroom is boring.

She took off my clothes, then hers. "You trimmed," I said.

"I lay out a lot," she said. "Can't have spider legs creeping out the sides."

On top of the blanket, Mallory on her back as I entered her. *Is her snatch bigger than Glynne's? Can't use a tape measure.* Pressed my dick along the top of her pussy, moving it side to side, brushing her clit. I scooched back to get the base of my pecker aligned with the bottom of Mallory's puss.

"What're you doing?" she asked.

"Playing," I lied. *About the same.* I returned inside her.

Afterward, "What're you going to do with all your stuff?" Mallory asked.

"Bring what I want, sell what I don't. How much was it to ship your car here?"

"About twelve hundred."

Not happening. She sat up, "Where are you and I in all this?" she asked.

"Well, I'd like to see if we can work things out," I replied. "We've been talking well and you know, laughing a lot. It's been good."

"Yeah, I think so too," she agreed.

"I think with some effort on both our parts, we can do better this time."

# # #

Isaac was at the apartment when I got back from the airport. "Well, you going to be a Hawaiian or what?" he asked as I closed the door.

"Aloha, motherfucker," I replied.

Sasha sneered from the couch. "What're you going to do about the lease?"

"I'll find someone before I leave Sasha, promise," I replied. "Wouldn't you love to live here, Isaac?"

He laughed. "Maybe. Holly and I are on a month to month now. You're here 'til June, right?"

Paula said, "Through June, yeah. You should, Isaac. Holly's fun and it'd be good to have another girl here."

"Let me talk to her," Isaac said. He looked back at me. "You and Mallory okay now?"

"Think so," I said. *Why'd you bring her up? Paula might've fucked me before I left.* "We had a great time together while I was there. Talked surprisingly well together. First time in a long, long time."

"When are you leaving?" Paula asked.

"Three weeks," I said. "I need to give my two weeks and a week to get all my shit together."

"You're going to have a going away party, right?" Isaac asked.

"Ladies?" I looked toward the girls.

"Of course," Paula answered.

April 1993 (Real World, Year 1)

Thursday evening, the doorbell chimed. Isaac, Holly and Porter walked in. "You didn't have to bring beer," I told Porter.

"Better too much..." he said, handing me a six pack.

"How often you going to get back this way?"

"Every few months, I imagine."

"Kind of expensive, don't cha think?"

"Not once they've completed the Trans-Pacific Highway. They're about a hundred fifty miles off the coast of California now," I said. "Once the Seattle exit is complete, the trip will take twenty-couple hours, so I'll be expecting to see you guys every once in a while."

The doorbell rang again. Paula opened the front door, Glynne walked in. "Hey, Glynne," I said. "Isn't Caprice coming?"

"She told me to tell you good luck, but she has to open tomorrow so has to be there at five."

"I'll let it go. This once," I said. "Beer?"

"Sure," she replied. We went to the kitchen.

Ameline, one of the front parcels, arrived with a couple cashiers from Haggen. Hank, Sasha and Tate sat on the floor of the dining area swapping SAGA stories. Paula, Porter, Holly and Isaac shot the shit in the living room. Glynne stayed in the living room while I floated from person to person, group to group.

Near ten thirty, the cashiers left, leaving Ameline behind. "You drove?" I asked her. *Nice butt. Flat chest. Too bad you're still in high school.*

"Yeah, I followed them over here."

"Let me show you the place," I said to Ameline. "You've seen the living room, obviously." I directed her to the downstairs laundry area, "One bathroom." Through the kitchen, dining room and upstairs, "Other bathroom." Pointing at the closed doors, "Paula's room, Sasha's room." I opened the door, "And my room."

Ameline followed me inside. "How did you get the biggest room?" she asked.

"Been here the longest." She flipped through my CDs.

She brushed her long, brunette hair aside, "You're going to Honolulu, right?"

"Yeah," I said. "I don't have a place yet, but Mallory's parents are going to let me stay there until we can find something."

"I've got a couple cousins on Oahu, over on North Shore. My parents said I might be able to stay with them this summer for a couple weeks. For a graduation present."

"You'll have to let me know if you make it over," I said. "I'm going to send a postcard back to everyone at Haggen when I get there with my address, you know, to rub it in."

"Looking forward to that," Ameline said. "Someone told me you had long hair before you started working at Haggen. Can't picture you with long hair."

"I've had some hair in my time. You should've seen me in high school. Wait, I've got my yearbooks right over here."

A knock on the door. "Come in," I said. Glynne opened the door. *You're still here?*

"What cha doing?" Glynne asked.

"Talking about Hawaii and high school," I replied. "About to bust out my yearbooks. Here, sit."

The three of us sat on the futon, me in the middle, showing off my high school pictures. Numerous laughs later, I closed my senior yearbook. "Not quite what I had before I started, but different."

"Kind of scary," Ameline said.

Setting my yearbooks on the floor, silence took over.

You can go, Glynne. Unless you both want to do me.

The quiet continued.

This isn't going anywhere. "Hey Glynne, what are you doing tomorrow?" I asked.

"Working at eight." I turned to my left.

"What about you, Ameline?"

"I'm on at nine."

Glynne sat silent. And sat silent.

Ameline, "I should get going."

"Oh, yeah. Cool."

Dammit.

Sasha and Paula were watching TV with Hank. "Night, guys," I said on my way back upstairs, after seeing Ameline out.

Right hand dug between her legs while I kissed a naked Glynne on the futon. Left hand squeezed her thigh, then her butt. She spread her legs, I scooted between them. *Get all the way to make it fair.* I rubbed my cock between her exaggerated labia. *Doesn't look good.* Twirling the head of my cock against her clit, I pressed against her. *More than an inch longer. Not that much bigger.* Donning a condom, I went at her. For five minutes.

"I'll let you know when I finally get an apartment," I said. "I expect you to write."

"All right," she said.

# # #

The day after arriving in Oahu, I phoned the promotion office after Mallory left for work. His secretary answered. "He's not in the office right now," she said. "May I take a message?"

"I was in three weeks ago and he'd ask that I give him a call when I was back on the island. I'm back now and wanted to let him know."

She paused briefly. "Oh, yeah. We've already hired for that position."

You did what? But he said... "Uh...um...okay. I was under the impression I already had the job, that's why I moved here."

"I can't speak to that, but we did hire someone for the assistant position last week. I could take your number and have him get back to you. He won't be in for a couple days, though."

"Um, yeah." I gave her Anthony and Cleo's number before I hung up. "Fuck."

To Mallory, "What am I going to do now? How are we supposed to afford an apartment?"

"We can stay here a while," she said. "Anthony and Cleo won't care. You'll find a job."

"I don't want to stay here. I feel like I'm imposing horribly, and I don't have money to pay for much."

"I've been looking for an apartment since you left and there's not a lot out there, unless we want to pay twelve hundred a month."

"For a one bedroom? You've got to be kidding."

"Anything decent starts at eight fifty," she said.

What the hell?

"We're probably going to be stuck here until you can find something."

Every time I suggested somewhere from the paper, Mallory said it was in a part of town where we didn't want to live.

How did I let this happen? Not working fast food.

I threw the paper on the coffee table. "Nothing?" Mallory asked.

"There's plenty if I want to flip burgers or get my masters."
Dammit.

"You said the promoter was going to call you back. Maybe the new guy won't work out."

What have I done?

# # #

Saturday afternoon Mallory had scheduled a couple appointments to look at apartments. "Anthony mentioned Liberty House is looking for assistant buyers," Mallory said in the car. "Is that something you could do?"

"Probably. What's Liberty House?"

"Like Macy's. They use the same computer system. You'd be helping the buyer with, well, whatever."

"Hey, I'll take anything. What do I need to do?"

"Anthony said he could talk to the gal in charge of hiring and get you an application."

"Seriously?"

Our second stop was a petite one bedroom in a secure building across the ditch from Waikiki. While it didn't have air conditioning, it was a corner unit with screened windows on both faces and a nook off the living area for a small table and chairs. The new washer and drier tipped the apartment over the line for us.

May 1993 (Real World, Year 1)

"You're in boys eight to twenty? Tamara's your buyer?" Mallory asked when I got home from training at Liberty House.

"Yeah," I answered. "How'd you know?"

"Anthony keeps me in the loop with all the buyer drama. Did you sleep okay last night?"

"Not so much, too damn hot. You?"

"Could we move the futon to the living room and change it back to a couch during the day? Maybe there'll be more of a breeze there."

"Can't hurt." We adjusted the futon to flat, put sheets over the cover and threw our pillows on it.

Naked, under a single sheet, I stroked Mallory's hand. "I started my period this morning," she said.

No sex then.

June 1993 (Real World, Year 1)

"Let's try doggie," Mallory said, turning over, getting on her knees. All the way inside her, she squealed and fell to the bed.

"Jesus! What was that?" I asked.

"That really hurt. We're going to have to try something else. I didn't think it would be as bad like that."

"Maybe on your stomach?" I pushed into her again.

"Oww! Stop. I'm sorry Jon," she said. "I can't."

You could blow me. "Is this the first time you've been in pain?"

"No, it's been getting worse for a while now."

"What's a while?"

"Before I left Washington," she said.

"Do you have a gynecologist here?"

"Not yet, but I'm sure Cleo knows someone."

# # #

"What'd the gyno say?" I asked Mallory the following week.

"She's sending me to some sort of women's specialist," she answered. "She said it could be a cyst or tumor of some kind or maybe some kind of cancer."

Cancer? "She doesn't think it's cancer, does she?"

"Probably not. Most likely it's a cyst. The speculum hurt so much I was crying the whole time and she didn't see anything wrong inside. They did a pap but my last one was clear, so..."

"Did you already make an appointment with the specialist?"

"Next week."

Then we can fuck again?

150

\# \# \#

In bed, a thin, cotton sheet over me, right hand found my dick. Immediately hard, the stroking began. Left hand grasped Mallory's back.

"Are you jerking off?" Mallory asked.

Now motionless. "I was."

"Stop it. You're shaking the whole goddamn bed." She twisted away from me, onto her left side.

Not going to help?

When Mallory was asleep again, I went into the bathroom, sat on the toilet and finished myself off.

\# \# \#

Over dinner the next week, "How was your first trip to the Distribution Center?" Mallory asked.

"Stupid as rocks," I scoffed. "All the stores send shit back to Oahu so we can put new prices on it then send it back to them? Ridiculous."

"But you got to wear jeans," Mallory offered.

"In an unairconditioned warehouse. Thought I was going to sweat to death. Who cares if I wear shorts there or not?"

July 1993 (Real World, Year 2)

On the futon, I ran a hand through Mallory's hair. "It hurts too much, Jon. I'm sorry," she said.

You could blow me.

"Can I stay on the outside?" I asked, rubbing my hard cock against her butt.

"You think you can actually do that?"

"If it's my only option."

She lifted her leg, my dick slid along the outside of her snatch. She reached down, cupping her hand while I ground into it.

"Don't trust me to stay out?" I asked.

"Thought it might feel good."

"It does." Three minutes later, I came in her hand.

"You think maybe we can do this instead of fucking?" I asked. *Beats jerking off in the bathroom.*

"Don't see why not."

# # #

Once in bed the following evening, I rubbed my dick against Mallory's butt the next night. She grunted, flopping onto her stomach.

Grabbing a *Penthouse*, I closed the bathroom door.

# # #

Eleven nights in a row I jerked off into the toilet after Mallory had gone to sleep.

# # #

"There's a message on the machine for you," Mallory said.

"Who is it?" I asked, taking off my tie.

"Some girl, Ameline. Who is she?"

"Ameline? One of the front parcels at Haggen," I replied. *A high school hottie.* "She said her parents were sending her for a graduation present. A couple of her cousins live up on North Shore. She leave a number?"

"It's on the message," Mallory said, returning to dinner preparation.

After listening to the message, I returned Ameline's call.

"Oh, hi, Jon. I hope it's okay I called. Mallory's not mad, is she?"

"Don't think so," I said, watching Mallory from the other side of the kitchen counter. "Thought you wouldn't be here until August."

"It's almost August," she said. "This week worked better. You going to have any time this weekend to get together and catch up? You want me to come into Honolulu?"

"Naw, let's meet in the middle somewhere. Where exactly are you?"

"Near Kuhuku," Ameline replied.

"There's a Burger King right off Kamehameha," I told Ameline. "You can't miss it."

"You're going to meet her at a Burger King?" Mallory asked after I hung up.

"It's easy to find," I said. "It's not like I'm taking her sightseeing or anything. Grab a bite, catch up."

152

# # #

Ameline sat by herself inside at Burger King. "How's everything going?"

"The promotion job fell through," I said. "Mallory's dad got me a job as an assistant buyer with Liberty House."

"Department store, right?"

"Yeah. I'm in boys eight to twenty."

"You like it there?" Ameline asked.

"Not at all," I replied. "The only decent part of it is being able to go to the distribution center once a week and get away from all the bullshit paperwork."

"What'd you expect?"

"I don't know what I expected but the title, assistant buyer, kind of made me think I'd be assisting the buyer. Mostly I answer the phone, file shit and work in the warehouse. Modified secretary is what it should be called. It might be okay if I didn't spend hours filling out shit by hand that would take a couple minutes if it was on computer. But fuckin' a, it pays the bills, so I should stop bitchin'. Anything new at Haggen?"

"Not a thing," she said.

Going to be a short conversation. "Anybody quit, get fired, beat up a customer?"

"Nope. Same ol'. You looking for another job, then?"

"Not yet," I said. "I should stay there for a while since Mallory's dad vouched for me and everything. I mean if I find something kick ass or someone wants to pay me a shitload, I'll quit in a second. I'm not expecting either."

"What else do you do here, besides work?"

"Movies, read, play games on the computer. What about you, now that you're all graduated?"

"Going to Whatcom in the fall and get my AA, then maybe U-Dub. Maybe Oregon."

"What for?"

"Nursing."

"Cool," I said. "Got any plans, or a bunch of lounging on the beach?"

"Mostly lounging," she said. "I brought a couple books I'm hoping to finish."

The conversation died.

"You want me to give you a ride back?"

"No," she shook her head. "It's way out of your way. I want to check out the mall before I head back, anyway."

"Well, get a hold of me if you want to go see a movie or if you make it into Honolulu."

"For sure," she said. "Good to see you. I'll be sure to tell everyone back at Haggen you're living the life."

"Thanks. Have a good vacation."

#   #   #

Mallory answered the phone when it rang late Sunday afternoon. She covered the mouthpiece, glaring at me, "I think it's Ameline. She's crying."

Crying?

She thrust the phone toward me. "What's up?" I asked.

"Oh God, Jon, I can't stand it here," she said. "My cousin is a pothead and his friends are always over smoking out in the living room. And his father walks around naked. I can't stay here another night."

Naked? "You have enough for a hotel?"

"No," she said.

"Okay. Have you called your parents?"

"I can't," her voice broke. "It's my mom's sister's kid and it'll be a huge deal. Is there any way I can stay with you and Mallory?"

Here? Why? "Uh…"

"I won't spend much time there. I won't be any trouble."

"Um…hold on a sec." To Mallory's scowl, "Would it be cool if Ameline stayed here a few days?"

"Why?" I gave her the short version. "Shit, Jon…"

"She's got no one else here," I said. "She can have the bedroom, you guys can go to the beach, and she'll be gone on Saturday."

"I'm not thrilled about it," Mallory replied.

Into the phone, "It'll be all right. Do you need us to come get you?"

"No, I'll take a cab."

"You sure? It's no trouble," I lied.

"No, it's out of the way and it'll be faster this way. What's your address?"

An hour later Ameline was buzzing from the ground floor. After repeatedly thanking us, she launched into the misery of her cousin's. "His dad came into the bathroom while I was in the shower. I locked the door, but it didn't work."

Mallory asked, "And what, went to the bathroom?"

"Started talking to me. And stayed even after I turned off the water and was trying to get out. I told him I needed to get out and he said, 'Go ahead.'"

"Wow," I said. "Scary. You really not going to tell your folks?"

"I don't think I can," she said.

Ameline settled in the bedroom, Mallory and I pulled out the futon for the night. "Thanks again for letting her stay with us."

"Did I have a choice?"

#   #   #

"I don't want to watch TV tonight," Mallory said Tuesday evening after dinner. "Can we play a game instead?"

"Do we have any games?" I asked.

"We've got cards," she said, looking through the hall closet. "And Uno."

"Brewno?"

"We going to get drunk, then?" Mallory asked.

"That is the point of the game."

After explaining the rules, the three of us sat around the coffee table in the living room as the dining room had but two chairs. The game didn't last long, but all of us were on our third bottle of beer before stopping.

"Okay," Mallory said. "I can't do that again."

"It's a little less crazy with more people," I said.

"Can we play something else?" Mallory asked.

"Any kind of card game you want," I said. "You girls play poker?"

Ameline shook her head. Mallory said, "We don't have any chips."

"We could play strip poker," I suggested.

"All right," Ameline said. "But each sock counts."

"And I get an extra because you both have bras on."

"Only one extra," Mallory agreed.

When I won the third hand in a row to win an article other than a sock, both girls quit. "This isn't much fun if we don't win," Ameline said.

"Just because you haven't yet, doesn't mean you won't," I said.

"Let's watch TV," Mallory said.

You didn't want to watch TV.

Sitting between the girls, my left hand rested on Mallory's leg. Ameline bumped my right arm, I moved it up to the back of the futon. Ameline scooted closer.

Did Mallory see that? I glanced at her out of the corner of my eye. *Doesn't look like it.*

My right arm fell onto Ameline's shoulders, left hand inched up Mallory's leg. Mallory reclined against the arm of the futon to a horizontal position, a sliver of panties visible up her shorts.

That an invitation?

I looked back at the television. Left hand continued its trek. Right hand crept onto Ameline's boob. No reaction.

Awesome. Both of them. Awesome.

Left hand pushed Mallory's panties aside. Right hand dropped under Ameline's shirt.

A light, quick snort.

No way. She's asleep?

I disentangled my hand from her pubic hair. *At least Ameline's still awake.*

Ameline got up from the couch.

Crap.

"You coming?" she whispered. Leaving the TV on, I followed her to the bedroom. She shut the door.

She lifted my face up from her breast. "Jon," Ameline whispered. "I'm kind of embarrassed to say this, but, well, I'm a virgin."

Why are you letting me do this to you? "Not a problem, Ameline."

Ameline naked, I kissed down her body. Past her belly button, Ameline pulled my head back up, closing her legs.

Why can't I eat you? Hand back on her snatch, letting one finger slip inside her, then circled her clit. She shuddered, squeaked. Back down her body, Ameline spun away, legs together.

But I want to. You're enjoying what I'm doing.

On my back, she mounted me. She kissed my neck, then my chest then returned to my neck. *Go ahead, you can suck my dick all you want.*

We continued kissing. Again, I ventured down toward her crotch. She pulled me back up.

Fuck this. I kissed her. "I should get to bed." *So I can jerk off.* "Good night."

I unfolded the futon, helped Mallory under the sheet, then lay on the floor and tugged one out.

156

# # #

Mallory apologized when I walked in the door Wednesday. "Sorry I fell asleep last night."

"No big deal," I replied. "Watched some TV and went to bed. How was your day at the beach?"

"We weren't there too long, a couple hours. What, we got there around ten or so and took off about one-thirty."

"Anything interesting happen?" *Like Ameline mentioning I groped her last night?*

"Laid out, didn't talk a much," she said. "Oh my God! She has got of ton of stretch marks on her hips. Was she bigger once?"

"No idea," I replied. "I hear puberty can have that effect on some people."

"Yeah, I guess. But I'm surprised considering how skinny she is."

Ameline wished us a good night after dinner and went into the bedroom. After the news, Mallory and I converted the futon to bed-form and pulled the sheet over us.

Ten minutes after I heard the first deep exhale from the other side of the bed, I discreetly put on my boxers and a t-shirt. The bedroom door wasn't completely shut so I pushed it open. "Ameline," I whispered.

"Yeah?"

"I take it you're awake, then?"

"Good guess."

"You mind if I come in?"

"Please do."

The mattress was on the floor, directly below the window. I sat on the edge of it.

"You want a backrub?" I offered.

"Sure." I repositioned myself atop her butt then lifted her sleep shirt over her head. I rubbed her shoulders, down her back, then stripped her panties off. I kneaded her butt, her thighs, her butt, her lower back then her butt again. I kissed her neck, moving down her back.

The bathroom door closed.

Ameline froze.

All the windows are open. "Okay, so then what about that one girl?" my loud whisper.

Ameline didn't answer.

Close to her ear, "Keep talking." I eased off her, taking up a foot away, against the wall, under the window.

"Oh, she's doing the same old crap," Ameline replied.

Better. "Didn't she say she was leaving?" I handed Ameline her panties.

She hurried into them before inching next to me against the wall. "Yeah, but she's still there." She pulled her oversized shirt over her head.

"And the front end manager is still the same ol' bitch?"

"Oh my God, the other day I thought she was going to hit one of the new cashiers."

"Why didn't she?"

"If they would've been alone," she said. "And the look on her face."

The toilet flushed. The bathroom door opened. *And Mallory knocks on the door...*

"We have to keep talking to sell this," I whispered to Ameline. *She's going to burst in here any second now.*

Ameline and I continued chatting another twenty minutes, rehashing the same events with the same people. I massaged her boobs over her shirt during our faux conversation.

I closed the bedroom door with an audible, "G'night." To the bathroom, scrubbed my face and teeth, then went to the living room. The form of Mallory's body under the sheet was still.

"What were you doing in the bedroom?" Mallory asked.

I started. "Oh, hey. Trying not to wake you up. Talking to Ameline."

"Why did you close the door?"

"Because you were sleeping. Were we too loud? I heard you go to the bathroom."

"No, I had to pee. Why was the door closed?"

"We didn't want to disturb you...I couldn't sleep because I was too hot. I went to the bathroom, the door was open, Ameline said hey so we shot the shit for a while. We shut the door in case we were talking too loudly. I think it was mostly me laughing more than the talking, but anyway..."

Monotone, "Uh-huh."

"Okay, if it happens again, I'll be sure to leave the door open so you can yell at me to keep it down."

"Yeah, good night." Mallory rolled over.

158

# # #

The three of us sat on the futon, dinner in hand, watching the news. "Should I get a cab tomorrow to take me to the airport?" Ameline asked.

"Naw," I said. "I can take you. I'll tell my boss I'm going out to the distribution center so they won't expect me at the office. No one cares when you show up at DC, so it's no problem." To Mallory, "Can you take the scooter tomorrow?"

She rolled her eyes. "Could you maybe have asked me first?"

Fuck you.

August 1993 (Real World, Year 2)

Friday morning, Ameline had the bathroom first so she could pack her toiletries then get ready. Mallory went in the bathroom as soon as Ameline was out. I pulled Ameline to the kitchen, still in a towel.

The water in the bathroom on, I set Ameline's towel on the counter and kissed her. Turning her around, I pressed my already hard dick against her, maneuvering it between her legs. Right hand wrapped around her hips.

Already wet? Terrific. Rub like that. That's peculiar. You didn't just... You're in her. Get out. I pulled back.

Divine. Just one more. I pushed back in a little.

Feels so damn good. She's a virgin. Get out!

"Sorry." Ameline grabbed her towel. *What a delightful pussy.* "No, really, I didn't mean to do that."

Ameline scampered to the bedroom, shutting the door behind her.

Can't I watch you dress?

Mallory left while I got ready.

Carrying Ameline's bags downstairs, "Sorry about that little incident in the kitchen. Seriously, I didn't mean to go inside you."

"Okay. Whatever."

"Ameline, honestly. You didn't say it was okay so it's not cool and I apologize."

"No big deal."

I could've stayed in you? "Do you ever go to the music store, Avalon, downtown?"

"Sometimes," she answered.

"It'd be awesome if you could pick me up The Cult import single of "She Sells Sanctuary." They have it there most of the time."

"Sure, if I make it down there," Ameline replied. "No problem."

"Plus, it'll give you a reason to write me."

I dropped her off at the terminal with a kiss then continued on to the Liberty House's distribution center.

#   #   #

"They find anything?" I asked Mallory when she's returned from the woman specialist.

"Endometriosis. Like she thought."

"Good, I guess. Now what?"

"They scheduled me for surgery on the eighteenth. In the hospital for a couple days and then bed rest for a week."

"But then you'll be okay?" I asked.

"Well, she said there's a chance of it coming back once it's removed. But at least we know what it is next time."

"That's a plus," I agreed. "Is there any way to keep it from coming back?"

"She said she's seeing more and more cases of it because women are waiting longer to have children. She said I probably wouldn't have to worry about it anymore if I got pregnant."

Not happening. Not with me. "What'd you say to that?"

"I said I wasn't planning on having kids in the foreseeable future, so we'll have to wait and see if it comes back."

#   #   #

Friday, a package in the mailbox with a Bellingham return address, a CD with a letter from Ameline:

Jon,

Thanks again for letting me stay there. It meant a lot to me that you and Mallory opened your home for me. I told my mom some of what happened at my cousin's but I left out a lot, too.

Here is the CD I think you wanted. If it isn't, too bad.

It was pretty shitty of you to pull that wham-bam no-thank-you-ma'am before I left. I really didn't want that to happen but apparently you didn't care about what I wanted, it was just about what you wanted. You said you didn't mean to but I think you probably did.

Sincerely,

Ameline

I didn't mean it. It was an accident. She accepted my apology on the way to the airport, didn't she? Can't let Mallory find this. I put the letter in the middle of my journal, then into the laptop's carrying case.

Later, Mallory asleep, I fashioned a letter on the laptop.

Ameline,

Thanks for picking up the CD for me, it was the right one. Next time you're in Avalon, tell them I said hi.

About the rest of your note, it was an accident and I'm really sorry it happened. I know you're a virgin and it was something that I wasn't expecting and I certainly didn't plan it. I am truly sorry and I hope you'll be able to forgive me.

Hopefully we can still be friends.

Jon

#   #   #

Mallory was still groggy when they wheeled her into her hospital room. Mush-mouthed, "You're here."

"Well, yeah," I said. "I'm not going to leave you alone after surgery. How shitty would that be?"

"What about work?"

"Went to DC and left early. There wasn't much to do. How'd it go?"

"She said she got it all but she was surprised at how much uterine tissue was everywhere. They had to spend an extra hour burning it all off."

"How do you feel?"

"Numb. They've got me on some good drugs," she giggled. "You should go home. I'm probably going to sleep the rest of the day."

"You sure?" I asked.

"Yeah. Thanks for being here, it's so sweet."

I kissed her on the forehead. "Call me if you need anything. I can be here in ten minutes."

# # #

Settling in on our couch, Mallory asked, "What'd you end up doing last night?"

"Got a movie from the video store, ate dinner, fell asleep." *Jerked off to bad porn.*

"I figured you'd go out for a beer."

"With who? I can drink by myself at home. It's cheaper too."

"Someone from work maybe?"

Like who? "I don't talk to anyone from work outside of work hours." *Have I ever gone out with anyone? Has anyone ever come over? You ever heard me on the phone with anyone?*

"Most people here are transitory. They get Island Fever after being here too long. Happens all the time," she said. "People are here for a couple years then pack up and move back to the mainland. A good friend of Cleo's had a successful business going, then, out of nowhere, up and left. Most people from the mainland are usually here about a year or so."

A year?

September 1993 (Real World, Year 2)

"How's that?" I asked, my dick barely inside Mallory.

"Good, so far. Go slow."

I eased the tip in, watching Mallory's face. She winced. "You want me to stop?"

"No, keep going," she said.

I backed up then in again. Then back and "Okay, I can't do this yet," Mallory said. *Probably mental.*

I removed myself. "You want me to eat you?" I offered. *Then you can blow me.*

"No," she said. "I've got to do some laundry."

Dammit.

# # #

Mallory stopped me on the way into the apartment, "What is your deal?"

"What deal?"

"Your attitude's been real shitty lately. It's getting old."

How about fucking me? "Nothing's different," I said. "I don't think I've been having attitude."

"Both Anthony and Cleo have brought it up on different occasions. You've been quiet when we go over there, you don't want to go to the beach. I swear to God I haven't seen you laugh in a month."

"Can we go inside?" I asked. Mallory closed the door behind us. "Maybe you're not paying attention when I laugh, Mallory. And you know I don't like laying out."

"You could do something else."

"Like what? I don't swim, surf or fish. What's there for me to do at the beach?" *Besides look at girls who might actually enjoy sex? It's depressing.*

"The next time we see Anthony and Cleo, can you at least try to act normal?"

"I'll make an extra special effort, okay?"

# # #

In the middle of journaling on my laptop after Mallory had gone to bed, I typed questions. 'Why am I here? What's keeping me here? Is there more good than bad?'

I opened up a new file and made a list.

Pros	Cons
Mallory	No friends
Anthony and Cleo	Hate the job
Nice evening weather	No leisure activities
	Too fat
	Too hot/too much sun
	No extra money
	Mallory

That's not real promising.

More questions. 'Can you fix anything? Do you want to? What are you going to do about it?'

I turned off the computer, set a *Penthouse* on the bathroom counter and dropped my shorts.

Don't offer to do anything, see what Mallory says. We'll never leave the apartment. And don't try to fuck her, see if she starts anything.

# # #

The following week I didn't touch Mallory; she didn't touch me. I didn't suggest getting a movie, going out to eat, anything. Neither did she. We stayed home, ate dinner, watched television. Mallory went to bed early, I stayed up and wrote.

# # #

Saturday evening I surprised Mallory by taking her to an expensive restaurant overlooking the beach on the far side of Honolulu. "I can't believe you're bringing me here," Mallory said.

"You wanted to come."

After we'd eaten, "You want to go for a walk?"

"Sure."

A few steps onto the beach, "You know, Mallory, I've been thinking a lot about things lately," I said.

Her smile evaporated. "Uh-huh."

"We've done better at the communicating thing since I've been here."

"I agree."

"But..."

"Of course there's a but."

"But, I haven't been happy in some time."

"Why haven't you been happy?" her eyes misting.

"I hate my job, you know that. I didn't come here for Liberty House."

"No, you came here for me."

You barely figured into it. I had plenty of play in Bellingham. "Not just you."

"Why not just me?" she countered. "You brought me to a fancy dinner to break up with me?"

"No, I wanted to come here. This is separate."

"What are you going to do? Move back?"

"Yeah, that's my plan," I said.

"You're fucking incredible," Mallory whispered. "We go through all this and now you're going to walk away."

"We've been trying, Mallory and I'm not happy here. It's got far less to do with us than it does with me."

"But you don't love me enough to stay here?"

Nope. "I have to try to get happier and I don't think I can do it here."

She spun away from me. "Well, fuck you." She walked toward the parking lot.

You going to leave me here?

The drive back to the apartment was silent.

"You want me to sleep in the bedroom?" I asked from across the living room, once we got inside.

"I'm going to go stay at Anthony and Cleo's."

The entire time she was throwing clothes in a bag, she muttered, "Can't believe you."

#   #   #

Friday night I called Mallory. "I found some of your stuff in the kitchen. But I already sold the scooter so I can't drop it off."

"I'll swing by and pick it up. When are you going to be there?"

"Can't go anywhere, Mallory. I'll be here all day, listening to music and reading." *You took the TV, remember?*

"Did you want to see my place?" she asked.

"Yeah, where is it?"

"A couple miles away, back toward Punahou."

#   #   #

Mallory arrived at noon. "You're sleeping on the floor?" she asked, looking toward the mound of blankets in the middle of the living room.

"One more night," I said.

She drove us back to her apartment. "How's the new roommate?"

"Seems okay," Mallory replied. "She's working this afternoon. Figured it'd be a good time to have you over."

Why? "That's too bad, I kind of wanted to meet her." *Love to picture you two fucking.*

"Local girl," Mallory said. "Works for her family at some restaurant."

Mallory's new apartment was bigger than ours, with an extra bedroom but no washer. "Is there a laundromat close?" I asked, turning on Depeche Mode's *Songs of Faith and Devotion* in her room.

"There's one by Cleo's office so I'll do laundry after work. You know what you're doing when you get back?"

"Staying with Mary until I can find a job," I replied, sitting on the edge of her bed. "You going to keep this comforter on your bed?"

"We have AC here." She sat down next to me. "Any idea what you want to do?"

"Not work at Liberty House or Haggen. Like to find a job in promotion but unless I can find something in Seattle, which I doubt, maybe get back into sound and lights shit."

"What about your feet though?" she asked, putting a hand on top of mine.

"I don't have problems if I'm moving around, it's the standing in one place."

Our clothes came off. Once inside her, I finished before "Condemnation" did.

"What time's your flight tomorrow?" she asked, putting her clothes back on.

"One," I said, doing the same. "Getting in at nine-forty. What're you doing for dinner tonight?" *Invite me to stay.*

"Going out with Anthony and Cleo," she looked at the clock. "I should run you back, I've got to go to the store before dinner."

#   #   #

Mary, Isaac, Holly, Ezra and Porter stood at the gate after I touched down at Sea-Tac Airport. Tears in my eyes, I hugged my mother. "Shit, guys, this is so cool. You didn't have to do this."

"Welcome back, schmuck," Porter said. "Thank Isaac for getting us all down here."

"I appreciate it so much," I said, hugging each of them in turn.

"I figured we should go to Denny's and hear about the Hawaii adventure," Isaac said. "Why'd you want to tell it over and over again?"

The group of us sat at a large round booth at the Denny's next to the airport. I spent the next couple hours describing my Hawaii experience.

"Is Mallory going to move back here?" Holly, Isaac's girlfriend, asked.

"Don't know why she would," I said. "She loves it there, has a good job and family."

"Yeah, but you're here now," Holly added.

"Don't think that's worth giving up a good job for," I replied.

Mary spoke up, "I'm sorry, guys, I'd love to hang out all night, but I've got to work tomorrow."

I thanked everyone again in the parking lot. "I'll let you know when I'm heading up to Bellingham," I said.

In the car on the way to Tacoma, Mary asked, "Any thoughts on work?"

"Not currently," I admitted. "I could probably get rehired at Western with the Athletic Department but it wouldn't pay much. And transportation would be a problem."

"See what you can find out and we might be able to work out something with the car."

Eight:
October 1993 (Real World, Year 2)

Mary loaned me her car so I could take a meeting at Western Washington University, who hired me immediately as they still hadn't found anyone to DJ the upcoming basketball season. They also said they'd be happy to get me more money for my services.

On my way out of town, I stopped at Haggen. Three cashiers I'd worked with were there. While catching up with a cashier gal, Ameline appeared. "Jon," she said. "What're you doing back here?"

"Moved back last week," I said. "Going to be doing the basketball games at Western this season."

"Living in Bellingham again?"

"Down in Tacoma with my mom, but I'll be staying with Porter between games."

She wrote her number on a paper bag. "Call me when you're up here," she said. "We can catch a movie or something."

We're okay now?

December 1993 (Real World, Year 2)

"Ameline wants you to spend the night with her?" Porter asked me Friday morning.

"Her parents are out of town this weekend," I said. "She's scared to stay in the house by herself."

"Why doesn't she have one of her girlfriends come over?"

"I've got a bigger dick?"

"You guys aren't fucking, though."

"Shit, I don't know," I sighed. "She's got a hot tub, if nothing else. But don't be surprised if I show up later."

After her shift at Haggen, Ameline asked me, "You still going to stay at my place?"

"I said I would, Ameline. That's why I'm here, remember."

Ameline's house was immaculate, not a magazine on the coffee table askew, pristine white couches, hardwood floors, simply yet elegantly decorated.

Why do you work at Haggen?

"Are you hungry?" Ameline asked.

"I could eat."

She led me to the kitchen, where she heated up some leftovers.

"Hot tub!" I exclaimed, putting my dishes in the sink.

"Is that the only reason you agreed to come over?"

"It's a good draw," I answered.

She showed me the bathroom, handed me a towel then went into her room to change. I put on a pair of trunks and waited in the living room, shirtless. She came out in a t-shirt and shorts.

Lovely. "A t-shirt?"

"It's cold outside," Ameline said. "I've got a swimsuit on."

She removed her clothes from inside the tub. *What a wonderful body. What stretch marks? Mallory's crazy.*

She sat across from me, I set my feet on either side of her. Her hands fell on my legs.

You're still mad at me, aren't you? "You and I all right?" I asked.

"Yeah," she said. "I was pissed at you for a while, but not anymore."

Why not? "Good to hear." I scooted next to her. My hands explored her body as we kissed. She stood up, I followed her.

Going to your bedroom?

"Too hot," she sighed. Leaning back against the hot tub cover, still halfway on, she kissed me again. Pushing her bikini top aside, I lifted her on to the side of the tub. I massaged her thighs, her back, kissed down her chest to her belly.

"No," pulling my head back to hers.

Why won't you let me lick your snatch?

After a few minutes, "I think my feet are warm enough now," I said, stepping out.

Dried and dressed, in the hallway outside her room, "Thanks for dinner and the hot tub," I said. "I'm going to go catch Porter before it gets too late."

"You're not staying?" she asked.

"Didn't figure you'd want me to."

"No, no stay," she declared. "I'm seriously scared being here by myself. Please stay tonight."

"You sure?" I asked. *Don't get you at all.*

"Yeah, I want you to stay."

I said I would. "Yeah, all right," I agreed. "Where should I set up?" *That couch sure looks nicer than the one at Porter's.*

"With me," Ameline uttered. "If that's still okay."

But I can't touch you? "Uh huh." *Doing her a favor, doing her a favor.*

In her room, I stripped down to my boxers. Ameline took off her shorts, but left her panties and loose t-shirt on. "You should know something," I started. "I've been known to molest girls while I'm sleeping."

"What?"

"Honestly, I've woken up with my hands all over girls before, so if that happens, push me away, no big deal."

"Uh, okay," she said. "Seriously, you aren't awake?"

"Well, not when I start," I answered. "I'll face the wall but I make no promises once I'm asleep."

In Ameline's single bed first, I faced the wall. She crawled in next to me.

Fuck, this is uncomfortable.

Pivoting, right hand went up Ameline's shirt, settling on her boob. I fell asleep.

That feels nice. Keep doing that. That's not her pussy.

I kissed her neck, her shoulders. She helped me lift her shirt off. Massaged her breasts while pressing my erection into her leg. She scooted her butt toward me. I pushed my underwear down, adjusting my dick between her legs. *I can come like this.*

I gyrated my hips, stimulating myself against her. My dick gradually repositioned to her panties. *Fantastic.* Increasing my thrusts, right hand approached from the front.

Soaked through her panties. Awesome. I continued thrusting against her undies.

Lift this...

Ameline shifted while wrenching my hand away, causing not only her panties to snap back, but my dick to fall away from the slippery bits.

I don't want in. Dammit.

Once I was completely displaced, Ameline settled into her former position. *You going to let me back there?*

The dick again reintroduced itself to Ameline's wet drawers, grinding into her. *Can't come on her panties, she's not on the pill. Is she?*

Right hand returned to add a friction ridge. *Am I going inside her a little? She'd kick me out if I was.*

I kept wiggling, she stayed motionless. *Did she fall back asleep?* I continued. *Not going to happen.*

"We should get some sleep," I said.

"Yeah," Ameline replied, sounding fully awake.

Underwear up, butt pressed against the wall, my hand returned to her boob before I fell back asleep.

# # #

Her room was bright, sunlight battering through the thin, white shades. I sat up, alone in Ameline's bed. *She left me here? What if I want to rummage through her stuff? Silly girl.* I found Ameline in the kitchen. "Wondering when you'd get up," she said.

"Why? What time is it?"

"Eleven-fifteen."

"Damn," I said. "I didn't mean to sleep so late. I told Porter I'd bring him lunch at work."

"You want anything for breakfast," she asked.

"Thanks, no. I'm good until lunch in what, twenty minutes? You going to be all right here tonight?"

"I think so," she said. "One of my friends is back in town today, so I can call her if I start getting scared or anything."

"I don't have another game until the thirtieth, so Merry Christmas. You going to be around?"

"We're going to visit my grandparents and won't be back until the second," she replied. Ameline walked me to the front door and gave me a little kiss. "Thanks again for staying with me last night."

Thanks for the blue balls.

# # #

Christmas Eve in Tacoma with Mary. "Is Isaac coming down to visit his parents?"

"Could be. He'll call if he's in Tacoma, for sure," I said. "Oh, I haven't told you about his plan to open an adult video store in Bellingham."

"Isn't he working at one now?"

"Yeah, but it's going out of business. He's buying up some of the better titles with Holly and looking for a place to open a new store."

"How are they going to finance it?" my mom asked.

"Don't know. Get a bank loan, maybe?"

She stared at me. "Do either of them have experience running a business?"

"Well, Isaac's been doing most of the day to day stuff where he is. I'm not sure what Holly's done in the past, but they think they can do better because right now, the owner doesn't bring in stuff people want."

"And they'd hire you to work there?"

"I haven't asked, but I hope so," I said. "The way they've been talking, seems like I'll be involved."

"How've they been talking exactly?"

"Like it's the three of us starting it. They always say 'we' when I'm there, so I assume I'll be part of it somehow."

"You know what they say about assuming?"

I rolled my eyes. "Yes, mother."

January 1994 (Real World, Year 2)

Ameline picked me up at Porter's Friday night. "How was the grandparents?" I asked.

"Not too bad," she said. "Where'd you want to go?"

Someplace dark. "I imagine your parents are home, so the hot tub's out?"

"They don't let my friends use it."

"You have anything you want to do?"

"Not really."

"Go up South Hill and see if we can find somewhere to park and talk." *Yeah, talk.*

Ameline drove toward south Bellingham. "You party on New Year's with the grandparents?"

"Uh, no. I think everyone was in bed by eleven. You?"

"I watched the ball drop," I said. "Should've been in Hawaii. Mallory said it was bigger than the Fourth of July and they went nutty cuckoo on the Fourth."

"You still talk to her?" Ameline asked.

"She calls every couple weeks," I said. "We're still friends. Hawaii just wasn't my thing."

She drove along Highland Drive across South Hill. "You hang out with anyone from the store away from work?" I asked.

"Not so much," she answered. "The other front parcel who went to Sehome and I used to pal around until I ended up naked in some guy's bed she'd introduced me to. We don't hang out any more."

Naked with a guy? You still a virgin? "Turn around," I said. "Right back there."

Ameline parked the car on a half-block, dead end street with no street lights or porch lights.

Moving to the backseat, I lifted off her shirt, she took off her bra. I played with her tits while undoing my pants.

Touch me. I tugged at her pants. She scooted out of them then climbed on top of me. *You going to fuck me now?*

Out of my boxers, I put two fingers under the elastic of her panties. She wrenched my hand away.

Not going to fuck me. But you're so damn wet.

My cock slid against her damp panties, Ameline pushed her hips against me. *Like that.*

I increased my speed. Ameline did as well. *You going to freak out if I come? You got to know I'll come from this. Don't freak out.* I came. And kept coming. My muscles continued contracting. *Jesus, that's a lot of spew.*

And I came some more. *Never came so much.*

"Thanks," I said. "Should we be worried about that?"

"I don't think so," Ameline said. "I started the pill after I got back from Hawaii."

You did?

"Hand me my bra?"

#   #   #

Walking into Red Robin, I noticed the hostess' butt. *Little bigger than I like.* The gal turned to greet me. It was Leila, former SAGA co-worker and month-long fling. "Jon, holy shit, how are you?" Leila asked.

You look good. "Fine," I said. "What are you doing here? I see you're hosting, but I thought you'd've moved away already."

"Me too," she sighed. "I was here part time before I graduated then ended up sticking around. Didn't you move to Hawaii?"

"And moved back," I said. "Doing games at Western again. Living with my mom in Tacoma and crashing on a friend's couch on the weekends. You know Porter?"

"I don't think so," she said. "If you ever need a place to stay, give me a call. I've got plenty of room and no roommates."

No roommates? "Thanks, Leila. That's really sweet. I will."

"Do I need to seat you or are you going up the bar?"

"I'm meeting said friend here, so I'll be up in the bar."

She walked with me to a booth. "I'll swing back by if I have a minute."

"Do," I said. *She wants me to stay with her? She'd at least blow me.*

Leila handed me her number as Porter and I were walking out. "Let me know next time you're up," she said.

February 1994 (Real World, Year 2)

Mary dropped me off at Porter's the next Thursday as she needed her car over the weekend. Mallory called me at Porter's Saturday afternoon. "Have you gotten my package yet?" she asked.

"Yes, thank you," I replied. "But where were the macadamia nuts?"

"What did you think of the pictures?"

"You didn't need to take a whole roll of your surgery scar."

"Uh," she stammered. "You haven't developed them yet?"

"I'm kind of broke so I'm going to try to get to it next week."

"You should do it today," she said. "It's not just my scar."

"You don't say?" *You drunk on your birthday?*

"Yeah, I think you'll like what's on there."

"Well, okay then."

"It's your Valentine's Day present. Keep them to yourself, okay?"

"No problem," I said.

On the bus to WWU, I pulled Mallory's freshly developed pictures out of their envelope. Mallory in a bikini. Her belly button. Another. Another. Mallory's boobs. I fumbled the pictures back in the bag. *Pictures of her tits? When did she get so fun?*

Throughout the game, I got a tingle in my belly every time I saw the envelope of pictures in my bag of CDs.

After the game, I quickly walked to Porter's apartment. *Maybe he went out tonight.* "How's the game?" he asked when I opened the door.

Drat. "We lost," I said. "Any fun stories of work?"

"Terribly slow today. What time do you need to be back in Tacoma?"

"Whenever," I said. "I have no life."

"I was hoping to meet a friend of mine in Seattle at noon, so we should leave no later than nine."

"Nine it is, then."

Porter and I shot the shit for half an hour before he went to bed.

The second Porter's door closed, I retrieved Mallory's pictures. Bikini, boobs, more boobs, butt, bush, pussy, fingers on pussy.

Fantastic.

#   #   #

The next Thursday in Bellingham, at Porter's, "Then my grandma says, 'How bout we make it a loan instead of an investment?'

"I asked if we can take a couple months before paying her back and she's like, 'Is six months okay?'"

"When are you guys planning on opening?" Porter asked.

"March first," I answered. "Is it going to be too much of a problem for me to stay here until the store starts making enough money for me to get a place?"

Porter raised an eyebrow. "The landlord is already suspicious. He asked about you the last time I saw him and I told him you stayed late sometimes. What about staying with Isaac?"

"They have a zoo in their apartment," I said. "What, three cats, a rabbit, a hamster, a shitload of fish, a lizard and who knows what Holly bought today? There's no way I'd actually be able to sleep there."

"That gal from Red Robin said you could crash with her, didn't she?"

"Leila? Yeah, I'll give her a call." *A lot to ask of a girl I'm not dating.*

On the phone with Leila that night, I detailed the video store I was opening with Isaac and Holly, my subsequent lack of finances and what was going on with Porter's landlord. "Oh sure, you can stay here as long as you want," she offered. "It's not a problem."

"You sure I wouldn't be pissing off a boyfriend or anything?" I asked.

"Nope, I live by myself and I'm so busy with work and everything else, I don't have time for a boy right now."

Maybe we can get frisky?

March 1994 (Real World, Year 2)

Arranging movies in the back of the store with Holly and Isaac, I said, "Mallory called me last night."

"I thought she didn't like porn," Holly said.

"She doesn't but she thought it over, and even though I'm not what she thinks of when she thinks of a porn store owner, she figured what I did, didn't change who I was."

"I think you've changed," Isaac joked. "Any minute now, you'll put on your silk button-up shirt, gain fifty pounds and slick back your hair."

"Fifty?" I queried. "I only need ten."

"She going to watch smut with you?" Isaac asked.

"She's not that okay with it," I replied.

"You haven't mentioned Ameline to her at all, have you?" Holly asked.

"Fuck no," I said. "She already went batshit crazy when Ameline crashed with us in Hawaii. I've said I've seen her, but hang out with her? No way."

"I'm still surprised she hasn't slept with you yet," Holly said. "She follows you around like a puppy."

"A virgin puppy," I countered.

#   #   #

After Porter informed me his landlord had levied an ultimatum concerning my presence there, I stuffed my clothes in my duffle bag, a backpack and a couple plastic bags. Isaac and Holly drove me over to Leila's. Standing in the living room, "Where should I put my bags?" I asked her.

"In the bedroom. You're living here now."

Guess so.

I put my bags against the wall, underneath the window overlooking the parking lot. *Her bed's tiny. Not sleeping there.* "Where should I put the sleeping bag?"

"Well, the couch isn't very long, so probably the floor."

"I can do that. Which floor?" I asked.

"I figured in the bedroom because we'll be going to bed and getting up at different times," she continued. "I work a lot of days so I'll be leaving before you and I like to watch TV while I'm getting ready." I unrolled my sleeping bag against the wall, near the foot of her bed.

"Leila, whatever works best for you. Thank you so much for helping me out."

"No problem," she said. "I think we'll have a good time."

Like a good time, good time? That'd be fantastic.

"Honestly, I'm not going to be around much," I said. "I work all day, every day so I'll only be here after ten-thirty."

"Well, I'm usually up until eleven-thirty or midnight so we'll see each other. But tomorrow I'm on in the morning so I'm going to bed."

# # #

Isaac and Holly picked me up the next morning. "You spend all night fucking?" Holly asked.

"Not going to happen," I said.

"I thought you guys used to be a thing," Isaac added.

"We did, but I'm sleeping on the floor."

"Damn," Holly said. "You don't even rate the couch?"

"Too short," I said. "And her bed's tiny, barely a single. I'd fall out sleeping by myself."

April 1994 (Real World, Year 2)

On the way to the store with Isaac and Holly, I reiterated Mallory's request to join her on vacation in Oregon. "You guys think you could handle the shop for a day or two in May?"

"Shit, Jon, you should take more time than that," Holly said. "Take a week. We can handle it. We're not that busy. Besides, you could really use some."

"Yeah, I know." *But Mallory probably won't fuck me.*

Talking to Mallory that night, "How about four days? Will that work?"

"You'll be okay being away that long?" Mallory inquired.

"Holly insisted I take some time off."

"That's awfully nice of her. Which four days?"

"Thursday through Sunday?"

"Sounds good. Is there anything in particular you wanted to do?"

Spend three days fucking and the fourth day sleeping. "Get away from the store. That's about it."

"Cleo told me about this great bed and breakfast in Portland. I'll look into it."

# # #

In Ameline's car after work, I detailed Mallory's upcoming vacation and my joining her for the weekend. *Tell me to fuck off now.* She asked, "You guys getting back together?"

No. "Not with her in Hawaii. She's coming over, we're going to hang out."

"Uh, yeah."

"Getting back together hasn't come up," I insisted. "I'm doing my thing, she's doing hers. She's happy there..."

"But why would you go on a vacation together if you weren't thinking about getting back together?"

To fuck, because you won't? "Honestly, we haven't talked about it. I left Hawaii because I was miserable, not because Mallory and I weren't getting along. You know we've stayed in touch since I left. We're going to Portland to hang out and have some time off. As for anything else, I can't say. You want to go somewhere?"

"I got to work early," she replied, before dropping me off at Leila's.

Leila sat on the couch, watching TV. "Leila, does going on vacation with Mallory mean we're looking at getting back together?" I asked.

"Sure looks that way from here," she said.

No it doesn't. "Well, if you were in Mallory's position?"

"I'd be figuring out if we should get back together."

Why? "Even if you were happy where you were with your job and everything?"

"Yeah, probably."

"Oh, fuck. Why?" I exclaimed. "That doesn't make any sense."

"It's a girl thing," Leila said. "Most of us want to get married, so we're willing to give up things to pursue someone who we want to marry."

We're not talking about getting married any more. "Even if you're already happy?"

"But being with you makes her happy," Leila said.

"That is fucked up," I replied.

"You're such a guy."

"She's happy with her life right now," I pointed out. "Don't get that at all."

After Leila went to bed, I called Mallory. "Um, is this vacation together to see if we should get back together?"

"Well, I've been thinking about that since I asked you to join me," she said.

Shouldn't you have figured that out before asking me? "Reached any conclusions?"

"Kind of. We've been doing well."

"I didn't think we were doing bad when I left," I interrupted. "I couldn't handle it there." *And some sex would've been nice.*

"You've said. No, I thought if we do okay while I'm there, I'll have to consider coming back there because you won't move back here."

"True, but you're still happy there, aren't you?"

"For the most part."

#   #   #

Returning to Leila's at 10:40, Leila stood in the kitchen. "Weren't you going out tonight?" I asked her.

"I did. We went over to that Mexican restaurant and got margaritas, but I had to leave because I've got to work in the morning," she said. "Want a beer?"

"Sure." She opened two beers, handing me one.

Five minutes later, Leila stood up from the couch, stumbling her way to the kitchen. "You want another?" she asked.

"In a minute or two."

"Okay." Fresh beer in hand, she joined me in the living room. Three extended swallows later, "Oh God! What time is it?"

"Eleven," I said.

"Shit, I've got to go to bed." She downed the rest of her bottle.

Guess she really can drink every boy at work under the table.

Leila headed toward the bathroom. "You staying up for a while?"

"Yeah," I answered. "I'm not tired."

She left the bathroom door open as she washed her face. "How was work today?"

"Not bad. Didn't make much money but we're getting more people finding us all the time. How about you?" I asked, from the bathroom's doorway.

"Same shit."

Leila exited the bathroom after peeing, joining me in the kitchen. "I wanted to let you know how much I enjoy you being here."

"Thanks, Leila. I don't think I'll ever be able to thank you enough."

"It's no problem." She threw her arms around me and squeezed me tightly, then gave me a big kiss. Another.

A minute of lip-locked frenzy before Leila declared, "I've got to go to bed." Leila kept hold of my hand as she walked into the bedroom.

Without turning on the lights, she walked around her bed to her closet, took off her pants, shirt and bra, put on a big t-shirt, then joined me in her bed.

I kissed her neck, ran my hands down her legs and slid off her panties. Squirreling under the blankets, my feet hit the floor while my tongue found her puss. Ten minutes in, she came loudly.

I continued until she squealed, "No more."

She gave me a peck on the mouth when I joined her above the covers. "I've got to get some sleep," she said, turning away.

Did you and Ameline set this up?

Four minutes later, Leila's breathing loud and steady, I crawled into my sleeping bag on the floor.

Leila will fuck me. Enough of this bullshit with Ameline. Mallory wants to get back together. But if Leila wants me...I'll cancel with Mallory.

# # #

Leila wasn't home when I got up the next day and was already asleep when I returned to the apartment after work.

Should I get in bed next to her? Might have to sleep there then. Talk to her tomorrow.

# # #

"How're things at the smut shop?" Leila asked, making breakfast.

"Getting new customers every day, so that's cool," I responded. "It'd be great if they'd rent more than one movie though."

"You haven't been open that long," she said. "Got to hit the store before work. You need anything?"

"I'm good, thanks."

Leila put her toast in a paper towel and left.

Didn't seem fake. Didn't talk about being naked though.

180

The TV was on in the apartment when I got back but Leila wasn't in the living room. "Shit, you scared me," she said, coming out of the bedroom, behind me. "I didn't hear you come in."

"Sorry. What're you watching?"

"Some sitcom."

"When do you work tomorrow?" I asked.

"I close, then I've got the weekend off, so I'm heading home for my sister's birthday this weekend."

"I get the place to myself? Party time."

"When do you have time to party?" she asked.

"Uh, maybe twenty minutes Friday night?"

"Have fun with that then. Good night."

Nothing's going on between us?

May 1994 (Real World, Year 2)

Ameline called me at the store. "What's going on?" she asked.

Aren't you done talking to me? "Same old shit," I said. "Leila's out of town for a couple days, visiting friends in Seattle."

"You want to get a movie after work?" she asked.

Didn't we try this last weekend? You left after twenty minutes, remember? "Sure. Why don't you pick something out and bring it with?"

"I'll swing by around ten," Ameline said.

In Ameline's car, on the way to Leila's, "What'd you get?" I asked.

"I couldn't decide so I brought a couple things."

Once we got in the apartment, "Which one you want?"

"I don't care, you choose," she said.

Shuffling them, I threw one in the VCR, then sat next to her on the moss green loveseat. Ameline snuggled up to me.

No more teasing. Done with that bullshit.

My right hand on her leg, she kissed me.

Maybe she'll let me come. Probably not. Don't push it. Maybe she'll let me come if you don't push it.

Standing, I removed her pants, exposing her butt. Kissed down her neck and back.

Stay in the living room. Slowly. Go slowly.

Behind her, my shorts dropped to the floor. *She's leaving.* Ameline stood still.

Maybe she'll let me come. I pressed my dick against her leg.

She knows I'm naked but she's still here. Hard, I pushed my hips into her. A quiet moan from Ameline.

That's new.

Ameline turned around, kissed me, took my hand, pulled me to the bedroom.

No way you're getting bottom. Can't come if I'm on top of you.

Flopping onto Leila's tiny bed, Ameline perched on top of me.

She took off her shirt. I took off mine. Right hand on a boob as she sat atop me. Left hand between her legs to assist my flattened pecker.

Lean forward. Can't move. She wiggled, my dick squished under her.

This won't work. Left hand remained between her legs, attempting to find a way to stimulate dick against her with no success. I pulled her toward me, kissed her and freed my dick. Right hand joined the fracas, holding the base of my dick. Left hand stayed near the head.

Can't go in. I ground against her. *Stay like this.*

Ameline sat back up. My cock went inside.

Shit! I stopped moving.

"Ummm," was the best I could muster. "I'm in you."

"Yeah, I know," she said.

"You okay with that?"

"Apparently."

WHAT THE FUCK! Tonight you're okay with this? Fuck her before she changes her mind.

Continuing inside her. *Incredible.*

Cautiously, I withdrew. *Divine.* I looked at Ameline's face. Her eyes were closed. No grimace. I kept moving.

Go slow. Enjoy it. Take your time. She'll like it more if you're slow. She'll want to fuck you again.

A minute later, "You still on the pill?"

"Yeah."

I came inside her.

Opening my eyes, the expression on Ameline's expression was peculiar; a mix of disappointment and relief with a splash of let me out of here. She said, "I should be getting home."

"You can stay." *Stay.*

"No, I can't," she said. "I told my mom I'd be home."

She stood up, wiped her crotch with her hand and went into the bathroom.

Too short, sure. It's been seven months. Give me another chance? I hopped off Leila's bed, retrieved my boxers, then went to the living room gathering Ameline's clothes.

When she opened the bathroom door, I held out her jeans and panties, "You okay?" I asked. *Not bleeding or anything?*

"Oh, yeah," pulling on her underwear.

"Sure you don't want to watch one of the movies?" *Cuddle on the couch?*

"I got to go," she stated.

At the front door, she asked, "When are you taking off with Mallory?"

"Tomorrow," I said. "I'll call you when I get back."

#   #   #

Our room at the bed and breakfast was on the top floor, a small balcony shadowed by ancient Maple trees overlooking downtown Portland. The room was elegant; a king bed against the far wall plus a single bed in its own alcove off the main room, distressed copper antique fixtures and a large, modern bathroom.

Returning from a dinner at an intimate Italian bistro, Mallory, with a glowing tan and slightly longer hair, lit scented candles she'd brought, took off her clothes, then settled face down on the king bed.

Still clothed, I sat on her butt and began massaging her back. Starting at her shoulders, I kneaded her butt for a couple minutes, but didn't go further south.

I want a backrub.

After a solid twenty minutes, "You're up."

"Dammit," Mallory groaned. "Alright."

I took off my shirt and assumed the position. "Lose the shorts," she demanded.

"You sure?"

"I'm not going to be the only one naked here."

She mounted my ass and rubbed away. "Uh, Mallory? How likely is it we'll be having sex tonight?"

"Pretty good."

"Things still hurt?"

"I don't know," she said. "Haven't had sex since you left."

Awesome. My face in the pillow, I smiled. "Haven't you put that vibrator in you to see how things are doing?"

"The vibrator stays on the outside."

Mallory kissed my neck and back. She remained seated on top of me as I rolled to face her.

Almost like Ameline last night. I was already hard but Mallory went down on me anyway. I pulled her up after five minutes and switched positions.

You need to come before anything happens. And she did.

When she'd finished climaxing, Mallory flipped onto her tummy. "You don't get as deep this way."

Not as deep? I'm not that big. I entered her cautiously at the invitation.

Does she expect me to come quickly? Is she going to know I had sex last night? She'll assume I jerked off this morning, right?

"Hold on," she said, rolling to her back. Mallory kept her hands on my hips. "Not too crazy, all right?"

I was slow. I was patient. And then I was done.

#   #   #

Sunday morning, in her mom's car, Mallory said, "I've had a great time this weekend."

"So have I," I said. *Would've liked sex more than once though.*

"You think we should give us another chance?"

"That's tough, Mallory. I still love you, but I don't want you to give up what you have in Hawaii."

"But that's my decision," she said. "Do you want me to move back here?"

"I do, but I'm in Bellingham for the time being, so you'd have to be okay being there. And you'd have to get over what I do."

"It doesn't bother me as much as I thought," she admitted. "Do you really want to try again?"

"I'm so much happier these days and I'd hate to think we gave up too soon," I said. "So yeah, we should try again. But only if you believe leaving where you are is the best thing for you. And I'm not so sure it is."

"It's still my choice."

"It is," I agreed. "Take some time and think about it. Get back to Hawaii before you decide anything, okay?"

Mallory dropped me off in Seattle, gave Porter a quick hello, kissed me and drove away.

"How'd it go?" Porter asked.

"She's thinking about moving back here," I said.

"Figured."
How did everyone else know what was going to happen?

June 1994 (Real World, Year 2)

Sunday evening, I stopped by Haggen after work, picked up macaroni and cheese, cereal, milk, butter and a pint of ice cream. I walked the rest of the way to Leila's. *This isn't too bad. Except paying with a credit card.*

On the phone with Ameline, "How's it going? Haven't heard from you."

"Not too bad," she said. "Been hanging out with a couple guys from work. Haven't felt like talking to you."

Why?

A second of silence. "Why's that?"

"The reason I came over to Leila's that night was to see if you'd still go with Mallory."

"What?" *You lost your virginity so I wouldn't see my ex?* "What what?"

"You never asked me not to see Mallory."

"If you wanted to be with me, you wouldn't have gone."

"Ameline, we talked about this already," I said. "Mallory and I wanted to see if we were able to be friends around each other."

"And, are you getting back together?"

Yeah. But if you wouldn't have been teasing me for months, we probably wouldn't be. Never would've gone with her. "Kind of looks that way."

"Well, good for you," her tone still hostile.

"If you didn't want me to see her, why didn't you say so?"

"You really don't get it, do you?"

Flustered, "Apparently not."

"Well, I got to go. Talk to you later."

July 1994 (Real World, Year 3)

Mallory returned my call at Leila's. "How're you and Isaac doing?"

Shitty. "We've barely talked since I told him I wanted to buy them out of the store," I said. "Not sure which is worse, his not talking to me or the constant barrage of shit I've been getting from Holly. Should be the other way around. We're signing the papers Friday."

"At the lawyer's?" she asked.

Had to bring goddamn lawyers into it. "Has to be official in order to change the shit with the state and the bank."

"So you'll be moving out of Leila's soon?"

Not if I can help it. "You're not moving here 'til October. I was hoping to keep cheap rent until then."

"But once the store's yours, won't you be able to afford an apartment?"

No.

# # #

I turned off the anime tentacle-porn when Leila stumbled through the front door. "Do you know how much I love having you here?" she exclaimed. "You are so easy to live with. I'm so glad you're my friend." She threw herself on the couch next to me and put her arm around me. "I am so lucky to have you for a friend." She kissed me firmly.

A blowjob tonight?

I slid off the couch onto the floor, taking her pants and panties with me. My face between her legs, she squashed my head as she came.

Returning to the couch, Leila continued kissing me.

Suck my dick already. I leaned away from her, she followed. A minute later, I pressed on her shoulders. She kissed my neck then pulled up my shirt, kissing down my chest to my belly.

Looking up at me, she asked, "What about Mallory?"

Fuck that. "What about her?"

"She wouldn't want you to do this," she said.

Who cares?

"I'm going to go to bed."

Of course you are.

She vanished into her bedroom.

Got to get the fuck out of here.

Nine:
August 1994 (Real World, Year 3)

Ezra met me at my apartment on the top floor of a new Garden Street multiplex. "You got any furniture?" he asked, looking around.

"Not yet," I said. "Mary's bringing me my kitchen shit from her garage and hopefully the papa san this weekend. Porter said he's buying a bed and going to give me his futon."

"You heard from Isaac?"

Have you? I shook my head. "His next door neighbor stopped by the store the other day and told me he and Holly had moved down to Tacoma."

"You two going to get past this whole store thing?"

"Doesn't look like it," I said. "I know I really hurt him but I had to do what was right for the business."

"When're you going to hire some employees?" Ezra asked.

"When the store can afford it. Not sure I can make rent until Mallory gets here to split it with me."

From the hallway, two feet away, "She's not paying anything now?"

"She's trying to save up money to move back," I replied. "And with all her medical bills, she can't afford to pay rent in two places."

"How is her health these days?"

"She's going back in for surgery on the twenty-second," I said. "Got to burn more shit out of her, I guess."

"That sucks. What is that, the third one in a year?"

"Yeah," I said. "You'd think her body would've given up pulling this crap by now."

"But seriously Jon," Ezra said. "You got to figure out how to hire at least one person because you're going to burn out man."

Already out. "Probably," I agreed. "But I'll be okay for a while."

# # #

Having finished my nightly macaroni and cheese with salsa prior to eleven, I put on the headphones to my portable CD player and opened up the sliding door to the deck. After throwing down a towel, I stretched out on the deck to watch for shooting stars.

Another surgery? If she's sick all the time, will that fly? She's going to be better by the time she gets here. What if she isn't? What if you keep not having sex? If it hurts her, it's okay not to fuck. But if she doesn't screw just because, then I'm done. Can't bail because she's sick. Too shallow, even for you. Satellite!

What about hiring someone? See how August finishes up. Looks okay so far but better wait. Can't keep doing this, Ezra's right. Got to start repaying my grandmother in September. Already? Shit.

October 1994 (Real World, Year 3)

Mallory stepped into the apartment ahead of me. "Bedroom's on the right," I said.

"Uh, Jon," Mallory stood in the living room. "How are we going to fit another chair in here?"

"What do we need another chair for?"

"If we have people over?"

We never have people over.

She turned to look at the kitchen. "Jesus, Jon, this place is tiny."

"But it's new and it has a deck. And we're on the top floor."

"How're we going to fit a Christmas tree in here?"

We need a tree? "There wasn't any furniture in it when I looked at it and my spatial ability sucks. That what you want to hear?"

She crossed her arms. "How long's the lease?"

"A year."

"Christ. A year from now?"

"August," I said. "It's cheap and neither of us have much, right? There's a storage room down on the second floor. We'll get something bigger this summer, okay? Can you handle it until then?"

She continued pacing through the apartment. "I'll have to, I guess."

I brought up her other bags from my truck, while she unpacked. "Are you too distressed about the apartment to have sex tonight?"

Smiling, "Have to want to kill you to not want some."

November 1994 (Real World, Year 3)

"Brought home a couple movies," I informed Mallory while she was cooking pasta. She scoffed. "One of them's for couples. Give it a chance?"

"I guess," she sighed.

After dinner, I threw on the "couples" title. There was some sort of plot but the acting was atrocious. The second sex scene ran identically the first; blow the guy, lick the girl, fuck in three positions, come somewhere on the girl.

Mallory spoke up, "How is this any different from any other porn you've brought home?"

"There's a story?" I turned it off.

"What about the other one?" she asked.

"Anal stuff," I said.

"I'll pass."

Figured. "Is there any part of porn you do like?"

She thought a moment. "The biggest problem I have is none of the guys are good looking. Some of the guys are tolerable but most are hard to look at. And their hairy asses and coming on the girls' faces. It's so degrading."

"I should bring home lesbian flicks?" I asked. *And then you'll want to fuck?*

"No, Jon, I don't like it. Something turned me off to it."

Someone force you to watch it? "What was that?"

"I can't put a finger on it," she said. "It's not like one event, but I've never been a fan of porn. It's oppressive and I kind of think it's wrong."

"Wrong?" *How is it wrong? It's fun.* "You haven't said anything about my subscription to *Penthouse*. You didn't seem to mind reading Forum with us." *And laughing at it.*

"That was funny."

"Yeah, it's just sex."

"I know," she admitted. "But I have a hard time with it. Most of the time I don't care but when I think about what you do, I kind of have a problem."

"Uh, okay. Did you want to tell me that before you moved back here?"

"I didn't think it wouldn't bother me...and for the most part it doesn't. I realize it's just sex, but there's still part of me that thinks it's bad."

Bad? Who did that to you?

December 1994 (Real World, Year 3)

"How are you and Mallory doing?" Mary asked when I was in Tacoma at Christmas.

"Not bad," I said. "She wishes you a Merry Christmas, by the way."

"Tell her the same from me," Mary added. "What does not bad mean, Jon?"

"She's been healthy since she got here, we're talking a lot about us and life and stuff. Still trying to get into a routine, I think, but besides that, things are good."

"You know, I'll have a real problem if you two end up having kids, split up and she moves back to Hawaii with them."

What? "We're not talking about having kids."

"But wouldn't it get rid of the endometriosis? I mean if you two do end up getting married. You are still talking about it, aren't you?"

"Talking," I said. "I think it'll be a while before we get into serious discussions about it. She wants to get a real job first and doesn't particularly want to stay in Bellingham."

"That could be a problem," Mary stated.

"I know. But I don't know if there's anything she wants to do around there."

"Where does she want to be?"

"Seattle, maybe California."

Mary's face dropped. "You think you'll move to California?"

"Who knows? I could probably get on with a recording studio, so I don't think it's out of the question. But for the time being, I don't think you'll have to fret about it any time soon. I'm not inclined to work for someone else these days."

May 1995 (Real World, Year 3)

Rachel, our downstairs neighbor, was sitting on the couch with Mallory, when I came home Wednesday evening. Mallory said, "Rachel invited us down to smoke a bowl. You interested?"

"If you are," I said. "Is Ross home?"

"He is," Rachel said. "But he's got a drug test at work in a couple days so he can't join us."

"They're drug testing to fuck with computers? Wrong in so many ways."

"I know," Rachel said. "I don't think Ross can pass it anyway. He smokes all the time."

"All the time?" closing the door to our apartment behind us.

"A couple times a week," she said. "When was the last time you got stoned?"

"Years," I said. "Three or four."

Mallory piped up, "I used to smoke a lot in high school but maybe only a couple times since then."

Ross was stuffing the bowl of a two-foot glass bong as the three of us came into their living room. "You're going to hang out and watch us get high?" I asked him.

"Yup," he replied. He passed the bong to his wife.

After three rounds with the bong plus a couple of pointless stories from Ross, Mallory said, "I should get to bed."

But this is fun. "Yeah, okay," I agreed. "Ross, Rachel, thanks for inviting us down."

"Our pleasure. We should do it again," Rachel said. "Maybe next time Ross can join us and stop with the stories."

"Definitely," I said.

Once we were back in our apartment, Mallory took my hand. "I forgot how horny I get when I get high."

"Horny, you say?"

"Oh yeah," she said, leading me to our room.

How much would it set me back to get her stoned a couple times a week?

June 1995 (Real World, Year 3)

Ezra, Jezzie, Ross and Rachel were over for a margarita barbecue. "We put a deposit down on a condo down in Fairhaven," Mallory told the girls. "It's probably five or six times bigger than this so we'll certainly have everyone over once we get settled."

"What's the rent?" Ross asked me.

"A couple hundred more, but it's got a view of the water, a block away from a video store and two blocks from the grocery store," I answered. "A little seventies in design but a ton of room. There's even an extra room off the carport."

"Don't know if we could afford more until Rachel starts working again," Ross admitted.

"Yeah, a hundred bucks extra a piece isn't too bad. But I think the kitchen's smaller than here. Can't open the stove and the fridge at the same time."

Out on the deck, I half-heartedly scraped the grill. *Too hot. Leave it open.*

Several minutes later I set the burgers and chicken breasts on the grill and pulled the lid. It didn't move. I tried again.

Stuck? Looking at the back of the grill. *Dammit.*

I stepped back into the apartment. "Ezra, could you help me real quick?"

"Can't you even grill a burger by yourself?" he joked.

I gave him the finger, found a couple oven mitts from the kitchen where Mallory was still blending margaritas and returned to the deck.

Ezra looked at the burgers. "You couldn't've burned them yet."

"I melted the building onto the grill."

"You're shitting me," he said. Looking at the back of the grill, "Oh my God, you're a dumbass. Give me one of those."

We pried the grill off the siding without disturbing the rest of the party. "Thanks." I whispered, "You know where to get some weed?"

"When did you start smoking?"

"It gets Mallory horny. I got to try something. We hardly fuck anymore."

"I knew a couple guys back in the dorms, but I haven't talked to any of them in a couple years."

"Maybe Sofia's boyfriend?"

"Because he's in a band?" Ezra asked. "Why don't you ask her? Or better, him?"

"I've met him, what, twice?" I replied. "And she'd probably want to know why I'm asking. 'Because Mallory won't fuck me?' Seriously? Sofia won't mind if you ask."

Ezra laughed at me. "You're pathetic. I'll let you know."

August 1995 (Real World, Year 4)

Mallory and I moved into a spacious Fairhaven apartment on the 1st. An extra/storage room off the carport with its own window and thermostat, the primary entrance to the right, opening onto a coat rack only entryway and twenty steps up to the left. The front door sat at the top of the stairs, next to the front door, a half bath, laundry room.

The wall from the staircase created such an angle on the main floor, Ezra and I hoisted the couch onto the deck from the carport, scraping it forcefully through the sliding glass doors.

The tiny kitchen shared a wall with the laundry room and opened onto the expansive living area, including a vaulted ceiling. Above the entryway staircase, another twenty steps led up to the bedroom. A half wall separated the stairwell from the bedroom. The master bathroom sink and mirror sat between the walk-in closet and the toilet plus shower cove.

"You realize we'll never be able to have sex if we have people over," I said.

"Why?"

"There's no door to our room."

"Like that'd stop you."

"You got a new job, Mallory?" Ezra asked, as Mallory cooked dinner for all of us.

"Ad sales for a paper down in Mount Vernon," she replied. "I've only been there a week now, but I should be able to make a lot once I get a regular client base."

"Commission then?" Ezra asked.

"Kind of," Mallory said. "Base plus. And health, dental, vision and a retirement plan."

September 1995 (Real World, Year 4)

"I've got to go in for a while tomorrow," Mallory told me Friday night after dinner.

"Wasn't the point of getting out of retail so you wouldn't have to work weekends?" I asked.

"Won't happen often, but I've got to finish up some stuff before Monday. I spent most of my time either on the phone or running around visiting clients last week. Do you have to give me shit about this?"

You bitch every time I got to cover a shift. "No shit," I said. "Asking."

"I'm not going to make enough this month as it is."

"I can cover things, Mallory," I said.

A tear started in her eye. "Only if I can't. I need to cover my own bills."

"I get it. Let me know," I said. "We going to pick blackberries on Sunday then?"

"Absolutely," she said. "Where are those pictures I sent you?"

"In the closet, in a shoebox. You want to see them?"

"No. I don't want one of your friends to find them."

"Why would my friends be rooting around our closet?" I asked.

"I don't know," she said. "They're embarrassing, I don't want anyone else seeing them, ever."

"Jesus, Mallory. I'm not going to show anybody, okay. You want me to move them out of our room?"

"Kind of," she said. "What if we need someone to housesit?"

Why would we need someone to housesit? We haven't gone anywhere since you got back.

January 1996 (Real World, Year 4)

"Look what I found at the mall." Mallory opened a bag and pulled out a long skirt.

I said, "Paycheck bigger than you expected?"

"I didn't want to say anything earlier because I didn't want to jinx it. I wasn't sure if the commissions were going to come through on this check or not."

"Excellent. Beer's on you?"

"Sure. Look what else I got." She showed me a pair of pants, three blouses and a bra and panty set.

"Could I see that on?" I asked.

"I thought I might surprise you with it."

She took off her clothes in the living room. Before she had a chance to pull up her new panties, I took her hand and led her to the couch, then spent half an hour getting her off.

My turn.

"I'm too hungry," Mallory said, standing up. "I'll take care of you later. Promise."

After a large dinner, I motioned upstairs. "Give me a while to get over feeling bloated," she said.

Upstairs, after getting ready for bed, Mallory was still feeling full. "You mind if I lay here?"

"Not at all," I said, entering her.

194

# # #

"There's an assistant manager position up at the outlet mall," Mallory informed me Saturday morning. "I'm going to go drop off a resume."

"It pay more?" I asked.

"About the same, but at least it's a steady paycheck. I hate stressing every month whether or not I'm going to be able to cover rent."

"I thought you loved that job."

"But the uncertainty is driving me nuts," she replied. "I'm not going to quit unless I get another job."

# # #

Mallory quit on Friday.

March 1996 (Real World, Year 4)

Sitting across from me at the Bellis Fair food court, Ezra's eyes, then his head tracked behind me. "Four o'clock," he whispered. "Go ahead."

I stretched and looked back to my right. "In the black tights?" I yawned.

"Wait until she turns around."

I twisted in my chair, pretending to stretch my back. "Me likey," I commented.

"I'd let her eat crackers in bed."

"Is that what you imagine when see a hot chick? The two of you in bed and her busting out a box of Saltines and you saying, 'Go ahead. I don't mind.'?"

He smirked. "Depending on what they look like, they're either straddling me or on their knees with me behind them."

"You picture them naked?"

"You don't?" wide-eyed. "I picture what they'd look like fucking me. If they have a great ass, doggie. Nice tits, facing me."

"I've never done that," I confessed. "I mean I appreciate what they're wearing and hope they look good naked. Because what if she's packing a couple slabs of liver between her legs? Don't want to be disappointed."

Laughing, Ezra said, "Ever since high school, when I see a cute girl, first thing is how would she look bouncing on me or under me."

"Huh. Maybe I'll give it a try sometime."

"You should," he suggested.

"So then, what's your perfect girl look like?" I asked him. As he opened his mouth, I continued, "Because I came up with a theory."

"Oh, do share."

"Your ideal partner is your first serious crush. If she was a blonde with big tits, that becomes your ultimate physical type. My ideal girl is a tall, skinny redhead with long, curly hair, small boobs, no hips, pale skin, nice hands and a scar on her face, like Kenna Anderson from junior high."

Ezra scrunched his nose. "A scar?"

"Well, that's not from her. That's Clare Grogan from the band Altered Images. Scars are hot. Kind of snuck in over the years. What about your first crush?"

"Shit, now that you mention it, I've always had a thing for girls with full, pouty lips and my first crush from back in middle school had these great lips."

"That's what I'm saying."

"Yeah, but the rest of it not so much. I dig big titties and my first crush had nothing."

"But how big are boobs in middle school, anyway? That could be a mother issue."

"Fuck you," Ezra replied.

"Umm," I began, "how often do you and Jezzie do the nasty?"

"Fairly frequently," he replied. "What about you and Mallory?"

"Fuck, every two weeks, if I'm lucky."

"Didn't you ever find some weed to horn her up?"

"Guess I don't know the right people," I said. "You're my closest link to the drug underworld and obviously you suck at it."

He laughed. "What, is she still having girlie problems?"

"Not that she's told me, so I have to imagine not. I know her schedule's fucked up and all that but still..."

"What about the rest of it?" he asked. "You guys talking marriage?"

"Nope. I think the last time it even came up was right after she moved back," I said.

May 1996 (Real World, Year 4)

Cute pussy. I came into my sock, turned off the VCR, the TV and the living room lights, went upstairs and joined Mallory in bed.

I touched her leg, she scooted away. *Doesn't the frequency of sex diminish after you get married? What's less than none? Is she happy never fucking me? Maybe. Stop asking to fuck all the time. Stop being affectionate. See how she likes it.*

# # #

After work the next day, I went to the gym without her, worked out for two hours before making my way home. "Why are you so late?" Mallory asked as I passed her in the kitchen.

"Went to the gym," I said.

"I didn't make dinner because I didn't hear from you."

"I can do mac and cheese." *Don't ask about her day, she never asks about yours.*

Once Mallory took her salad to the living room, I started boiling water. She turned on the TV and ate. I sat on the opposite end of the couch with my food and focused on the tube.

She's not going to talk to me, is she?

Another show came on, Mallory took her dishes to the kitchen. "I'm going to go read a while," she said, heading upstairs.

"Okay," I nodded, remaining on the couch.

Two hours later, I went upstairs. Mallory was under the blankets, reading. I washed my face, brushed my teeth and got into bed. She turned off the light, "Good night."

"Night," I replied, turning away from her.

This is pathetic.

# # #

I followed Mallory home from the gym. *Surprise me, Mallory. You know it's NOID. Let's fuck on the deck. Anything. Between the buildings. Whatever.*

"I'm too tired to make dinner," she said when we got out of our vehicles. "You want to get pizza?"

"Sure," I said.

After we ate, Mallory went upstairs to read. *She'd probably fuck, if I went upstairs. I am not initiating this. I'm not doing all the work.*

She was asleep by the time I jerked off in the downstairs bathroom.

# # #

Two weeks later, I woke to the sound of Mallory getting ready for work. She slammed a brush on the counter, then turned away from the mirror to face me. "Why have you been such a dick lately?"

"Didn't think I was being dickish," I said. *Mimicking you.*

"That's bullshit, you know damn well what you're doing." She walked into our closet, emerging with a light jacket.

"This is the way you get girls to break up with you so you aren't the bad guy, huh?"

Pretty much.

Walking toward me, "Why do you think I came back here, Jon?"

"So we could try again."

"I thought you were going to marry me!" she bellowed. "But it's pretty fucking obvious that's not going to happen. You've decided we're not getting married, so you tuned out."

"I never said that."

"But that's what you've done. And that's a seriously fucked up way to handle things, Jon. If you knew this was over, say so. I'm a big girl, I can handle it. But instead, you're an immature prick who makes me do it.

"Fine. Fuck you, I'm leaving."

She stormed down the stairs from the bedroom, the door slammed in the entryway, shaking the entire apartment. *Scary.*

At the gym after work, I took my time between machines, spent an extra twenty minutes on the treadmill, did extra crunches. It was six when I drove back toward the apartment. *What if she's there? She might kill me.* I pulled into Ezra's driveway across the street instead.

"I'm scared to go home," I said. "I don't want her to beat the shit out of me."

He chuckled. "If you see lights on, come back here. How'd she put it?"

"The immature cock, excuse me, prick, combined with I'm a pussy for making her break up with me."

"Well, did you?"

"I mean, you know it's been going downhill for a while and I sort of gave up a month ago or so," I said. "Too much work to save a dead relationship."

"But you could have said something to her when you figured that out," he said.

Wanted her to.

The living room light was on, but her car wasn't there. "Mallory!" I yelled from the entryway. No response.

At the top of the stairway, I looked into the bathroom. A stack of her clothes was missing from atop the drier. "Mallory?" I called. Nothing.

The kitchen seemed as I'd left it as did the living room. From the bottom of the stairs to our bedroom, "Mallory?"

Silence. *Thank God.*

Most of her toiletries and a fair amount of her clothing were missing.

# # #

A message on my machine the next night; Mallory was staying with old roommate, until she found a place and wanted to stop by tomorrow to grab some more stuff and didn't want me there.

No problem.

# # #

Mallory phoned a couple days later at the store. "Uh, hi," I said. *You couldn't've left anything at the apartment, it's empty. You found your naked pictures and swiped those too.*

"Hey, uh, Jon, I was hoping you could help me move a bed into my apartment."

Why would I help?

"I wouldn't ask if there was anyone else."

"Well..."

"I'll make dinner. How does cacciatore sound?"

"Better than mac and cheese," I said.

Straight to Mallory's after work, a lean one-bedroom with a skeletal kitchen, boxes stacked everywhere. There wasn't anything on the stove. *You haven't started cooking yet?*

"That your truck out there?" I asked.

"Yeah," Mallory replied. "I'm still not done getting everything out and I just got home."

You said you needed a little help. "Here," I took one of the bags of groceries from the counter and put a couple things in her fridge.

"Let's finish getting stuff in here," she said. "There's not enough room in the kitchen for both of us."

The next twenty minutes we unloaded the U-Haul. "You sure there's nothing I can do to help?" I asked. *I'm ravenous.*

"Could you make the bed?"

"Sure," I replied, rolling my eyes away from Mallory's view.

After I'd settled her down comforter, I went back into the living room and turned on her stereo. "You told Anthony and Cleo already?"

"They want me to move back there. But I like my job and my boss and I signed a six month lease here."

"They think I'm an asshole?"

"No," she said. "Anthony said he hopes you grow up someday. Cleo wasn't quite as friendly."

"Figures. Your mom?"

"She wants me to be happy so if we weren't going to work out then it was time to move on. She's always liked you, you know that."

"Okay, but I figured Anthony and Cleo liked me more."

"She said she saw it coming and wasn't surprised."

I didn't see it coming. "Well, how many times have we broken up now, three?"

"Guess it is three now. Mom didn't see us getting married. Didn't think you had it in you."

Neither do I. "You know what's funny?" I asked. "I'm more attracted to you when we're not together. You seem stronger, got your shit together, more confident. I mean, you got an apartment in a couple days. I'm impressed."

"Thanks. I feel good about where I'm at with everything. I'm glad you and I can still talk. I'd be disappointed if we lost our friendship as well."

"Yeah, me too."

We sat on the floor of her living room and ate dinner.

She took our plates to the kitchen then sat down in the one piece of furniture she had, a papa san chair. "Can I join you?" I asked. "My ass is falling asleep down here."

"If you can fit."

Pressed against each other, "You have tomorrow off? Maybe unpack more?"

"I don't have a day off until next weekend," she said. "Hopefully I'll do some every night." I worked my left arm from between us, my hand settling on her leg.

"So you'll be done in July sometime?"

Mallory pivoted, her left hand to my belly. "Maybe," she whispered. Passionate kissing, wild groping, clothes strewn about and a feverish breaking in of the new bed.

Both of us spent, we lay motionless for some time.

Why can't we fuck like that when we're together? Can't stay here, she'll take it wrong.

I got up, picking up my clothes on the way to the living room. Mallory followed me. "Thanks for that. I needed some hot sex."

"No, thank you. For the dinner. And the sex."

June 1996 (Real World, Year 4)

The next week, the phone rang at nine-twenty. *Who's calling me this goddamn early?*

Mallory sobbed into the phone, "Can I come over?"

"Sure, yeah. What's going on?"

"I got fired."

"Oh, shit. Yeah, come over."

Ten minutes later, I met her downstairs in the carport. She started crying as she hugged me. "What happened?" I asked when we'd gotten to the living room.

"I got written up last week because I'd messed up with the deposit and I could've sworn I closed the safe last night when I left. But when my manager got there this morning, the safe was open so she had to let me go. I mean I don't blame her but what am I going to do? Now there's nothing keeping me here.

"That job was the only reason I didn't move back to Hawaii, and now..."

I looked at the clock, 9.45. *Got to get to work.* "Is there anything I can do for you?" I asked. *You need money?*

"I don't know," she said. "Oh, shit, are you opening today? You should go."

"I'm doing a fund-raiser cruise thing after work tonight, but call me late if you want to talk more, okay?"

"Okay," she sniffled.

"You'll be fine," I said. "Things will work out."

There was a message from Mallory on the answering machine telling me to call her when I got in, regardless of the time. "How you doing?" I asked. *You sound better.*

"Awesome," she said. "Cleo's going to bring me on at thirty-thousand plus travel and vacation so I'm moving back at the end of the month."

"What about your lease?"

"I talked to the manager this afternoon and explained what happened. She's such a sweet woman. She felt bad for me and said she could rent the apartment, no problem. I'm going to be out of here on the twenty third."

"Damn," I said. "Someone sure lit a fire under your butt."

"I have a big favor to ask."

This should be good. "Yes?"

"Could I put some of my stuff in your storage until I can arrange to have it shipped over?"

"No problem, I've got tons of room."

A pause. "And..."

"Uh huh. Didn't figure that was a big enough favor."

"I can't get a flight until the twenty seventh, so could I stay over there until the twenty sixth? My mom can take me to the airport so I'll drive down but I can't handle her giving me crap about losing my job for four days."

Understandable. "Well, on one condition."

"Which is?"

"Butt sex with the lights on."

"The lights on?" she asked.

"You've never let me watch. I want to see..."

"Maybe."

"Good enough."

# # #

Mallory had dinner waiting for me when I walked in. She handed me a beer. "I could certainly get used to this," I said. "Nothing to do today, huh?"

"Nope," she answered. "You'd have to support me, though."

"Yeah, well, never mind."

We sat on the couch and watched TV while we ate.

Lifting my shirt, "Do I look darker?"

She studied me for a second. "How many times have you gone?"

Apparently not. "Five times," I replied.

"A little bit, maybe."

"I'll have to stay in longer," I said.

"Probably not a good idea. You burn pretty quick in those things."

"Well, obviously fifteen minutes isn't making enough of a difference."

"You're right about that," she said. "Have you jerked off while you're in there?"

Have you? "No. I hadn't considered it. Why, have you?"

"Yeah," she said. "Something about being all warm and naked. I mean I spray the bed down after I'm done so no one gets my stuff on them."

"Wow," I said. "How many times have you done that?"

"Pretty much every time I go."

You're horny twice a week? "Why don't you ever jerk off around me?" *That could've helped.*

"I don't feel like it, so I don't."

#　#　#

The morning of the 26th, I rolled over and draped an arm across Mallory's belly. Whispering in her ear, "You going to pay up?"

"What?" Mallory asked, her eyes still closed.

"The butt sex with the lights on."

"I said maybe."

"I guess you can weasel out of it that way if you want, but I'll lose all respect for you, if you do."

"Okay, fine then."

"You want me to lick your snatch first?"

"No, go ahead," she said.

In the shower, after, we washed each other's backs.

"Call me when you get there," I said, down in the carport.

"I will," she responded, arms around me. "You know I love you," she whispered.

"I love you, too."

Ten:
January 1997 (Real World, Year 5)

Sofia's friend, Wren, a tall, slim, sandy blonde dancer who'd joined us last summer at the bar, stood in the doorway of Sophia's door. "Yes," she said.

"Hey, Wren." *Still hot.* I took a step toward her. She didn't move.

"Have we met?" she asked.

"We were at the Three B together last summer, right before you and Sofia went to Scotland." *I played with your hair... Sofia got pissed about it...* "Didn't she tell you I was coming over?"

"I don't think so," Wren replied.

"We're going to see her ex-boyfriend's band, and Sofia's not going to be back until ten because she's at some event in Mount Vernon." Wren stood firm. "I'm not going to wait in the car." I pushed the door open, walking past her.

"How do you know Sofia?" she asked, remaining near the door.

"I met her our first day at Western. So what, we've known each other ten years now? How would I know your name if I wasn't a friend of Sofia's?"

She stared at me a second. "Lucky guess?" She came into the living room. "Did we really meet last summer?"

"We did." *Wanted to jump you. Still do.* "At Sofia's birthday. We were sitting close to the stage all night."

"I remember Sofia's friend Ezra and someone else. Was that you?"

"I imagine," I said. *Glad I made an impression.* "Jon."

"You're Jon?" Wren asked. "You own the porn store, right?" *Christ.* "I do."

"How is it running a porn store?"

This again? "Like a business," I replied.

"But don't you get a lot of weird people coming in there?"

"Not really."

Sofia opened the front door. "You guys ready to go?" she asked.

"Born ready," I replied.

Once at the Three B, Wren and Sofia found us room at a booth next to the pool tables. Wren sat down next to me, flipped her hair out of her face and asked, "Why aren't there more people here?"

It's not Seattle? "Still early," I said. "It'll fill up around eleven, eleven-thirty."

Sofia returned from the backstage area. "My ex's band already played. They switched times with the other band, car trouble."

Are we leaving?

"What's the plan, then?" Wren asked.

"Already paid the cover," Sofia said. "Might as well stay."

The girls left me at the table to watch the beer when the band took the stage. During the second song, Wren came back, grabbed my hand, insisting I join them.

The three of us went back to the table a couple songs later. I sat next to Sofia, Wren on the other side of the booth. An attractive young man asked Wren to dance, she declined, then went to the bathroom.

"How long have you known Wren?" I asked Sofia.

"A couple years now," she said. "We met through a friend of mine in Seattle, at a Scottish dance exhibition down in Skagit County."

Wren squeezed into the booth next to me. "Why are you two sitting here like bumps? Let's dance." We did.

Wren took my hands while dancing. *Is she flirting with me? Way out of my league.*

Back to Sofia's, shortly after two. "Can I hang out?" I asked. "Not sure I should be driving quite yet."

"Not a problem," she answered. "You want some water?"

"Probably a good idea," I said, following Sofia to the kitchen.

Wren returned from the bathroom in a pair of grey sweatpants and a tight navy blue t-shirt, and sat in the corner of the couch opposite me. B cup breasts, slender hips, toned butt. *Damn. Perfect body. Like Kenna all grown up.*

Sofia lit two three-wick candles, then sat in a chair across from us. "I'm not keeping you guys up, am I?" I asked.

"Not at all," Sofia answered. "We usually stay up talking at least a couple hours when we get back from the bars."

"Still need to do that," Wren said. She stretched out, her legs falling across my lap.

She is flirting. Go to bed, Sofia.

Over the next hour, the gals discussed mutual friends, work and family. Wren got a blanket from the closet and resumed her position on the couch.

Seriously flirting.

"You still going up to Baker in the morning?" Sofia asked Wren.

"Oh yeah," she replied. "I'll try not to wake you up when I go. Should be back around six."

"What time you leaving?" I asked.

"Seven or so," Wren replied, rolling to her back.

Sofia headed to her bedroom. "Good night you two."

"Night," we said. Wren turned off the light next to the couch.

"You want I should go?" I asked.

"You don't have to," she said.

Then I won't.

I started massaging her right hand. Then her left. *Long, delicate fingers.* "You should be getting to sleep," I said. "Close your eyes."

I blew out the candle next to the couch then rubbed her temples, moving my hands into her hairline and back down across her face. *So sexy.*

"You asleep?" I whispered.

"Nope," Wren replied. "You look uncomfortable like that."

"You were supposed to relax," jockeying into the negative space behind her as she rotated to face away from me. *Should I kiss her? She offering her neck?*

My head on her shoulder. *She'd move away if this wasn't okay.* Repositioning, ending up with my mouth on the nape of her neck. I kissed her, then nibbled, then sucked. Wren sighed. *Awesome.*

"I don't think is a good idea," Wren whispered.

"Probably not," I said, sitting up. "Sofia won't be too happy with me. She was pissed when I played with your hair last summer. Don't imagine she'd be too thrilled by any of this."

"She was?"

"She bitched to Ezra, so I heard about it."

"Hmm. You two ever slept together?"

I chuckled. "Uh, no."

"Why's that funny?"

"Never thought about Sofia like that," I said. I kissed Wren solidly. She held my face, returning the kiss. She pulled me to her, positioning herself beneath me.

Wren, "You still too drunk to drive?"

"Don't think so," kissing her again.

She pushed my right shoulder. "You be on bottom," she said.

Likes to be on top? Spectacular.

We traded positions. My fingers ran through her hair, across her back to her hips. She continued to kiss me, her fingers stroking my hair and neck. Left hand skittered across her butt. *Not so fast.*

"Sorry," I said. "I'm trying to be gentlemanly here."

"Don't let it happen again." She smiled.

"Never." *She's perfect.*

Wren kissed me again. "What're you thinking?" she asked.

"Nothing."

"Liar." She lifted my shirt and kissed down my chest to my stomach. "Does that help you remember?"

"Not so much," I said. *You can keep going.* She nibbled on my belly. "I really enjoy kissing you," I said. "Is this going to be a one night thing?"

"Simply the fact that we're discussing it, kind of makes it seem like it isn't, don't you think?"

Stay cool. No big grin. Fantastic. "Yeah," I replied. "Sorry for keeping you up so late."

She sat back up, still straddling me, placed my right hand on the back of her neck. "Feel that?" she asked. "That's a spine."

"But I should still let you sleep." I got up, pulling the blanket with me. "Lay down." She did. I tucked the blanket around her, finishing with a kiss. "Have a good time tomorrow. If you have nothing going on after you get back, give me a call. Sofia's got my number."

#   #   #

Tuesday night on the phone, "How was snowboarding?" I asked. *Why didn't you call me before you left Sunday? Wanted to see you again.*

"Not bad," Wren replied. "You ever go up to Baker?"

"I'm a danger to myself on flat land. I know better than to zip around with trees and shit around," I said. "Sofia said you work for a dentist. You clean teeth?"

"Hell no," she said. "I work in the office, with the patient files. I'd never want to have to dig around in people's mouths. How'd you get into the porn business, anyway?"

After my made for TV version, Wren told me of a long relationship that had ended a year ago, with a guy in her dance program at the University of Washington.

We've been on the phone for two hours.

"My mom got remarried and is up near Anacortes with my step-sister."

"How often you make it up here?" I asked.

"Every couple weeks," she answered. "More often until Baker closes."

"You thought about moving closer to your mom?" *And me?*

"I couldn't leave the city. Part of the charm of Bellingham is that I don't live here."

Could I live in Seattle? Need to sell the store. Plenty of jobs in Seattle. Could finally work in audio production...

Our conversation continued until Wren asked, "Do you think we would be better as lovers or friends?"

Lovers. "Well, we seem to get along well, I'm attracted to you, so I'd have to say lovers."

"I'm thinking friends," she countered.

Dammit.

"I've never been this open or honest with a lover before."

That's sad. "But doesn't that make a stronger relationship? To be open and honest?"

"Maybe," she replied. "But don't take me saying that as a limit. It's what I was thinking about what's going on with us."

That you'd rather be friends? Swell.

"When are you going to be down this way?"

"My buddy Neal is having a birthday party next weekend over in Redmond. I think Sofia's going. You should join us, if you can."

"Maybe," she said.

# # #

Ezra and I were sitting in the Quarterback Sports Bar with a beer in front of us waiting for the game to start. "Do you believe in love at first sight?" I asked.

"Oh, Jesus," Ezra sighed. "What happened?"

"Seriously, do you?"

"Not really. You're not talking about Wren, are you?"

"It's not like first sight, but I've been getting the feeling she might be the one," I said. "I'm always thinking about her. Hell, I smile when I think about her."

"You mean like now?"

"Yeah, like now," I replied. "Haven't you heard about people who knew they'd met their soul mate from the first time they talked?"

Ezra tilted his head. "You're serious?"

"Yeah."

He took a deep breath. "I'm sure it happens. Things going that well?"

"I'm not sure where I stand, honestly. Last night she was talking about being friends instead of lovers, but she didn't say that's all she wanted."

"Hunh," he grunted. "How would things work with her in Seattle?"

"I'd have to move down there eventually. She's not interested in leaving. I can sell the store, no problem. A couple people have asked about it."

"Sell the store?"

"It's not like I'd do it next week or anything," I said. "But it's crossed my mind."

February 1997 (Real World, Year 5)

Each time the doorbell rang Neal's split-level in Redmond, I looked. *Where's Wren?*

"What's this I hear about you and one of Sofia's friends?" Neal asked me.

"We spent a fevered evening on Sofia's couch last weekend," I replied. "Talked a few times since. I'm staying with her tonight."

"Oh you are, are you?"

"With any luck," I said. "Assuming she shows up."

"Ezra lent Sofia his car to go meet her," Neal said.

Sofia escorted Wren in to the living room half an hour later. Wren smiled at me. "Which one's the birthday boy?"

Ezra, standing next to the fireplace, bumped Neal forward. "Right here."

"Happy Birthday," Wren said, holding out an envelope to Neal.

"Hope it's money," Neal said.

"Great. Now I all look like shit because I didn't bring a card," I said.

"That's not why you look like shit," Neal said.

Neal opened the card, thanked Wren, then took her and Sofia on a tour of the house. Ezra and I went downstairs to the game room and joined Jezzie next to the ping pong table. Twelve minutes later Sofia sat down with us.

Where's Wren?

Ezra and I played a game of ping pong before I headed upstairs. Sidling up to Wren in the kitchen, "How's things?"

"Dandy," she answered. "Where'd you run off to?"

"Playing ping pong downstairs."

"Is that where Sofia is?"

"Think so," I said.

She touched my arm as she left the kitchen.

Can't we talk?

Finding Ezra and Neal, "What do you think of Wren?" I asked, glancing at the stairwell whenever someone appeared.

"She's all right," Neal said. "Haven't had much of a chance to talk to her. Been flitting around all night."

"She has?"

"Yeah," Ezra said. "Bopping from room to room, chatting with everyone."

Except me.

I found Wren playing doubles ping pong with Jezzie, Ezra and Sofia. The game finished moments after I arrived downstairs, and Wren and Sophia immediately returned upstairs.

When I found Wren twenty minutes later, she had her coat on. "Sofia, can you point me out of here?" Wren asked.

Neal asked, "You taking off too, Sofia?"

"No," she replied. "I'm with Ezra and Jezzie."

Outside, I listened to Sofia's directions, then asked Wren, "Am I still welcome at your place?"

"I wouldn't tell you it was all right, if it wasn't," she said.

At Wren's, she led me up a steep staircase, past the living room. *Where's your roommates?* She closed her bedroom door behind us. *I'm staying in your room? Hot damn.*

"Where's the bathroom?" I asked.

"On the right," she said.

Wren was stretching on the floor in a tank top and nylon shorts when I returned to her room.

Am I sleeping on the floor? "Where do you want me?" I asked.

"In bed with me, silly," she replied.

Kick ass.

"Where were you thinking? The floor?"

"Didn't want to assume," I said.

Wren stood up and kissed me. We climbed into bed. She pulled a joint out of the drawer of her night stand. After a draw, she offered it to me.

"No, thanks," I said.

"You okay with me smoking?"

"Your house."

One more pull before putting it out and kissing me again. The light off, Wren snuggled up to me.

Don't rush things. No pussy play tonight.

Wren kissed up my neck to my mouth, then nibbled on my bottom lip. She ran her fingers through my hair as she climbed atop me. My hands ventured down her back, stopping above her butt. I ran my thumbs along her hipbones, across her thighs. Over, onto her back, dragging me with her.

Our hips pressed into each other. I took my shirt off, then kissed her boobs through her cotton shirt. Pushing the shirt higher, I kissed her bare stomach and the edge of her ribcage. Back to her face, then her ears and her neck.

"We should get some sleep," she suggested after half an hour. "I'm meeting a friend of mine for breakfast. You want to join us?"

"Sounds good," I said. *Introducing me to friends? Awesome.*

# # #

Back in Bellingham I called Mary. "Hi, Mom. How're things?"

"The same," Mary replied. "How's the store doing?"

"Strong lately. Been able to spend some afternoons writing since I hired a manager." I paused. "I've got news. I met somebody."

"That's great, sweetie. How did you meet?"

"She's a friend of Sofia's," I said. "Her name's Wren, she lives in Seattle, works at a dentist's office."

"Seattle?" Mary asked. "How's that working then?"

"Well, she's up here every couple weeks or so. I figure I could move down there this summer or so."

Long pause. "When did you meet her?"

"The end of January, so what, almost three weeks now?"

"What about the store?"

"A couple people have inquired about buying it, so I shouldn't have too much trouble selling it. I'm sure I can find something in Seattle, either at a venue or a studio."

Another long pause. "Isn't it a little early to be thinking about moving and giving up the business?"

Not at all. "I think she's the one," I said.

"Oh," Mary said. "Maybe you should wait a while before you make any big changes in your life?"

Why? "I couldn't get anything done too quickly anyway. Besides, I haven't mentioned any of this to Wren yet. I don't want to scare her off. I know it's quick, but still..."

#   #   #

"Why didn't you call me back last night?" Ezra asked me.

"Down in Seattle, at Wren's," I responded. "What'd you need?"

"Jezzie and I were going to the movies and thought you might want to join us. Jezzie's friend Phaedra came with us, and we thought you two might get along."

"What'd you see?"

"*She's All That*," he sighed. "I was outnumbered. Maybe if you'd've been here we could have gone to *Payback*. How's Wren?"

"All right, I guess," I said. "We were getting all hot n' heavy, both in our undies, and I head south. And she stopped me and pulled me back up."

"You try again? In the morning?"

"Naw," I said. "Maybe she was bleeding or whatever."

"She blow you?"

"No," I said. "I mean I want to take things slow, but we haven't talked about not doing anything, so who knows what's up?"

"She coming up for Valentine's Day?" Ezra asked.

"I had Neal make reservations for us at some restaurant down there. Maybe I need to buy her dinner before she'll suck my dick?"

# # #

Monday I mailed Wren a note telling her I was looking forward to seeing her on the fourteenth. And another on Wednesday. And a mix CD of sappy, emotion-laden songs on Thursday.

# # #

I offered a single red rose taped to a bar of chocolate to Wren when I picked her up. "Thanks," she said.

"You mind driving?" I asked. "I've got a general idea of where we're going, but you'll probably be able to get us there faster. You listened to the CD I sent?"

"Oh, uh, not yet," she replied. "Got it this afternoon."

After dinner, we went back to her house, again bypassing the roommates, straight to her bedroom.

# # #

Wren called me late the next night. After minutes of small talk, Wren declared, "I think it'd be better if we were just friends."

Didn't we already have this discussion?

She asked, "What do you think about that?"

"Can't say I'm happy about it. I've been under the impression we've been doing all right as more than friends."

"You're dating other people, aren't you?"

"No." *You're awesome.*

"Why not?"

"Because I don't tend to date. I'm more of a serial monogamist." *Unless I'm cheating.*

"You don't seem like a monogamist to me," Wren stated.

Because I want to lick your snatch?

"I think you should date," she said.

"But I don't want to see other people, Wren. I'm happy the way things are." *But we could fuck.*

"We'll work better as friends." I didn't reply. "You still there?"

"I'm still here. I don't think you've given us much of a chance."

"Really, Jon, you're not considering my feelings with this. I'm going to bed now." And she hung up.

*She's seeing other people? She's so cool. What's wrong
with me?*

# # #

Wren called the following Thursday. "I thought we were still
friends," she said. "Why haven't you called me?"

"We are still friends, Wren," I said. "I'm having a tough time
with our new status. And even though you're calling us friends, it
hasn't changed the way I feel about you."

"Well, you should've called so we could talk about it."

"But if we're friends now, then I wouldn't call you about us."

"That's silly," she said. "You could've called to be friendly,
even if you didn't want to discuss us."

"I could've, but I talk to Neal what, once a month? Maybe?
Since I just saw you, I don't feel due to call you for a while."

"That's not very nice."

"But true."

March 1997 (Real World, Year 5)

Ezra stopped by the apartment early Sunday afternoon.
"How was Wren's party last night?" he asked.

"Her mom's, yeah," I said. "Not bad. She hung out with me
and Sofia some, showed us around. Eventually the three of us left
and went over to another friend of hers before Sofia and I took off."

"Nothing interesting?"

"Well, Wren called me at three last night and apologized for
us not having any alone time. Then she called about half an hour
ago and said she wanted to get together and is going to stop by in
about an hour or so."

"That's why you're cleaning?"

"And the dishes stink," I answered.

"You don't have time to go on a bike ride, then?" Ezra
asked.

"Not today. Tomorrow, if the weather holds?"

"Fuck the weather," he said.

"Fine. Five?"

"No pussying out," Ezra said.

My apartment was respectable when Wren entered. A
quick tour ending up on the living room couch. Wren described her
morning in Anacortes with her family, her plans to make it up for

the last day of the season at Mount Baker and a new boy Sofia was interested in.

"Are you and I okay?" she asked, an hour in.

"Yeah," I said. "But if you're asking if I've stopped being attracted to you, then the answer's no."

"Oh."

"Until you tell me there's no chance of us being anything more than friends, I'll still pursue you in a more than friendly way."

"You know Jon, I'm vacillating emotionally from one day to the next and I don't want to mess with you. One day I feel this way, the next day I feel completely different. Not just us but everything. If I were you, I'd run from someone as flaky as I am these days."

But you're terrific. "I already told you, I'm not running."

Wren crawled across the couch, nuzzled into me. "I want you to stop with the gifts, okay? I don't feel like I can return the favor and I feel guilty. Please stop."

"You don't have to get me anything," I said.

"Enough already," she stretched to kiss me.

"Okay, no more presents."

Fifteen minutes later, Wren asked, "What are you thinking?"

"It's kind of scary," I said. "Should probably keep it to myself."

"That's not fair."

"I was thinking I could fall for you in a major way." *Already have.*

"That's what I was afraid of," she said, sitting up. "Monogamy is the furthest thing from my mind right now. I can't imagine being in a serious relationship...I'm really enjoying being single. And I don't want to hurt you. Why aren't you seeing other people?"

"Not interested in other people," I said.

"You should work on that. I got to go."

"Should I call you later?"

"You can, if you want."

I want.

# # #

Wren's black Jetta sat in front of Sofia's apartment Saturday afternoon. "Ezra and I are going riding up at Lake Padden. Want to join us?" I asked both gals.

"We're making dinner for Sofia's new boy," Wren answered. "I don't have a bike here, either."

"You should bring it up," I said. "Ezra's meeting me there in fifteen minutes. I got to get going."

Wren got up. "I'll be right back," she said to Sofia. She closed the door behind her. "I want this to be fun between you and me," she began. "If it's work, then it's too much like a relationship and I don't want to do that."

I invited you to go on a bike ride. "What constitutes work, Wren?"

"You know, if you're in Seattle, stop by. If I'm up here, I'll see what you're up to. If you feel like calling me, call me. And I'll do the same. But we shouldn't have to feel like we have to call each other."

"Okay, but I'm never going to stop by uninvited," I said.

"Why not?"

"I don't want to drive an hour and a half to find you hanging out with another guy, so I can drive back home feeling like shit. I won't put myself in that situation."

"Should I worry that you'll have some girl over if I drop by?" she asked.

"No, I've already told you, I'm not interested in seeing other people. You can stop by whenever, it's not a problem. But don't expect it from me."

#   #   #

The following Friday night, in my bed, Wren's snuggle led to a kiss, then another, then her shirt coming off and her grinding on my thigh. Left hand slid under her panties and diddled a while. She took her underwear off.

I stopped. "I need to tell you something," I said.

"What?" she whispered.

"I've had genital warts," I said. "Haven't seen any in a long time, but there's still a chance you could end up getting them."

Wren sat up. "What's a long time?"

"Shit, I don't know. The last time I was treated was more than five years ago, but I wanted to let you know."

She sat silent. Ten seconds, then twenty. "When was the last time you were tested for HIV?

"About six months ago," I said. "You?"

"Last month. I'd die if I got an STD, so I get checked at least twice a year."

"I've got condoms."

"The moment's been ruined."

Not for me. "Am I ever going to get the chance to go down on you?"

She said, "There's always a chance."

"Yes, but a point zero zero zero one percent chance doesn't do much for us mathematicians," I replied. I rolled away from her. She ran a hand across my back and kissed my neck. She pulled me to her. We kissed a while before I went under the covers, kissing to her belly.

Wren gripped my head again. "Not tonight."

Right.

#   #   #

Ezra and Jezzie arrived at my apartment at five on Saturday, a pizza in hand. "Phaedra isn't coming, I take it?" I asked. *Liked the way she looked. Long fingers, light eyebrows.*

"Why didn't you tell us Wren was coming to the movies last night?" Jezzie asked.

"I didn't know," I said. *Seriously uncool.*

"Phaedra was pretty uncomfortable once she showed up."

"Yeah, me too," I said. "Then she fell asleep in the middle."

Jezzie looked aghast. "Did she really?"

"Yup. She insists I date other people then shows up unannounced like that."

"She around tonight?" Ezra asked.

"Maybe," I said. "Told her we were watching a movie, so who knows."

Wren called with about ten minutes left in the film. "What're you doing?"

"Finishing the movie," I replied. "You heading up this way?"

"Having breakfast with the family in the morning and then I'm meeting a friend of mine to do some shopping tomorrow afternoon."

"Okay," I said. "Then I'll talk to you sometime this week?"

"If I came up to spend the night, would you keep me up?"

"Not if you didn't want me to." *I can come quick.*

"Well, maybe I'll stop by later. You don't have anyone over there, do you?"

"Ezra and Jezzie."

"Maybe I'll stop by."

Wren knocked on my door long after Ezra and Jezzie had walked home. "Are they still here?" she asked, not fully stepping into the entryway.

"They left around nine," I said.

Wren told me about the party she'd attended that afternoon while on our way upstairs. Shirtless, under the blanket, she asked, "Why are you so eager to go down on me?"

"Because I want to be that close to you," I said. "And I want you to feel good."

Nibbling her neck, her boobs, then continuing to her belly. *She's going to stop me.* She didn't.

Pressing my tongue against the top of her panties, Wren stayed still. *Any second now...* I continued my teasing through her underwear, occasionally slipping under the side elastic.

She's going to let me!

Pulling her panties to the side, I ran my tongue across her clit. *Finally.*

I licked and sucked, nibbled and played. A finger inside, circled her clit; she barely responded. Fifteen minutes in, I gave up. *You could tell me what you like.*

"Thanks," I said, moving next to her.

"I should get to sleep," she said.

# # #

Wren didn't wake me when she left Saturday morning but the phone ringing at eight did. With a gravelly voice, "Aren't you skiing?"

"We're going tomorrow instead," Sofia answered. "Get up and come to breakfast with us."

"Fuck, fine. I'm up now."

At a diner across town, Ezra and Jezzie were sitting with Wren and Sofia when I arrived. "Go-od morn-ing," Ezra sang.

"Fuck you."

"You need coffee?" Sofia asked.

"I'll be good in a few minutes," I replied. "Most likely."

After breakfast, we made plans for me to pick up Sofia and Wren at seven and meet up with Ezra and Jezzie to check out the new smoke-free pool parlor in Fairhaven.

After a couple hours at the pool hall, Sofia got out of my car. Wren sat silent in the passenger's seat. "Still going skiing tomorrow?" I asked her.

"Yeah," she answered. "Heading up at six."

"I'd love for you to stay with me, but it's more convenient for you to stay here, huh? What do you want to do?"

"I don't care."

If you don't care... "Then stay here," I said.

"Fine." Wren hurriedly opened the door, out and up the stairs to Sofia's without looking back.

What the fuck was that about?

I drove the long way home. *Utters four sentences to me all day but gets pissed when I don't beg her to stay with me? Fuck that.*

A message from Wren on the answering machine when I got home. "Call me at Sofia's when you get home. We should talk about the weirdness in the car."

Not going to talk about this while you're at Sofia's. Should finish that porn from yesterday.

Threw pants and underwear in the washing machine before returning to my masturbatory haven on the couch. A knock on the door.

Goddammit.

I ran, halfie bobbling, upstairs to put on a pair of sweats. When I opened the door to the carport, Wren was walking back to her car.

"Wren."

She turned around, aggressively walked to me, held my head and kissed me. "Why are you being such a butthead?"

Me? What are you talking about?

She walked up the stairs to the living room, removed her shoes and coat and continued up to my room. "Tell me," she continued, "why are you being a butthead?"

"I don't know what you're talking about."

"You do too," she said. She stood next to the bed and took off everything save her panties. She crawled into bed. "You're being poopy. Why?"

"Really Wren, I haven't thought I was the least bit of an ass today."

"Well, you have been. Total butthead. Come here."

Under the covers, I covered her body with kisses, tossed her underwear away and ground my boxers covered cock against her. *She's going to let me fuck her? Awesome.*

I continued grinding, she kneaded my ass. I stretched for the night stand but couldn't reach.

"Hold on a sec," I said, moving off her.

"You're trying to have sex with me because I'm drunk and high, aren't you?"

What? "Not at all," I said. *If you're so fucked up, how'd you drive here?*

"You shouldn't be trying to take advantage of me like this."

What? Taking advantage of you? How do you get that?

"I'm going to go to sleep now," she said.

Who the fuck are you?

She rolled away from me.

"That's not what I was trying to do, Wren," I said. *Want to fuck you. Nothing to do with your mental state.*

"Go to sleep," she whispered. "I got to get up early."

Dammit.

#   #   #

Tuesday evening Sofia called me. "You should call Wren," she said. "She's still upset about whatever happened this weekend."

"Oh," I said. "Did she fill you in on everything?" *Maybe you can decipher what's going on?*

"No, but this is exactly why I didn't want you two going out. I don't want to be in the middle of stuff with two of my friends. I'm not taking sides and please don't tell me what's going on, just call her."

"I never wanted you in any of this, Sofia. I'll call her right now."

"Thanks."

Wren didn't answer the phone but called me back late that night. "I already told you I'm not interested in anything if it's going to be work."

"You mentioned that, yes," I replied.

"You shouldn't have expectations from me, Jon," she continued. "If you do, we should call this whole thing off."

No, no, no. "I don't want that, Wren. I had a hard time this last weekend, we didn't talk much, you were doing stuff with other people and I felt kind of ignored."

"See, you're expecting things from me."

For you to talk to me? I asked, "You going skiing again this weekend?"

"Yeah, I'm staying at my mom's because my step-brother is coming with me."

Shit.

# # #

Friday evening, at Sofia's, Wren led me out to the front walkway. "I've heard you want more than a casual thing," she started.

You heard? I told you. "That's certainly my ultimate goal. But you're seeing other people and I know I can't have that with you now, so casual is what I'm trying to do."

"How do you know I'm seeing other people?"

"You've mentioned it," I said.

"Oh." She thought a moment. "I don't want to keep having discussions about our relationship. That's too much work."

"Okay." *I can NOT talk.*

"Do you know what a Movado is?"

"Nope."

"It's a watch. They run about twelve hundred dollars. The next time you talk about us, you're going to have to buy me one."

"I can do that."

"I don't think you can," she said, before breaking into a smile.

"You don't want a bike or a computer? You want a watch?"

"Yup. Next time you talk about our relationship."

"Done," I said. "You heading back down to Anacortes tonight?"

"Yeah. Sofia and I are going to the Three B for the Clumsy Lovers. You should come."

"Can't," I lied. "I've got to take care of some stuff at the store. You guys have a good time." I turned to leave.

"You're not going to kiss me goodbye?"

I kissed her, then returned to my apartment.

# # #

Wren stopped by Sunday night. "I had a couple minutes before I need to head back," she said, sitting next to me on the couch.

"Thanks for stopping by," I said. "You have a good time on the mountain?"

"For the most part. Would've liked to have spent less time helping my stepbrother, but he's a beginner."

"He get better?"

"Not much," she said. "We'll need to take another newbie with us next time we go. You do anything?" Wren snuggled up to me.

"Worked. Neal was up so we hung out last night. That's about it." We kissed a while.

Wren leapt up. "You got to go?" I asked. She led me up to the bedroom.

This is all right.

Tinkered with her snatch before planting my face in it. A couple minutes in, Wren pulled me up.

You don't want to fuck? Let me finish.

Face between her legs again licked her for a couple more minutes. Her breathing faster and shallower, she pulled me back up.

"Why do you keep taking me away?" I asked.

"I enjoy it, but I don't want you to spend all your time down there," she responded. "Not that you can't go back..."

Wren took my left hand and put it on her pussy. After jostling her bits, a finger, then two entered her. *Can I get her to squirt? Come hither motion.*

I beckoned her puss. A moan. I rubbed with palm and massaged with fingers. Wren got louder and louder.

She's going to squirt. Hot damn.

Wren squealed, yanking my hand out of her. "Too much," she panted.

Not enough...you didn't come.

After catching her breath, she stood up, got dressed. "I need to get home."

April 1997 (Real World, Year 5)

Wren, newspaper in hand, joined Sofia, Ezra, Jezzie and I at the Old Town Café for breakfast. While Ezra, Sofia and I talked about this and that, Wren read the paper, continuing to do so after our food arrived.

After brunch, Wren gave me a cursory wave and walked away with Sofia.

What was that about?

Sofia called that afternoon. "You want to go to the mall with me?" she asked. "I've got to find a couple things."

"Wren take off already?"

"Yeah. She wondered why you were in such a bad mood."

Me?

# # #

Saturday afternoon I called Ezra. "Last night could've gone better," I started.

"At least Wren didn't show up this time," Ezra said. "It looked like everything was going all right."

"Yeah, Phaedra seems nice and all, but it wasn't like we were going to get to know each other while you, Jezzie, Sofia and her ex are sitting at the table with us."

"Stop being such a pussy then and ask her out."

"I can now," I said. "Now that we've had some sort of interaction." My phone clicked. "Hold on, I've got another call."

"Call me back later."

Wren was on the other line. "My mom and I are fighting," she said. "We're going sailing tomorrow but I don't want to hang around here tonight. You want to go see a movie?"

"Sure, but I'm stuck at the store until nine-ish. That work?"

"Yeah, *Go!* is playing at Sehome Cinema at nine-thirty," she replied. "Can you make that?"

"Might be close, but I think so. Why don't I meet you there?"

"I'll be at your place at nine-twenty."

Doesn't make sense.

Wren's car wasn't outside my apartment when I returned at nine-thirty. *Where is she?*

I called her pager when I got inside. She knocked on the carport door at nine-fifty.

"I was here at nine-twenty and when you hadn't shown up at nine twenty-five, I left," she said.

"By the time we get there, we'll have missed at least half an hour."

"Sofia's watching *The Nutty Professor* with her new boy," Wren said. "We should go over there."

You don't talk to me around other people. "Why don't we hang out here a while?"

She sat on the couch. "What's going on with your mom?" I asked.

Wren went into great detail about their relationship and how things came to a head this afternoon. "We should stop by Sofia's and see what they're doing," Wren said.

"Why don't we get ice cream?"

A gal was locking the door as we pulled into the Baskin-Robbins parking lot. "Apparently, they close at ten fifty-five," I said.

"I'm sure Sofia's still up," Wren said. "Let's stop by."

"How about, let's leave them alone? If she wanted to see us, she would've called."

Back at my apartment, she asked, "What do you want to do now?"

"You want a backrub?" I offered.

"I guess." I led her upstairs. Eight minutes in, she said, "I want to ask you a question but I'm not sure I want the answer."

"You want me to lie about it?" I asked, continuing to rub her back.

"No, you won't know which way to lie."

Seriously doubt that. "I can probably figure it out," I said.

"I don't think you can."

"Give me a little credit." In a falsetto, "What are you reading now?" Pause. "Zombie by Joyce Carol Oates." Again in a falsetto voice, "Are you expecting a backrub after this?" Pause. "It'd be nice, but no, I don't expect it. I offered, you didn't." She didn't react. "Does it bother me that we'll never sleep together?" Pause. "No, actually, it doesn't."

"I never said that," Wren said.

"Not in so many words but that's what you meant. You said if you got an STD, you'd die. Your life would be over. That's as good as saying it'll never happen."

"That's not what I meant."

"But that's definitely the way it came across," I said. "Did I answer your question?"

"Not at all," she said.

"You going to ask me then?"

"It'll keep."

We kissed.

You going to sleep with me tonight then?

She took off her shirt but each time I tried to unsnap her pants she dismissed my hand.

I knew what you meant.

Wren put her shirt on at two thirty. "I need to get back."

May 1997 (Real World, Year 5)

Through the throngs of bodies in the beer garden downtown, Ezra handed me a cup. "Didn't Sofia come with you?"

"She was waiting for Wren, said she'd meet us here," I replied. "Did Neal say whether or not he was coming?"

"He can't get up here until tonight."

"What time are we meeting everyone up on campus?"

"They wanted to do some night golf, so nine."

I made my best horrified face. "We're going to miss the finale of the block party?"

"Who's playing?"

"No idea."

Wren spun me around to hug me. "Happy Memorial Day!" she said. "I haven't seen you in ages. How've you been?"

"Not bad, you?"

"Packing my shit up to move out this week. Finally," she said. "Sofia said she's moving into your complex in July."

"Two doors down," I nodded.

"I'm going to get beer," she announced, moving away.

Ezra, "She certainly was friendly."

"I know. Can't believe it. There's people around and everything. Maybe if I ignore her more, she'll be nicer to me."

An hour later Ezra and I said goodbye to Sofia and Wren. Wren hugged me and slurred, "How can you leave me for Frisbee? Stay."

"I've already said I was going," I replied. "Neal came up. It'd be rude to ditch him. If you want, call me when you get back to Sofia's."

"You should stay with me," she whined, then turned back to Sofia.

Home from Frisbee golf after eleven-thirty, no messages on the machine. *Guess you're not calling.*

Shortly past midnight the phone rang. *Jesus Wren, what if I was trying to sleep?*

"Hey Jon," Sofia said.

Sofia? "What's up?"

"Wren wants to come over to your place but she's had too much to drink. Is there any way you can come get her?"

Drunk enough to fuck me? "How much is too much?" I asked.

"She's in the bathroom throwing up."

Nice. "How do you know she wants to come over here?"

"She keeps telling me to call you. Can you please come get her?"

So I'll have to deal with her puke?

Sofia opened the door to her apartment, then the door to her bathroom. "I'm meeting Ezra and Jezzie at Denny's," Sofia said. "She's all yours."

Wren raised her head out of the toilet. "I want to go to Denny's."

"Why don't we stay here until you feel a little better," I said.

"I feel fine," she mumbled, then retched. "I want to go to Denny's," Wren said again. "I'm hungry."

I'm sure.

She sat up, looked me in the eye. "I'm hungry."

Wren and I squeezed into the booth with Ezra, Sofia, Jezzie and Sofia's new boy. Wren ordered an egg and toast then fell asleep on my shoulder. "I can't thank you enough, Sofia," I said.

"You are so welcome," she replied, with a smile. "Hey, she was asking for you."

"You could've told her I was already asleep."

"Could've..."

After eating, I led Wren to my car then upstairs, undressed her leaving her panties on. By the time I'd brushed my teeth, Wren's breath had turned to a slow, deep rasping.

You could've not fucked me at Sofia's.

June 1997 (Real World, Year 5)

"How's your new place?" I asked Wren on the phone Saturday afternoon.

"Haven't unpacked much," she said. "Still got stuff in my car from my house. Too tired to deal with it now. Are you going to be down here tonight?"

"Uh, no," I said. *Why would I be down there?*

"Why not?"

"Because I have no reason to be there." *Do you want to see me?*

"If you were around, you could help me unpack."

"I could. You want me to come down and help?"

Her voice quieted, "If you're going to be here."

"The only reason I'd have to come down would be to see you."

"Oh."

"Say it."

"Say what?"

"Say you want to see me. If you invite me down, I'll come." No response. "If you want me to come down there, you'll have to ask me."

"I'm not playing that game," she said.

226

"Wren, look. I already told you I'm never going to just show up. You're the one seeing other people and I'm not interested in knocking on your door and finding someone else with you. I'm not coming down without an invitation."

"Well, if you're not going to be around," she said. "Then maybe I'll see you later this week. I'm going rock climbing in Canada with a friend of mine this weekend."

"All right then. Good luck with the unpacking."

She hung up.

"You couldn't just invite me!?!" I screamed at the phone.

# # #

Thursday night, minutes before midnight, a knock at my front door. *Who the hell is that?* Wren's black Jetta was in the driveway. *Why's she here? Supposed to be rock climbing with some guy.*

At the door, "Hi."

"We got rained out as soon as we got there," Wren explained, walking in.

"You were going to stay the entire weekend. What else happened?"

"The guy I was with was getting on my nerves. I couldn't stay there any longer. I think he's wants to be more than friends. I'm not interested in him that way."

Why did you agree to spend the weekend with him?

"Were you already in bed?"

"No. I've got to open the store tomorrow, my manager's going out of town this weekend."

"You mind if I stay here tonight?"

"Not at all."

In bed, I fondled her for twenty minutes then propped myself up on one arm. "Why don't you ever touch me?" I asked.

Wren hesitated then answered. "It's not you, it's me."

Bullshit. "Okay, I can almost buy that, except seeing as you're sleeping with other guys, I kind of got to figure it's me."

She opened her mouth to speak but didn't.

I continued, "I figure you're physically attracted to me since we hang out together and get somewhat intimate on occasion. But it's been months and you still haven't touched me, so I'm having a tough time figuring out what's going on."

"I've got a lot going on, Jon," she said.

Not right now. "Okay," I said. "I should get to sleep. Night."
Why am I still doing this?

# # #

My alarm went off at eight forty-five. Wren opened her eyes then reached for me. "Stay here with me."

"Can't," I said. "Got to shower before I head out."

"You're the boss," running a hand down my back. "You can be late. Stay."

"Not today." I hopped in the shower. *You could join me in here.*

Wren stayed in bed while I dressed.

"You sticking around today?" I asked.

"No. I should head back."

You were supposed to be gone all weekend. What do you have to do?

Downstairs, I poured a bowl of Rice Chex, turned on the TV and ate. Dressed, Wren came downstairs. "What are you going to do then?" I asked her.

"Go visit my mom," she said.

"Tell her hi from me."

# # #

My phone rang at seven o'clock on Saturday. Wren asked, "Were you going to be down here tonight?"

"No, I weren't," I replied. "If you invited me down, I'd love to see your place."

"I know you're not going to be strolling by, Jon," she said. "But since I'm calling you and seeing if you're going to be around Seattle, that means I want you to come down."

"But that's not what you're saying. Why don't you ask me if I'll come see you instead of hinting about it?"

"Asking you to come here would be work and I told you I don't want to work at this."

"Bullshit, Wren," I said. "If I want to see one of my friends, I invite them over. That's not work, it's being friends."

Silence. More. "You know, I'm expecting things from you that I'm not getting."

Someone who'll jump through hoops for you? "What are you expecting then?"

"I wanted to hang out with a friend in my new house and I wanted that friend to be you."

"Then ask me to come down and I will. You only have to ask." Again, silence. "It's easy. Say, 'Jon, want to hang out over here tonight?' Easy."

"Why are you being like this?"

"We've been over this, Wren."

"Fine, I'll guess I won't see you tonight then."

"Guess not."

She hung up.

# # #

The door to the store opened at twelve-thirty, Sofia stepped in. She leaned over the front counter to me. "Will you please go down and visit Wren?"

"Now she's having you bug me about it?"

"She's not," Sofia replied. "I'm asking you. Please. She says she's not going to come up this weekend if you're around. I don't know what's going on with you two, and I don't really care, but we've got tickets for the Highland Games out in Ferndale already, so will you go down there. Please?"

"I will, as soon as she invites me."

"She's invited you."

"No, Sofia, she hasn't," I said. "She's asked me if I was going to be around Seattle. That's not an invitation. I don't have plans to be in Seattle for any reason, so I told her unless she invited me, I wouldn't be there."

"Wren says she's been asking you to come visit her but you won't."

Of course that's what she's said. "She hasn't invited me. I've already been over this with her. She has to ask me, not beat around the bush. I'm more than happy to see her, but I told her months ago, I wouldn't show up without being invited and she still hasn't asked me."

I turned to my manager, who had been listening to our conversation. "What have I been saying about not being invited the past week?"

My manager grinned. "From what you've said to me, she keeps asking if you're going to be in town."

"Would you take that as an invitation?" I asked.

"No," my manager said. "It's not the same."

I spun back on Sofia. "It's not me being a dick, Sofia. I'm sorry if she's screwing up your plans but this is all on her, not me."

Sofia shook her head. "Could you call her and try to work things out? Please? For me?"

I sighed. "I'll call her, okay?"

"Thank you," Sofia said and left the store.

The message I left on Wren's voicemail asked what she was doing later and to call me to clear the air.

A smidge after four, the store phone rang. My manager handed it to me. "It's a girl."

"You called?" Wren said.

"I'd like to see your new place," I said.

"You going to be around?"

"No, but if you invite me, I'm more than happy to drive down tonight." My manager shook her head. I rolled my eyes at her then took the phone around the storage shelves, away from the retail floor.

Wren sighed heavily. "Why don't you come down here?"

"You need to invite me, Wren. If you're not doing something with someone else, invite me."

"I'm getting busy here, let me call you back."

"I'm taking off in about an hour," I said.

My manager laughed as I hung up the phone. "Still didn't invite you?"

"Not yet."

Wren called back at five-thirty. "Hey," she said. "What're you doing?"

"About to walk out the door," I replied. "What's the plan?"

"I'm having dinner with a friend of mine."

You could've told me that earlier. Unless you made plans since we last spoke. "Well, maybe I shouldn't come down then, disrupt your evening and all. And if I come down after, it'll be late and then what's the point? To tuck you in?"

She asked, "Why not?"

I didn't answer right away. "It's not worth the three hours of driving to see you awake for ten minutes."

"Let me see how concrete these plans are and I'll get back to you."

"Call me at home then."

I sat by the phone until six-thirty. *This is stupid.*

I rode my bike along the Boulevard trail. *Why am I even bothering with her? Treats me like shit more often than not. Never talks to me when other people are around. Won't touch me.*

When I returned to the apartment, there was a message on the machine. "Hey? Are you there?" The caller ID noted the time as 6:38.

No directions? No plan? Not helpful.

After putting a Boboli pizza in the oven, the light on the answering machine blinked. *When did that happen?*

"I'm going to be here for another half an hour so call me." It was Wren. She'd called at eight. It was 8:10.

At eight-thirty, I returned her call, going straight to voicemail. "Hey Wren. Sorry I missed you earlier. I waited until six-thirty to hear from you then went on a bike ride before the sun went down. I'm about to eat dinner and I still need a shower, so I'm going to skip coming down tonight. Maybe some other time. Talk to you later."

Two minutes later the phone rang. "I can't believe you," Wren said. "After everything you've been saying about wanting to see me and my apartment. Now you're not coming."

"Are you back from dinner yet?" I asked.

"No, I haven't gone yet. It's going to take you an hour and a half to get here."

"Exactly," I said. "That would make it what, ten-thirty or so? Not much point in me coming down any more."

"Jesus," she sighed. "Fine. Have a good weekend then."

"Yeah, you too." *Don't imagine I'll be seeing you.*

#   #   #

Tuesday, eleven forty-eight, my phone rang again. "I'm having trouble getting to sleep," Wren said.

I responded, "So you called the most boring person you know to try to help?"

"I talked to someone else last night before I fell asleep and I didn't want to talk to them two nights in a row."

"Did you want me to tell you a bedtime story to help you get to sleep?" I asked.

"Do you have one there?"

"No, but I can make something up."

"Talk to me a while," she said.

"Anything in particular you'd like to talk about?" A long pause. I whispered, "Are you asleep now?"

"What's going on with us?"

I replied, "What do you mean?"

"What do you mean what do I mean?"

"That question doesn't make sense to me, Wren."

"Are we still dating?"

"I didn't think so," I said.

"Why don't you think so?"

"Well, because of the little psycho-adventure a few weeks ago and the fact that we haven't spoken since. Since you were in town after that and didn't call, I figured we were done."

"The reason you don't want to go out anymore is because I didn't call you when I was up one weekend."

"It's everything, Wren," I said. "Guess you owe me a watch."

"What?"

"Remember that little bet you made me about me owing you a watch if I talked about us? You owe me a watch now."

"I wasn't serious about that," she replied.

The hell you weren't. "You seemed pretty serious. And I haven't said anything about us since, have I?"

"I don't get you, Jon. Just because I don't call when I was in town..."

What? "Do you really want to get into this now?" I asked.

"Might as well," she replied. "I don't understand any of this."

"Do you have any idea how it makes me feel to beg you to see you alone? It makes me feel like shit. The one night you come up and we are actually alone, all you talked about all night was going over to Sofia's. Even when we were out driving that night, you wanted to stop by Sofia's. Do you know how that makes me feel?"

My voice louder. "You never come up to Bellingham to see me. You see me when you're here but you've never come up to spend time with me. You come up to see your mom, or go rock climbing or go do something with Sofia but you have NEVER come here to be with me!

"I've never been able to take you out to dinner in Bellingham, Wren. Not once. You won't let me plan like that. The one time you said you were coming straight here you went to Sofia's first and the three of us went to dinner.

"Most relationships are built on communication or sex and, well, we're not having sex, so when we're not communicating... really, what's the point?"

Wren said, "The reason I come up there so often is to see you. Why do you think I've been there almost every weekend? You're the one who never comes down here to see me."

"You said we're not supposed to work at this. This was supposed to be casual and easy. You've always had some other reason to be in Bellingham. I haven't needed to be in Seattle, so I haven't come to see you. If I were to come there just to see you, that'd be work, right?"

"So it's work for you to come and see me?" she asked.

Are we even talking the same language? "For one minute, listen to what I am saying! Take what I am saying at face value and do not read one thing into it!" I paused.

Tell her it's over. Slam down the phone. Tell her you're sick of her shit. Tell her to fuck off. "I forgot what I was going to say."

Silence.

"That's it then?" she asked.

"Guess so." *You're not going to address anything? Going to let it go? Amazing.*

"This isn't helping me get to sleep."

"Sorry about that. I'm going to go."

#   #   #

The next morning I emailed Neal with a synopsis of my conversation with Wren. After stopping off at the gym, I walked across the street to Ezra's.

"Did you tell her all that?" he asked after I told him the story of the prior evening.

"Yeah, I couldn't believe it," I said. "I'm surprised the neighbors didn't come over I was yelling so loud."

"Damn, Jon, that's impressive. About time. Wren's been leading you around by the dick for far too long."

"Yet somehow never touching it..."

#   #   #

The following day I got an email from Neal:

LOST

One spine. Last seen 3-4 months ago during encounter with strange woman. Last seen wearing shreds of dignity. Has eluded capture many times. Owner misses spine and is willing to bend over backwards for its return.

Dear Editor,

Please cancel the above ad scheduled to run in next week's "Tits and Bigger Tits" Singles Edition. It seems that the spine found its way home after a long and humbling journey. It is a little worse for wear but it still fits. Both the owner and his friends are delighted to see it and will take better care of it to make sure it doesn't run away again.

Thanks,

Neal & Ezra

#   #   #

Friday evening while sitting at my computer logged into a chat room on Yahoo!, an instant message popped onscreen from Wren. *She knows my screen name?*
I opened it.

"Do you forgive me for all of the things you think I did to you?"
-- Wren

I burst into laughter and didn't reply.

July 1997 (Real World, Year 6)

Thursday, following Sophia's birthday dinner at Olive Garden, Ezra and Jezzie and I huddled around my computer upstairs at my apartment, investigating a photo editing software program I'd purchased. "Hello?" a female voice called from downstairs.
"Is that Sofia?" Jezzie whispered.
"I don't think so," I replied.
Wren's head popped up above the half-wall of the staircase, "Here you are!" She walked the rest of the way into the bedroom, a full glass of white wine in her hand.
"Here we are," I said.
Too loudly she asked, "What're you doing?"
"Showing them a new program I got today."
"What is it?"
"For editing pictures," I replied.

"Cool," she said, sitting on the papa san chair next to the computer. She didn't cross her legs, providing me a clear view of her panties.

Must you? "Where's Sofia?" I asked.

"Home. I told her I wanted to come over and see you. I found some wine and here I am."

Great.

Ezra spoke up, "We should probably get going. Early day tomorrow." He and Jezzie wished us good night before seeing themselves out. Wren sat in the office chair in front of the computer and started tinkering with the picture on screen. I remained on the bed.

"What're you going to use this for?" she asked.

"I'm tired of asking Sofia to scan pictures for me, so I'm going to buy a scanner and clean them up myself."

She spun in the chair to face me. *Don't stare at her crotch, look at her eyes. She's fucking with you. Let it go.*

Wren stared at me. "How are you, Jon?"

"Same," I replied. She took my hand then put my index finger in her mouth. *Why are you doing this?* Another finger. *You're not going to do that with my dick. Not falling for it.*

Wren moved next to me on the bed, her right breast visible through the sleeve of her sundress. *That's fucking mean. Don't fall for it.*

"What did you have at dinner?" she asked. "I wasn't paying attention."

"Angel hair with marinara," I said.

"That's right." She laid across my lap, still clutching one of my hands.

You've got to be kidding. How much have you had to drink?

She put my hand on her stomach. "You should've come to the Highland Games with us. It was so much fun."

You didn't invite me. "I heard."

She sprung up. "I got to pee."

Wren came out of the bathroom and sat next to me again, putting her left leg over my lap. *Why are you doing this?*

She kissed my neck, then nibbled. *Dammit.*

I kissed her. *Bad fucking idea. She's not going to fuck you. She won't touch you. But she'll let you touch her.*

Wren lifted off her sundress. I took off my shirt. "Why are we doing this?" she asked. "You really think this is a good idea?"

Not at all. "No," I said. "I've got no idea why we're doing this, but we've always been physically attracted to each other so there's that."

"Do you want me to go?"

"Yes!" I replied. "It'd be much better if you left now."

She kissed me. "You want me to go?"

Yes. No. Yes. "I do."

She kissed me again. "You think I should?"

Leave already. "Absolutely. No good can come from this."

On top of me, she kissed me passionately. *Don't do this, it's stupid. She feels nice.*

Left hand under her panties, two fingers slipped into her. I pushed her to her back and kissed down her body. I ate her until she came. *Get her drunk every time she's over.*

I rejoined her at the pillows. She kissed down my chest to my belly. *Finally.*

She returned to my chest. *Bitch.*

Wren shuffled under the sheet. "I've been thinking about getting into a committed relationship again," she said.

Got to ask. "With me?"

"No," she replied. "You're too single."

I couldn't hold back my laughter. "Really? How do you figure?" I asked, still laughing.

"You're still looking to date other people, so you're too single." I couldn't get the grin off my face.

"Okay," I managed. "Anything else keep me out of the running?"

"You have unrealistic expectations for a relationship," she said.

Like wanting to spend time with the person I'm dating? "Like what?" I inquired.

"I think you want too much from the other person. You're looking for perfection and that's not realistic. Nobody's perfect, Jon."

"You're right," I said, able to straighten out my expression. "No one is perfect."

"And you know you have trouble communicating," she slurred.

You have trouble listening.

"Can we talk more about this later?"

"If you want, but you're going to need to go to Sofia's."

"Why?"

"I've got to get up early," I said. "I'll walk you over there if you want."

"You're really kicking me out?"

"I am."

"Tomorrow's the Fourth, you aren't working."

"I give my employees the day off every Fourth so I cover it."

She put her sundress back on and left.

Eleven:
August 1997 (Real World, Year 6)

Saturday morning Sofia called. "Hey Jon," she said. "I wanted to let you know that I have to leave your birthday party at nine."

"Shit, Sofia," I replied. "You'll be leaving right when Neal, Ezra and Jezzie get here. Why you got to take off? There can't be anything more important than being with me?"

Sofia whispered, "Wren's coming up tonight." I didn't reply. "She's not sure if she's invited."

"She's not," I said.

"Why not?" Sofia asked.

Because she's psychotic.

"Neither one of us has any idea what's going on. Has she done something wrong?"

I paused. "Nothing out of the ordinary."

#   #   #

Wednesday afternoon, a coffee shop downtown, on an overstuffed couch with no table, I waited for the last interview of the day. *Rebekah. Worked for an airline. Why does she want to work at a porn store?*

A young lady came in, dressed well above Bellingham casual, looking around. *Must be her.* I summoned her over.

"Jon?" she asked.

"You must be Rebekah." She offered a long-fingered hand. "Have a seat." *Red hair. Lovely hands. Please don't be dumb.*

She sat in the chair across from me and adjusted her skirt. *Were those her panties?*

"Why do you want to work for me?"

"I've been looking for a while and when I saw you were hiring, I figured since I liked movies and hadn't worked in a video store before, I should give it a shot."

"You realize we're mostly adult movies, right?"

She nodded. "I've rented there a few times."

And you like porn? If only you were taller...

Two scripted questions later, "Why are you in Bellingham?"

"After seven years at the airline, I was sick of it," she said. "My brother moved to Vancouver and I looked around and saw that Western has a good environmental sciences program, so I quit and moved here. Once I finish my AA at Whatcom CC, I'm hoping to get into Western to get a degree."

"And then what?"

"Not sure exactly, but I've always wanted to be a marine biologist."

"We should get back to the questions," I said. "Our ability to provide excellent customer service is critical to the foundation of our store. As a result, employees are required to watch at least two adult movies a week. Is this going to be a problem, either with roommates or significant other?"

Rebekah smiled. "I'm not seeing anyone right now and I live by myself, so I should be good to go."

Not seeing anyone? Great. She re-crossed her legs, another flash of her white panties. *Sweet. She doing that on purpose?*

Wrapping up the interview, I offered her the job.

#   #   #

At the store the following Friday, "How long did you stay at the bar last night?" Rebekah asked me.

"A little after one," I said. "You close the joint?" *You looked great. Too bad you're a smoker.*

"Until the lights came up," Rebekah replied. "Who were you were with?"

"Oh, Sofia?" I snorted. "Been friends since my first day of college." *Something going on here?* "You go to the Three B all the time?"

"Only Thursdays," she answered. "Live bands are too hit and miss."

"Agreed. You ever go out to watch the meteor showers?"

"No, but it's supposed to be best in August, right?"

"It is," I said. "I used to watch them from my deck but I think I'm going to go down Chuckanut to get away from the lights."

"When are you going?"

You want to join me? "If it stays clear, I'll go tonight."

"Well, if you go, give me a call and let me know."

She flirting?

On the phone with Rebekah after the store closed. "Not a cloud in the sky," I said. "You still interested?"

"You think we'll see some?"

"Absolutely. A couple, at least."

After finding my apartment, Rebekah joined me on the papa san cushion at a lookout on Chuckanut Drive, focusing at the night sky. "How long have you smoked."

"I don't much," she replied. "Only when I drink. You don't?"

"Smoked cloves for a couple weeks in college. Played soccer growing up. The two don't mix. How long have you had your tongue pierced?" I asked.

"Right after I moved to Bellingham, about four months now."

"Why'd you get it?" *Better blowjobs?*

"I always thought they looked cool, so as soon as I wasn't working someplace where it was absolutely forbidden..."

A couple minutes later I suggested, "Don't look at a certain spot in the sky, you can catch more in your peripheral vision."

"I'm having some trouble since I don't have my glasses on."

"Don't you wear contacts."

"I do, but they were burning so I took them out when I got home and forgot to grab my glasses when you called."

"How well can you see? Are the stars fuzzy?" I leaned over her. "Am I fuzzy?"

"You aren't but the stars are one big blur. I thought there'd be more big, blazing lights."

Kiss her. Don't kiss her. Rebekah looked at me. *Don't kiss her. Remember Brodie. What if she's not into you? She'll quit.*

I stared at her a second longer, then laid back down.

Don't do that again. "Should we take off then? I mean, you're not going to see anything..."

"Wait. Let's stay a little longer."

Four minutes later, "Yeah, okay," Rebekah said. "I can't see a thing. Let's go."

Taking the cushion out of my car in the carport, I said, "Sorry you didn't see anything."

"It was my own fault," Rebekah replied. "Thanks for taking me with you."

# # #

"You going back out tonight, Jon?" Rebekah asked me at the store the next day.

"Wasn't going to," I said. "It's overcast, so I'll probably stay home."

"You ever use your foosball table?"

"All the time," I said. "Why? You think you can beat me?"

"I'm not that bad."

"Any time, sister."

"I'll stop by after dinner."

Two games of foosball with Rebekah scoreless, I played one handed. "This isn't fair!" she exclaimed. "You're still beating me."

"It's my table, I shouldn't suck. You want to do something else?"

"No, I'm going to beat you."

No you're not. "Should I start playing with my feet?"

"Damn," she said. "No more." She threw herself on the couch. "Swear to God, I'm going to beat you one of these days."

"You know where I am." I sat next to her, then kissed her. She kissed me back.

Doesn't taste like smoke. A redhead! Stop now. This is bad.

I pulled back. "We shouldn't be doing this. You're an employee and it can't end well."

"What do you mean?"

"Well, we could end up getting married, but if we didn't, we'd be looking at an ugly break up. Either you break up with me and quit, or I break up with you and you quit. Either way, I still have to hire someone else.

"And if we start dating, the other employees will most likely think I favor you with better shifts, less discipline, whatever, whether I do or don't.

"And there's the issue of sexual harassment."

Rebekah scoffed. "You're not harassing me. This is very mutual."

"Now it is," I said. "But if we break up, you could be angry enough to file a sexual harassment suit, or something to do with coercion. And if we were together long enough, you could make a claim on the business because we'd been together.

"That's why I don't date employees."

Rebekah thought a moment. "I could sign something saying this was consensual and that I won't sue for the store. Like a pre-nup."

You'd do that? That's so cool. "Maybe you could. I'll need to check with my lawyer. But for now, I think it's best if you take off."

Sighing, "Yeah, all right."

# # #

Rebekah came by my apartment at ten-thirty the next evening. "I'm not going to show you any sort of favoritism at work, so don't think you're going to get any," I started. "There needs to be two relationships, our working and our not working and we have to do our best to keep them separate."

"I can handle that," she said. "Do you have the pre-nup?"

"My lawyer told me it's good enough if I write it up," I answered. "Should have it done tomorrow. And you'll need to come with me to get it notarized."

"No problem."

"You're okay with all this?"

"Yeah, I pretty much figured I'd have to agree to it or we wouldn't get together."

You want to be with me that much? Kick ass.

The kissing started up. My hands went up the back of her shirt. *Just because she works in a porn store doesn't automatically mean she's not like Ameline or Wren. She might be teasing.*

Rebekah raised her arms, I lifted off her shirt. *Maybe not.*

I kissed down her neck, she laid back against the arm of the sofa. *Leave her bra on.* I nibbled over her lacey, white bra.

She unclasped it, tossing it to the floor. *Great boobs. Didn't look this nice clothed.*

To her belly. She raised her butt off the couch, pushing her pants off. *Going to eat a red-bushed pussy. Go slow, enjoy it.*

Tracing my tongue across her abdomen, I ended up at the top of her plain panties. Nibbling one hipbone to the other then down her leg. Rebekah opened her stance, I licked back up to her underwear. My tongue against the cotton, I covered her with my mouth. Rebekah pulled her panties to the side.

"Not yet," I whispered. *She wants me to? Awesome.*

"No. Now."

Readjusting her panties, "I'll get to it. Don't worry." My tongue ran underneath the sides, not touching her clit. She pushed toward me, I backed off.

"Oh, all right," I said, pulling her panties off. I paused. *Red pubic hair. Stunning.*

Her breathing grew louder and her legs pressed firmly against my head after three minutes of oral attention. Rebekah backed away from me while I continued my lapping. *I can keep going, it's great here.*

Rebekah stood up. *Maybe we can do this again sometime?* She took my hand and led me upstairs.

"You're wearing too many clothes," she said, sitting on my bed.

"All right," I replied. I took off my shirt, sat next to her. We kissed, she pulled me on top of her, tugging at my shorts.

You want to fuck? This won't go well.

"Before we go any further, I've got to tell you a couple things."

The HPV debacle confessed, Rebekah asked, "Not much of a chance I'll pick them up then, is there?"

"Don't think so. My ex never got them after four years."

Rebekah shrugged.

When I pulled a condom from the nightstand, "I'm on the pill," Rebekah said. "And I hate condoms."

"Me too, but I'd feel better anyway. Besides, it's been a while…"

"How long?"

"Almost a year now." *Almost a virgin again.*

"No way!" she exclaimed. "I'd never make it a year. Damn. Been about three weeks for me."

Three weeks?

She asked, "You haven't had sex in a year?"

"Yeah, but it's different for guys. Girls can always get laid."

"Not with who you want to sleep with," she said. "Sure, if you'll fuck anyone, you can always find a taker, but if you have any sort of standards…"

"I'm up to your standards?"

"Not if you don't hurry up and put that thing on."

I pushed into her.

My first redhead. That's so nice. Oh shit. Not so fast. Oh shit.

Thirty-three seconds in, I came.

"Christ, I'm sorry. I swear I can last longer."

"Don't worry about it." *Like that's going to happen.*

"Next time, at least ten minutes, promise." *If there's a next time.*

"I believe you."

You do not.

"I need to get home though," she said. "My cats still haven't been fed. I wasn't planning on all this."

#   #   #

Sophia's front door opened slowly. "Wren's here," Sofia whispered.

"I don't mind," I said. "Bringing your chairs back."

She relinquished the doorway. Wren entered the living room as I set the chairs next to the dining room table. She rounded on me. "What have I done to piss you off so badly?"

"Uh, we talked about this a while ago."

"I can't believe that you've turned on me like this," she continued.

Sofia went upstairs to her bedroom, leaving us in the kitchen.

"I never expected you to be so cold from all the things you said to me in the beginning and when we were in bed together. You invited me to your birthday party and then took it back. That's really fucked up, Jon."

No, I didn't. "I did?"

"Yes, you did. I even joked about the present I got you. Don't tell me you don't remember," she hissed.

"Honestly Wren, I don't remember inviting you to the party. If I did, then I'm sorry. It's uncool if I invited you then said I didn't want you there. But I don't remember inviting you.

"I would've been uncomfortable if you would've been there. It was my birthday party and there's no reason I should be uncomfortable."

"Why would you be uncomfortable?" she asked. "Is it because you're seeing someone else? Because if it was, then you should've told me."

"No, it has nothing to do with someone else," I said. "I just didn't want you there."

"But you're the one who said at the beginning of this, you wanted us to be friends, no matter what. And now all of a sudden, you flip-flop and don't want to talk to me at all."

I replied, "You know, I stopped calling you a couple months ago and stopped e-mailing you as well. The only time we got together was when you got in touch with me. And once that stopped, well...

"I don't feel any animosity towards you any more Wren, but I've got no interest in us being friends. I know we'll see each other because of Sofia, and I hope we can be civil, for her sake anyway."

She scoffed. "I don't decide I don't want to be someone's friend unless something big happens."

Looking her in the eyes, "Over the last six months, you've said time and time again we don't have anything in common and it's taken me all this time to reach the same conclusion. Since we both feel this way, there doesn't seem any reason why we should keep trying to be friends."

Wren straightened up. "But that's not what you said when this first started."

I hesitated, shrugged my shoulders, then replied, "I was wrong." I closed Sophia's door behind me. *And fuck you too.*

September 1997 (Real World, Year 6)

"Five movies at a time?" Rebekah asked me, flipping through the stack of porn titles beneath the television in my bedroom.

"They help me fall asleep," I said.

She looked around at me. "Sure they do."

"It's true. Most of them bore me, so I have to bring home five or six at a time to see if there's one I can watch all the way through."

"You don't jerk off to them?"

"If they're good, I will. But the majority are the same shit. Suck me, eat you, fuck in three positions and come somewhere, usually the face."

"You want me to turn something on?" she asked.

"Whatever you want."

Rebekah put a movie in the VCR, took off her clothes and climbed in to bed next to me. The movie began as Rebekah climbed on top of me. "You want to see what's going on?" she asked.

"Probably should. It is our job and all."

Rebekah got on all fours, facing the television. A gal was already sucking a cock onscreen. "Bet he eats her next," I said.

A couple minutes later, a close-up of a pussy being licked. "Now three positions."

"You're kind of taking the fun out of this," Rebekah sighed.

"Fine," I said. "Here." I repositioned her to her back, propped up so she could see the TV then planted my face between her thighs.

"That's better," she said.

After Rebekah came, I finished up inside her. "Was I right?" I asked, moving alongside her.

"Two positions, then he came on her tits," Rebekah answered. "Can we talk for a minute?"

"Absolutely," I said. *You don't want to watch porn while we're fucking?*

"I've been thinking about us and I don't want to get into anything serious right now."

You don't? You've been over here almost every night. Aren't we a couple?

"Oka-ay," I said. "What does that mean, exactly?"

"I think we should be free to see other people, if we want."

Dammit. "You got someone in mind?"

"Not at all," she said. "I want to keep things casual. But I want us to be able to talk about stuff honestly. That's one of the things I like best about us, we talk so easily together."

That too. "I'm okay with the honesty thing. But please keep in mind, if you ask me a question, I'll answer truthfully. So make sure, absolutely sure, you want to know the answer."

"What do you mean?"

"Say you ask if I've ever been with a guy. Do you really want to know whether or not I have been?"

Immediately she asked, "Have you?"

You didn't think that through. "No, but that's not the point," I said. "If I'd answered yes and it wasn't to see what it was like but I considered myself bisexual and wanted you to join me in a three-way where the main focus wasn't you. Well, would you really want to know?"

"But you're not, are you?"

I sighed. "No. But there could be some questions you don't want to know the answer to. I'm just sayin'…

"And about other people, I think we need to let each other know if that's going on so we don't show up and things get all ooky with someone else being there and all."

"Okay," Rebekah replied. "Are you seeing anyone else right now?"

"Uh, no. You?"

"Nope."

That's good. "Were you going to spend the night?" I asked.

"I was hoping to, yeah. That okay?"

"Absolutely. As long as you don't mind leaving on the porn."

"Not at all," Rebekah said. "You should know, I jerk off every night before falling asleep."

"No way. Even if you've just had an orgasm?"

"Yeah. It relaxes me."

"Every night?" *Bullshit.*

"For the most part."

"You touching yourself right now?" I asked.

"See for yourself." Her hand made little circles on her mound.

Cool. "You want any help?"

"Not tonight," she said. "But keep asking."

#   #   #

The following week, I was at Rebekah's large windowed, undersized studio overlooking downtown she shared with two cats. "I can't believe you wrote me up," she said.

"I told you from the beginning, I wouldn't give you special treatment. And I won't. If anyone's more than twenty minutes late, they get written up." I held up a pack of cigarettes from the dining room table. "Thought you only smoked when you were drinking?"

"Mostly I do," she said. "Every now and then if I've got a lot of homework or a test."

"How long you been smoking?"

"A couple years, I guess. I don't smoke that much."

"Hey man, whatever."

"Does it bug you that much?" she asked.

"Like you're coming back from the bar all the time. That's the thing I hate most about going out is I have to shower when I get home to get the smell off me."

"My clothes don't smell, do they?" Rebekah hugged me.

"Some, but I think we can take care of that." I lifted off her shirt. She sat on the edge of her futon, still in the couch position. She took off her bra while I pulled off her pants and panties.

"Goddamn, your boobs are fantastic," I said, kneeling on the floor.

"I think so too," Rebekah agreed. "Wouldn't trade them for anything."

"Please don't." My shorts down, I ran my cock around the entrance to her pussy. Rebekah put a finger in her mouth before rubbing her clit. My dick, now hard, crossed her threshold. A couple thrusts later, I removed my dick from her and guided it lower, against her butt.

"You mind?" I asked. *Please don't mind.*

Her eyes still closed. "Not so far."

Rebekah continued playing with herself. After adding saliva to the mix, I slinked into her ass.

That is so cool. Red bush, dick in her ass, rubbing her clit. Three fantasies at once. As the head of cock disappeared, Rebekah gasped then convulsed.

Motionless, "You okay?" I asked.

"Oh...yeah...that was...intense." She caught her breath. "You need to take that out now."

"Do I have to?"

"I'll let you back in later."

"Promise?"

October 1997 (Real World, Year 6)

Home from the Three B on Thursday night after 1am. "I got to shower," I said to Rebekah, opening the carport door.

"Mind if I join you?"

"Not at all," into the tub. *Damn, you look good naked.* Rebekah rinsed her hair as I massaged soap across her boobs.

"Did you notice?" she asked.

"Did you shave again?" cupping my hand over her pussy.

"I did, but I didn't have a cigarette tonight."

"You didn't, did you?"

"It's been two weeks now."

Kick ass. You doing that for me? "How're the cravings?"

"Not bad. I keep gum around now and it hasn't been bad at all."

"Good for you," I said. *And me too.*

# # #

Rebekah took the plate of pasta I handed her. "Thanks for cooking tonight."

"No problem. If you hate it, it's not my recipe. Mallory used to cook this all the time."

"Smells great." On the couch, the television on. "This is really good," she said, through a mouthful of noodles.

Lowering the volume on the TV, "Since we're being all honest with each other and everything, I saw a friend of mine talking to this cute girl at the gym last night and I'm going to ask him about her."

Rebekah's face fell. "Really?"

"She might have a boyfriend or whatever. Wanted to let you know before anything happens."

She put her plate on the coffee table. "Are we breaking up?"

"No, not at all. You said we should see other people, so I figured I'd keep my options open."

"But you're still okay with us?" Rebekah asked.

"Oh yeah," I said. "I saw my buddy talking to a cute gal and I know he's gay, so I figured I'd ask about her."

Rebekah sat silently for a minute. "I know I said we should see other people, but I don't really want to. Do you?"

You don't want to see other people? "No. I wanted to make sure I had other options in case you were." *Fucking Wren.*

"I don't want to get into some hardcore committed thing, but I don't like the thought of you being with someone else."

"I feel the same," I said.

"Can we keep doing what we're doing and not see other people?"

"I can. Can you?"

"Yeah."

\#   \#   \#

"You wore the same costume last year?" I asked Rebekah as I followed her up the stairs to my bedroom.

"It's still in great shape," she answered. "No one in Washington's seen me in it."

"I guess the real question is, why did you keep it?"

"It's cute," she said. "What time do we have to be at Sofia's?"

"Seven or so."

She took off her shirt, then mine. "We've got time."

Naked, Rebekah got out of bed and went to the sink. "How long's it going to take you to get ready?" I asked, still in bed.

"Fifteen, twenty minutes."

Rebekah dumped her purse on the bathroom counter, lifting up a white container. She stood in front of the mirror, "Oh, I guess I forgot to take my pill."

I sat up. "What?"

"Looks like I forgot to take my pills," she replied.

"Pills? Plural? What'd you mean? More than one?"

"Uh..." her voice quieted. "Looks like I've missed the last three days."

"Three days?!? How the fuck could you forget three days in a row?"

Silence.

"Why did you let me come inside you if you haven't been taking your pills?"

"I forgot."

What? Are you stupid? "Forgot!?! You forgot?" Standing up, I advanced on her. "Forget a day, sure. Two days maybe, but probably not. Three days! What the fuck? Are you trying to get pregnant?"

Almost inaudibly, "No, I forgot."

Or do you want a kid?

Glaring at her, "How long have you been on the pill?"

She didn't look up. "About seven years."

"And you just forgot...three days in a row?"

A tear dropped down her cheek. "I'm sorry."

"Fat fucking good that's going to do us." *Begged me to stop using rubbers. Need my head examined. Fuck.*

From the closet, I said, "Hurry up, we're already late."

A loud sniff behind me. "Yeah."

My ill-fitting retro clothes on, my wig of straight brown hair properly adjusted, I sat downstairs, waiting for Rebekah. Half an hour later she appeared; white face paint with a large, blue mouth and eyebrows, a purple afro wig, a red foam nose, a puffy black and white polka dot shirt with a big tie, baggy blue jeans, purple socks and polka dot sneakers. *Impressive.*

"You ready?" I asked.

"Yeah. I'm sorry."

Not waiting for Rebekah to catch up, I walked one building over to Sofia's. "About time," Ezra called from the couch.

Sofia came up while I was at the fridge. "I almost thought you weren't coming."

"Wouldn't miss it, sweetie," I lied. "Got behind schedule, sorry. Did we fuck anything up?"

Rebekah sat down by herself at the dining room table.

"No," Sofia replied. "We've been talking about whether to go to Rumors or the Three B."

"I'll vote for Rumors," I said.

"Cute costume," Sofia said to Rebekah.

"Thanks."

Wren was talking with a guy I didn't know, in front of the balcony door. A harlequin, Wren was in a form-fitting, all-white jumpsuit with a frilled collar and dance shoes. Her white face paint was accented by black, diamond shaped eyelashes painted onto her cheeks. No wig, her thin hair slicked into a ponytail.

Wren strolled into the kitchen. *You going to ignore me?*

Putting her hand on my lower back, she opened the refrigerator. *Guess not.*

"Nice costume, Jon," she said.

"Yeah, you too." I squeezed past her and stood next to Rebekah. As Wren came out of the kitchen, beer in hand, I said, "Wren, this is Rebekah. Rebekah, Wren."

Rebekah, "Hello."

Wren offered a half-hearted nod to Rebekah. Then to me, "You going to join us at the bar?"

"Don't know," I replied. "Depends."

"Oh." Wren returned to the other side of the apartment.

Ezra crossed the living room. "How was that?" nodding toward Wren.

"Stupid," I said. "Same ol' Wren." *But she's hot tonight. And I'm here with Baggy Purple Hair.*

"Don't let her get to you," Ezra said to Rebekah. "She's, well, you know already."

"Pretty much what I expected," Rebekah replied.

After an hour of discussion of which bar would be more entertaining, Sofia declared we were heading to the Three B. "I think we're going to bug out on you, Sofia," I said. "I can't handle another smoke-fest and I'm kind of tired. Long week."

"That's too bad," Sofia said. "Thanks for coming, you guys. We going to do breakfast tomorrow?"

"Call me," I said.

When the front door of my apartment closed, Rebekah said, "I'm going to go."

"Yeah, okay."

She retrieved her stuff, then stood in front of me. "Can I have a hug?"

I hugged her firmly, then stayed in the living room as she walked down the stairs to the carport. *Fuck.*

The porn didn't put me to sleep right away. *She want to have a kid? Is she that irresponsible? After seven years? Has she been planning this since she told me to stop using rubbers? If she wanted to get pregnant, why tell me at all? She would've just gotten pregnant, right? So it wasn't intentional, it was irresponsible. Grossly irresponsible. Can I be with someone like that? She's a redhead who loves sex. Jerks off every day. Let's me fuck her in the ass. Wants to have a three-way. What if she is pregnant? Should I marry her? No. We'll abort or adopt. She'd be so fucking hot pregnant. Adopt. Sleeping with a pregnant redhead. So hot...*

# # #

The following morning, "Sorry for being such a dickhead last night," I said to Rebekah. "If you say it wasn't intentional, then it wasn't intentional. If you end up getting pregnant, we'll deal with it." *But if it wasn't intentional then you're either a ditz or a flake.*

"You're not mad anymore?" she asked.

"A little, I guess," I said. "I wish you would've told me before I came inside you last night, but nothing to be done about it now. However, I'm not going to be able to come inside you anymore."

"You want to stop having sex?"

"I didn't say that. Guess it's butt sex until your period. When should you bleed?"

"Probably next weekend."

"C'mon," I said. "You can handle taking it in the ass for a week."

"Funny."

November 1997 (Real World, Year 6)

While riding around town two weeks later, I stopped by Rebekah's apartment. "I've got good news," she said as she opened the door. "Finally."

"Thank God." I let out a huge sigh as I set my bike down in the entryway of her apartment. "Though I've got to admit, I was starting to have some fantasies about you with a big belly."

"I don't want to be fat."

"You'd be pregnant. Totally different," I said. "And you'd lactate."

"Eww." She went into her bathroom, leaving the door open.

"You'd be a hot pregnant chick."

"Not any time soon," she replied.

Glad to hear that.

I stood in the doorway, watching her pencil her eyebrows brown. "Why do you do that?" I asked.

"You can't hardly see them without it," she replied.

"I know, it's really sexy. I think it looks better without the color."

"I don't see how. I look like I don't have any without it."

"Pshaw. It's hot," I added. "Do I need to worry about you taking your pill?"

Rebekah turned away from the mirror. "No, Jon. I don't know what happened, but that was the first time I've forgotten like that."

That you know of.

"I don't want kids, all right?" she insisted.

# # #

At my mom's by myself for Thanksgiving. "What's Rebekah doing for Thanksgiving?" Mary asked.

"Down in Portland, at her parents'," I replied. "Her brother picked her up yesterday and they drove down together. You never did tell me what you thought about her."

"Well..." Mary hesitated. "We didn't talk a lot when I was up there. Maybe if she would've joined us at the craft fair, I could've gotten to talk to her more."

"Okay, but you must have formed some sort of opinion."

Mary asked, "She's going to Western?"

"No, Whatcom. Going to transfer to Western next year after she gets her AA."

"And how old is she?"

"Twenty-seven."

"Oh, I figured she was younger. And she's just now attending community college...what's she been doing since high school?"

"Uh, hanging out...working. She was at an airline in Alaska, then moved to Bellingham to go to school."

"And have you two discussed children?"

Far too much. "It's not a high priority for either of us right now."

"When it came up at breakfast, I got the impression she didn't want kids at all."

When did it come up? When I went to the bathroom? "Certainly not while she's in school."

"Of course not," Mary sighed. "What she told me was she didn't know if she'd be having children."

That's a relief. "Okay..."

"I want grandkids, Jon. You're my only child, so if you end up with someone who doesn't want kids, I'm going to be seriously disappointed."

"What if I was gay?"

"But you're not."

I could be.

"And I haven't been pressuring you about it, have I?"

"Uh, no."

"You need to know, it's a big deal for me. You might not understand now, but once you have kids of your own, you will."

"All right," I said. "Besides the kid issue, what did you think? You like her at all?"

"From the little time I spent with her, sure," Mary replied. "But honestly, she seems, well, immature."

Immature? Really? "Are you saying that because she's late to college?"

"There's that," Mary said. "And her clothes..."

"She does most of her shopping at Value Village, but I don't pay well."

"Boots, baggy jacket and t-shirt. It's an interesting look."

"So, what? You telling me you don't like her?"

"No, please, Jon. She seems fine, and if the two of you are getting along well, that's great. I'm telling you what I got from the hour I spent with her."

"We get along and she doesn't treat me like shit," I said. *Like Wren.* "I don't know if we're going to get married, it's been three months. It hasn't come up."

"You asked me what I thought, I've told you. I don't have much to base my opinion on yet."

# # #

Across the street at Ezra and Jezzie's when I returned from Tacoma on Saturday. "How's Mary?" Ezra asked, handing me a beer.

"Doing well. Hates Rebekah, though."

"What?" Ezra sat on the other end of the couch. "Why?"

"Thinks she's immature."

"Huh." He took a sip of beer. "Do you think so?"

"I can see where my mom's coming from, but I haven't thought of Rebekah in those terms. I mean, sure, she took a while to go to college, but did it help that I went straight from high school? I sure as shit didn't go to school to own a porn store."

"And look at you now," Ezra snickered. "A regular Captain of Industry."

"Maybe not Captain. Sergeant? Private?"

"Why don't you wait until Rebekah is out of school and then see how things are?"

"Makes sense. Oh, shit, apparently Rebekah said something at breakfast about not wanting any kids and Mary tells me she's expecting to have grandkids."

"I was getting the same thing from my mom," Ezra said. "But now that my brother's hitched and looking to start a family, takes all the pressure off me."

"Must be nice," I grinned. "I think Mary's head will explode if I end up being sterile."

December 1997 (Real World, Year 6)

The fourth circle past the baggage claim area, I spotted Rebekah. "Sorry," throwing her bag in the back seat. "The plane took off late."

"Not a big deal," I kissed her. *She didn't pencil her eyebrows. Sexy.* I pulled into traffic. "How was Christmas?"

"Good. Mellow," she said. "There was still a lot of stuff in boxes, so we got a baby tree after I got there. Went out to dinner on Christmas Eve because Mom didn't want to go through all the kitchen stuff."

"You end up jerking off while you were there?"

"Once, in the shower. Couldn't help myself. Took me less than two minutes."

"Know how that goes," I said. "You know, you could've called me while you were there. Would've been nice to hear from you." *You pissed about our conversation on the way to the airport?*

"I didn't want to be too clingy," Rebekah replied.

Yup, guess you are. "You should call if you want to call, Rebekah. And I'll do the same. I couldn't call because you didn't leave me your parents' number. I don't think we absolutely have to see each other every day, that's all I meant."

"That's not how it sounded."

"I'm sorry then. We okay?"

"Yeah, we're fine."

An extended silence. I broke it. "Thought you should know, I'm going to France for the World Cup with Ezra and Neal this summer, for a couple weeks in June."

"Okay..." Her eyes narrowed.

"Ever since we started talking about doing it, it was going to be the three of us going to a bunch of games in France. But Neal found a villa so we're looking for more people to join us."

"Would you give me that kind of time off?"

"We could work that part out. It's more the cost that's an issue."

"How much would it be?" she asked.

"If there's eight of us, three hundred or so for the house, I already bought my ticket, that was around seven hundred, plus food and trains and tickets for games while we're there."

"I can't afford that," Rebekah said.

"I could help you. But I couldn't cover all of it. Probably stuff while we're there."

"Nope, there's no way. But you should go and have a good time."

I will.

Close to Bellingham, I exited to a rest stop. "You got to pee?" Rebekah asked.

"Nope. Can't wait any longer." I parked as far away from any overhead lights as I could get. We climbed into the backseat.

Butt on the floorboard, I licked her pussy. "Please, please grow this out," I said, pulling on her pubic hair.

"Can we talk about this later?" pushing my head back between her legs.

I raised up and pressed myself into her. "You don't have to keep it, but I want to see it. Please?"

Rebekah worked her clit. "If you shut up about it already, I will."

"Done." I pulled my dick out of her.

"Not right now. It's so cute you always try to put it in my butt," she said.

Cute? Never thought of it as cute.

"Hey, I got to try," I said, re-entering her puss. "Sometimes it works, and sometimes is better than no times."

January 1998 (Real World, Year 6)

Looking up from my writing, I asked Rebekah, seated across from me at a deli downtown, "Where do you see yourself in a couple years? Five years? Ten years?"

"I haven't thought much about it," she replied, keeping a finger on the paragraph she was reading.

Nothing? "Brew on it for a couple minutes." *Please prove my mother wrong.*

"In two years, I guess I'd like to be at Western and finishing up the program there," she said. "After that? Shit, I don't know. Get a job?"

Not married? Not see the world? A job?

"What about you?"

"I hope I can keep the store open for the next five years, maybe ten. I'd like to get the book published. Go back to Hawaii, maybe to Europe again. Maybe not, depends on this summer, I guess. Maybe get married.

"In ten years? Shit, uh, I'd like to have a collection of pinball machines, learn how to fix them. Maybe go back to school for a degree in electronics. Write another book." *Be married.*

"Wow, Jon. You sit around and think about this all the time?"

Don't you? "Nope, just came up with most of it. Except finishing the book. I want to finish it and see if I can get it published before the end of this year. With any luck..."

February 1998 (Real World, Year 6)

Rebekah didn't answer her phone. *Where is she?* I put on my jacket and shiny shoes and walked to the end of the driveway. *They're not going to hold our table. Hurry up!*

I looked at my watch again. *We're late.*

Rebekah pulled up. "Sorry, I know I'm late."

"It's Valentine's Day," I reminded her, closing the door. She pulled back into traffic. "Why didn't you have me pick you up?"

"I wanted to drive," she replied. "I've got a surprise for you."

"You wearing anything under that skirt?" I asked.

"Nope."

Kick ass. "Can I see?"

"Not while I'm driving. Later."

Once out of the car at the Cliff House, I said, "You look nice." Rebekah was in a black button-down, thigh-length dress, patterned with miniature white flowers, woven black leggings and combat boots.

"So do you," Rebekah replied.

Seated in the bar area, fifteen minutes late for our reservation, "I think I cut myself shaving," Rebekah said, adjusting in her chair. "It's annoying the shit out of me."

"Your leg?"

"No," she whispered. "My snatch. That's why I was so late. Took a lot longer than I thought."

"You had a lot to get rid of. What time did you start?"

"At five," she said. "Gave myself an hour, but obviously I needed more time."

How could it take more than an hour to shave and put on that little bit of make-up?

A grin crossed her face. "Oh, I have another surprise for you after dinner."

"What? More than a smooth snatch?"

Rebekah smiled her answer.

Hairless is enough.

I paid the bill and looked at Rebekah. "Are we leaving?"

"Yup."

Rebekah got into the car and opened up the glove compartment. She handed me a blindfold. "Put this on."

Awesome.

She backed out and drove.

We're heading downtown. She turned right. *On State Street.* She turned left. *Holly Street.* "We going to The Royal?"

"Shit," she said. "How did you know where we were?"

"You've only turned a couple times," I replied.

Rebekah continued driving, turning right.

Cornwall, probably. Right again. Right. Right. Left. *Shit, we're nowhere.* Long straightaway. Left. Right.

"You know where we are now?" she asked.

"Not at all."

"Good." She continued driving.

We going to someone's house? A park? Bowling? She shaved and isn't wearing underwear. She must want to screw. A park then. Maybe we're meeting someone for a threesome. She brought up a threesome a couple weeks ago. Does she know some cute girl I haven't met? Or a boy? Too many dicks. A girl.

The car stopped.

It's time. Rock n' roll.

"Stay there," Rebekah said. "I'll help you out." Her door closed, then mine opened. "Give me your hand. You still don't know where we are, right?"

"I'm guessing a parking lot because of the cement, but other than that, no clue."

"Walk slowly, okay?"

As we walked across the cement, somewhere close, a female voice, "Come here, stay out of the way."

Rebekah replied, "Thank you."

A couple giggles fading behind me.

"Stop," Rebekah said, dropping my hand. A stifled swoosh. She took my hand again. "Step up."

My footfalls echoed over muted street noises. *A tunnel? Which park has a tunnel?*

"Don't move," she whispered.

What's she fiddling with? Her purse?

"Step forward."

Carpet?

Rebekah took off the blindfold. "Surprise!"

In the middle of a hotel room, "This is awesome, Rebekah."

"Did you know where you were?"

"Not at all. This is great."

"Sofia let me in to your place and I got your all your bathroom shit."

"This is so fucking cool. Thank you."

She held up a camera. "I thought we should take some pictures."

Anyone joining us?

Rebekah plopped down on the bed, lifted her skirt and looked between her legs. "That's swollen isn't it?"

"What are you...? Oh, your left lip? Yeah, it's not very happy, is it?"

"Do you see any cuts or anything?"

Examining her labia closely. "Nope, nothing. Red and swollen, though. What did you use, soap?"

"Same shaving cream I've been using for years." She got up and unbuttoned the top button on her dress.

"Wait," I said. "If we're taking pictures, I want to go from dressed to not. Hopefully this'll be enough light," I said. "If I use the flash, it'll wash you out."

"Do you know of someplace that develops pictures like these?"

"I guess we could try somewhere and hope they don't look at them."

Rebekah put the camera back in her bag. "Doesn't our manager's boyfriend work at that place in the mall?"

"Think so. He'd probably do it for us. As long as you wouldn't mind him seeing them."

"As long as it's only him, I won't mind."

Probably make copies for himself. Can't blame him.

The roll of film exhausted, both of us naked, Rebekah slathered lube along my cock, her pussy, then sat on me. A couple thrusts in she stopped. "It really hurts. The lube's not helping." She climbed off.

"Maybe the vibe?"

"Fuck it. Let's try again in a while."

You're going to fall asleep.

I turned on the television. Rebekah was asleep before the first commercial.

# # #

Morning, sporting a raging stiffie, I asked, "How's your snatch?"

Opening her eyes, "Seems okay." She felt around. "Feels normal. Look at it."

I pulled off the covers. "Like nothing ever happened."

"No way." Rebekah sat up, looked between her legs. "What the hell?" She poked and prodded her left lip. "You want to go try out the Jacuzzi tub?"

"Absolutely."

In the parking lot, loading up her car, Rebekah asked, "Did you know which hotel we were at?"

"No idea. How did you end up getting us out Meridian like that?"

"Went into a couple parking lots downtown. Thought it'd throw you off."

260

"It did," I put my bag of shit in the backseat of her car. "This was remarkable, Rebekah. Thank you."

"Happy Valentine's Day."

"You, too. And what, now you're off to work?"

"Yup."

"Damn, your boss is kind of a dick."

March 1998 (Real World, Year 6)

Saturday night, Rebekah and I on my couch, the movie's credits rolling, she asked, "Do you feel like we're moving forward?"

No. "As opposed to backward?" I said. No reaction. I turned off the TV and tried again. "Like, are we going to be moving in together? That what you see as the next step?"

"Kind of," she said. "I mean, if we're not going to get married, is there any point to keep seeing each other?"

We like to fuck each other? I paused, "Guess not."

"Do you think we'll get married?"

No. Another pause. "I haven't considered it seriously. We're having a good time together, right?"

"Yeah," she said. "But..."

"How's this, if I wake up one day and know that I don't want to marry you, I'll tell you right that instant? Right now, I'm kind of going along and seeing what happens. Marriage isn't out of the question, but it isn't something I'm considering. It hasn't even been a year."

"Naw, you're right. But promise you'll tell me if you figure out you don't want to keep going."

"Promise."

April 1998 (Real World, Year 6)

"You want mustard?" I asked Ezra at Archer's Ale House.

"Pretzels without mustard? Blasphemy," he said. "How's the store doing?"

"Same ol' shit. You quit your job yet?"

"Not yet," he replied. "Thinking I might want to get my master's next fall, so I should keep working until then."

"Shit," I murmured. "Rebekah got accepted to Western."

"Good for her. Huxley College, right? Be an enviro-freak?"

"Or something," I said. "Doesn't have much of an idea exactly what field she wants to get into."

"What's that look?" Ezra asked.

"Now she's going to be in school for two more years."

"So?"

"I don't know if I can handle two more years of her at school, trying to figure out what to do with her life." *And the boys she'll meet.*

Ezra gave me the eyeball. "Things not going well?"

"It's not that," I said. "They don't seem to be going. It's been what, eight months now? It doesn't seem like we're doing anything. And two more years of school? Two more years of a holding pattern before we could become a real couple? I don't know."

"Do you love her?"

No. Maybe I will. I could. Don't now. Love her body and fucking her. No.

I stared into my beer. "My first reaction is no. But maybe I could. I'm not sure I know her well enough to be sure one way or the other." *Every conversation is work or sex or music.* Shaking my head, "I don't think we've ever gone to the grocery store together."

"Bullshit," Ezra said. "I've run into you two at Fred's."

"Yeah, but I'm talking full-on grocery shopping, not picking up beer or tampons. We've never done things like that because our schedules are completely opposite."

Setting his beer on the table, Ezra asked, "What're you going to do?"

"Wait and see, I guess."

"You think that's fair to her?"

"What if she's the one? Took four years to realize Mallory wasn't it, and we were living together. Rebekah and I don't see anywhere near that much of each other."

"You should talk to her about it," Ezra said.

"And tell her what?" *I don't love you but I want to keep fucking you?*

"Let her know your concerns and see where things go."

"Talk to my girlfriend? That's insane."

May 1998 (Real World, Year 6)

Sitting across from me at Stuart's Coffee House on Sunday morning, Rebekah looked up from her textbook. "Why don't we do this every weekend?" she asked.

"Seems like one of us is always doing stuff in the mornings," I replied. "Or we don't want to get out of bed."

"True," she nodded. "Is Ezra going to meet us?"

You could talk to me. "Maybe," I replied. "He wasn't sure what Jezzie wanted to do today."

I pointed to her book. "How much you got?"

"A shitload," she said.

"You want to come to *Gladiator* with me and Sofia anyway? I hear it's kick ass. All sorts of blood and gore."

"Yeah, but I can't. I've got to get this reading done."

"You can't take a couple hour break?" *We don't get many afternoons together.*

She shook her head. "Don't go being a bad influence on me. I'm already behind on this. I've got a test this week and two chapters to finish before tomorrow."

Then why'd you go out last night?

"Can you let me read for a while?"

"Sure."

I sat silent, sipping my iced mocha and people watching until Rebekah looked up from her book. "What time's the movie?" she asked.

"One-thirty. You change your mind?" *Come with me.*

"No," she said. "It's getting loud so I'm going to head home and try to get caught up. Call you tonight?" She put her books in her backpack, kissed me and left.

#   #   #

Almost asleep, in my bed. Rebekah, her head on my chest, whispered, "I don't want us to break up, like, ever."

Your orgasm was that good? "Now why would you say that to someone who is commitment-phobic?"

"I don't mean like that," she replied.

Then like what?

"Everything's so easy with us. I want it to always be like this."

How's that different?

She squeezed me.

"Uh huh. I'm probably not going to call while I'm in France," I said.

"I didn't think you would," she replied.

Why not?

"Ezra said he didn't think you'd have a phone where you're staying."

"There's that," I said. "And I know I'd ask about the store and I want to get away from it for a couple weeks."

"I get that. It'd probably be expensive, too."

"I imagine."

She scooted up, hugged me, then turned away.

# # #

I asked my manager at the store, "How's everything going?"

She stopped counting the deposit and looked at me. "Can you have a talk with Rebekah about her attitude before you go on vacation? She's starting to drive me crazy."

Attitude? "What kind of attitude?"

"She acts like she's in charge when you're not around. Telling everybody what to do. She's done it to me more than once. I'm worried she'll be insufferable while you're gone."

"She has?"

"Yup. A couple employees have mentioned it to me. She told one of the employees the store will be hers next summer."

Is she crazy? "What? She said that?"

"She figures you're going to propose around Christmas and then she'll be in charge," she said.

Rebekah in charge? Not ever. "Wow." I sighed. "I mean, marriage hasn't come up. Ever." *Did it? Did I miss it?*

"That's how girls are, Jon. You guys have been going out almost a year now. It's what most girls expect."

"That's horseshit. Just because we don't fight, doesn't mean we're getting married."

"Can you talk to her?" my manager asked. "I don't feel comfortable saying anything because you two are dating."

"Oh, I'll talk to her." *And stop this bullshit.*

June 1998 (Real World, Year 6)

On the sixth day in France, walking to the bar to watch a game, Ezra held me back from the rest of the group. "Dude," he started. "You really ought to give Rebekah a call. Call and say hi. You two have been going out a long time now, and she deserves to hear from you."

"We discussed it before we left," I said.

"It'd be a nice thing to do and there's no reason for you to be a dick about things, is there?"

"All right. Fuck. I'll call her after the match. She's probably not home now."

Rebekah answered on the third ring. "You said you weren't going to call."

"Thought I'd surprise you." *And get the creeps off my back.* "How's everything going?" *You pissing off the other employees?*

"Fine," she said. "Nothing very interesting. How's France?"

"Stellar," I replied. "Haven't made it to a game yet, but hopefully tomorrow. Been watching in one of the bars here. The people here are surprisingly friendly, even though we are so disgustingly American."

She chuckled, "How's that?"

"We're loud, don't speak the language and dress funny. Stick out like sore thumbs. But almost everyone's been kind and generous. The guy who owns the villa we rented took us on a tour of the town when we got here. You want me to bring you back anything?"

"Ooh, what about some wine?"

"Kind of a given, isn't it? Anything else?"

"Naw," Rebekah answered. "Wine's good."

"You guys having any issues at the store?"

"Nothing we haven't been able to work out. Just have a good time, will you?"

"Oh, I am."

"You should go. This is probably costing a fortune. I'll see you when you get back."

"Yep. See you then."

I opened the door to the villa. "There! I called her," I declared to the group, all seated around the kitchen table. "Will you leave me the fuck alone now?"

Ezra, "Doubt it."

#   #   #

"How are you feeling about Rebekah, anyway?" Ezra asked me as the two of us left the bar the following evening.

Not much. "Shit, I don't know," I said. "I feel bad that I haven't missed her. But I think I'd've had a shittier time if she'd come with us."

"Hmm. The whole clingy thing?"

"Yeah," I answered. "She's changed all these things, quit smoking, removed her tongue stud, stopped wearing makeup. And

I mean it's great for me, but it seems like it's for me, not her. I don't want to be her everything. I got my own shit."

"Any more about marriage?" Ezra asked.

"Not after the bullshit at the store." I paused. "I don't think I'd marry her, Ezra. We're too far apart where we are in our lives and I don't want to wait for her to catch up." Shaking my head, "Jesus, that sounds awful."

"Sounds like the truth. Can't help that." Ezra paused. Then, "Try imagining life without her. Do you think your life's better with her in it or not? If you can't envision moving forward without her, then you should marry her. If not..."

#   #   #

Sunday morning, waiting for a table at Old Town Café, I filled Rebekah in on the trip, Jezzie's piss-poor attitude the entire time, culminating in my not speaking to her by the flight home.

Our food arrived. Halfway through my first eggs benedict I asked, "How're you feeling about us these days?"

Rebekah looked up at me. "Pretty good. Don't you?"

Eggs Benedict on my fork, "Well, I thought a lot about us the past couple weeks."

"And?" Rebekah put her orange juice down.

"I said I'd tell you if I didn't think we'd get married..."

"And now you don't?"

"No," I said.

A restrained chuckle. "I was thinking the same thing."

Don't believe you. "You were?"

"Yeah. After we talked about all the work stuff before you left, I thought about our relationship and reached the same conclusion."

"What do you see as our biggest problems?" I asked.

"Well, it's not any one thing, it's everything."

"What do you want to do about it?"

She shrugged. "Guess we should probably break up."

"Probably," I said. "You going to quit?" *Don't. Don't want to have to train someone again.*

She tilted her head. "Not unless you want me to. I don't want to have to find another job. I can still work there even if we aren't a couple. Not like we work together much anyway."

"True. But I don't want you to be uncomfortable."

"I'll let you know if it's too much for me to handle."

Finished breakfast, drove back to my apartment. "You got anything inside still?"

"I don't think so," she replied. "If you find anything, bring it to the store." She got into her car and pulled away.

Shit, that was easy. Single again? Should ask out that girl at the gym. Why was that so easy for her?

Two hours later Rebekah called. "You forget something?" I asked.

"No. I've been over this a couple times now so, uh, why don't you think we'll get married?"

"You know, Rebekah, I never felt that we made a mental connection. Knowing what the other is feeling and thinking. I mean, a little, but I've never felt it with us. What about you?"

"I kind of do, yeah. Do you think if we were together longer, you could maybe get that connection?" Her voice cracked. "I mean, did you really give us a fair chance?"

"Um, well, it's been almost a year now. So, yeah, maybe." *Fair chance? Did I?*

"Do you think you might be willing to try to make that connection?"

"What're you thinking?"

"Hanging out and see what happens. Unless you hate me now."

"No, not at all," I said. "It's more a matter of still seeing each other if we're not going to get married. Don't want to waste our time."

"But it wouldn't be a waste if we end up staying together." *Guess not...* "What do you think about seeing if you can get that connection with me?" *If we can still fuck, I'm in.*

"Worth a try," I answered. "So, uh, what does this do to our break up?"

"We're still broken up," Rebekah said. "But we're going to wait and see if you can figure stuff out."

Doesn't help. "No sex, then?"

"Is that what you want?"

"Not particularly," I said. "That's never been a problem for us."

"That's for sure," Rebekah said. "We should date a while and see how things go."

"Uh, okay. But what if I don't ever get there?"

Rebekah was silent a moment. "I kind of figure if I get hurt now or later, it doesn't matter too much. But I'll think I could end up regretting it, if I don't make an effort."

Makes sense. "I get that," I said. "Okay, since we're dating now, what're you doing tomorrow?"

"Coming over?"

July 1998 (Real World, Year 7)

I called Mary. "Thought you'd like to know, Rebekah and I broke up."

"What brought that on?" she asked.

"I didn't feel the mental connection with her I'd been hoping for."

"Well, that is important. How're you doing with it?"

"Enh. After we broke up, she convinced me to try and see if we could get that connection, so now we're dating instead of being a couple."

Mary hesitated. "What does that mean?"

"Haven't noticed much of a change," I said. "We're still sleeping together, but she's been spending the night in her apartment more often. Only been a couple weeks now."

"She still coming to your birthday party?"

"As long as that's okay with you," I said. "Since Sofia and Ezra aren't staying down there, I'm sure they'd give her a ride back to Bellingham."

"Whatever you want, Jon. I can't say I'm overjoyed the two of you are still dating, but I want you to be happy."

"Thanks for that," I said.

August 1998 (Real World, Year 7)

Ezra let himself into my apartment to find me eating a bowl of cereal on the couch. "Hey," he said. "Jezzie and I are going up to Lake Padden this afternoon. You want to join us?"

"You running?" I asked.

"Yeah. Only two laps. You interested?"

"I can do two, if you keep a snail's pace."

"No problem." He looked toward the stairway to my room. "Rebekah here?"

"Nope," I answered. "She's in Arizona at her parent's for a couple weeks." I put my bowl down. "Had my first blind date yesterday."

Ezra looked at me quizzically. "Blind date?"

"Rebekah and I are broken up, remember?"

"She know you're going out with other people?"

"No, but she's probably going to give me the heave once Western starts anyway."

"Probably," he said. "Who set you up?"

"A gal that works at my bank, Lucy." I stopped talking.

"Okay dickhead, what happened?"

"Oh, you want to know now, huh? Well, Lucy knows this gal who works at another bank downtown, so I stop by and we walk to that little café on Magnolia, next to the Federal Building.

"She's cute, nice body, a couple inches shorter than me, thick black hair. We order, she asks what I do for a living and I tell her. The rest of the lunch she barely talks, hardly looks at me. I walk her back to her bank and that was it."

"She didn't know you own a porn store?"

"If she did, she suddenly figured out she didn't want to hang out with the owner. Figured Lucy would've told her what I did before she agreed to go out with me."

"You'd think..." Ezra agreed.

#   #   #

"Looks like you survived your parents," I said to Rebekah as we stuffed my car with pillows. "Jerk off?"

"A couple times," she replied. "But I didn't have a lot of time to myself, so I didn't think about it too much."

You touch yourself every night. How could you not think about it? "That's good, I guess." I got into the car. "You remember your contacts this time?"

"I did."

At the lookout on Chuckanut, Rebekah asked as we laid the papa san cushion on the cement, "Wasn't it a year ago the last time we did this?"

"Almost to the day," I replied. "Because it was about a week after I hired you."

Covering ourselves with a couple light blankets, we stared up at the night sky. "There's more clouds than I expected."

"Yeah," Rebekah said. "It was clear at my place."

We watched the sky for twenty minutes, saw two brief flashes then Rebekah said, "I think I need a snatch licking."

"Here?" *That'd be awesome.*

"No," she said. "Let's go."

In bed, I had my face between her legs, sliding the purple vibe rhythmically in and out of her, then quickly across her clit and returning it to her pussy. After a couple fruitless minutes of swirling my tongue around her clit, she asked me to put the vibe in her rump.

"Talk dirty to me," I said, inching the vibrator in.

"I can't," she replied. "I'm concentrating."

"Tell me how it feels." I kept licking her. "Say you like it in your ass." *Talk to me.*

I stopped again. "Something. I'd like to hear you talk to me for once."

"I don't want to."

"Why not?"

"Fuck this," she said. "I'm not in the mood anymore."

Did someone make you?

She pulled the vibe out.

Next to her, motionless, wordless. My stomach gurgled. "I got to take a dump." I went to the downstairs bathroom.

Returning to my bedroom, "You want to talk?" I asked, climbing into bed. *Was that a sniffle?*

"There's nothing more to say," Rebekah replied.

I tried. What the fuck was all that about? She pissed I wanted to do something different? Or that I had to shit?

Nodding off, I jolted awake. *Is she crying?*

The noise again. *Jesus, she is.* "What's the matter, Rebekah?"

She sniffed loudly. "Sorry. I thought you were already asleep." A deep breath, "I was thinking about us and started crying."

Not about the talking dirty? "You want to elaborate?"

"Not really."

"You going to be okay?"

Another sniffle. "Yeah. It's nothing."

Then why are you crying?

September 1998 (Real World, Year 7)

"Rebekah said she wants to date a girl?" Ezra asked.

"Swear to God," I replied.

"Rebekah going to leave you for her?"

"Doubt it. Rebekah only saw her for a couple minutes after this gal interviewed me for one of the local magazines. Then gives me her number in case I had any questions. I called her the next day and we talked for about half an hour."

"You are so full of shit."

"Went out for Thai food last week."

Ezra guffawed. "Have you told Rebekah yet?"

"Hell, no," I replied. "I mean, she's attractive and if she wanted to go, I'd hop right on that. But she's twenty-three and doesn't act like she's interested in old men. Besides, she's going off to Chile next quarter. Can't imagine she'd want to get involved with some dude she interviewed and had dinner with once."

"Then why she'd go to dinner with you if she wasn't interested?"

"She hadn't been there before and I'd raved about it. She wasn't interested, Ezra. I didn't even get half a signal from her. She acts like she's found a new friend in the porn store guy."

"I don't know, man."

"And she doesn't think Loveline's funny. How could we ever make it work?"

October 1998 (Real World, Year 7)

Rebekah called. "How're classes?" I asked. *Any cute guys you're going to dump me for?*

"Interesting," she said. "Pretty sure my Bio class is going to take most of my time. Two weeks in and I'm already a chapter behind.

"What do you think you'd do if I told you I didn't want to see you anymore?"

"Not much," I replied.

"I don't think you're going to realize what you have until it's gone."

Want to try me? Have at. "Okay. Are we breaking up now?"

"No," she said. "Wanted to let you know what I've been thinking about."

But you're not going to do anything?

\#   \#   \#

"Did you make one of these?" Ezra asked, the official display contest judging sheet in his hand.

"I did," I said.

"Should I try to guess?"

"You'll probably figure it out."

Reaching the back of the store. "That's got to be yours."

Dammit. "Why do you say that?"

"Dr. Fuckenstein's lab? C'mon." He nodded toward the doll on a table, covered with a sheet, a disproportionate bulge standing straight up, surrounded by full size scissors, a knife and bottles of colored liquid.

"I can't say," I replied.

"Am I the only judge for this contest?"

"I've already had a customer give me scores, and a gal from the bank is stopping by later so we can have a completely impartial judge."

"I'm impartial," Ezra said.

"But you're still my friend. There could be the appearance of favoritism."

"But I don't like yours best."

"Thanks."

Ezra finished filling out the form and handed it to me. "You can't count the votes," he said.

"I'm not going to cheat. Besides, I'll leave the forms for the employees to look over if they want."

"Which one was Rebekah's?"

"That one." I pointed to the thirty by thirty piece of paper taped to the counter with the store's name and a short catch-phrase.

"Oh," Ezra said.

"She blamed her classes for the lack of effort."

Dropping the deposit at the bank, I went to Lucy's desk. "You still stopping by to judge the display contest down at my store?"

"When is that?" she asked.

"Today."

"Today? Shoot. I've got to pick up my husband right after work because we're heading out of town for the weekend. I'm sorry, Jon. I can't do it."

"No problem," I said. "You think one of the tellers might be able to help me out?"

"Maybe," she said. "Go ask them."

I approached the least conservative looking gal. She had plans.

Moving to the next teller, "Hey, Ava. What're you doing after work today?" I asked.

"Right after work? Nothing. Why?"

"Lucy bailed on me and I need a judge for a display contest I've got going on down at my shop. It'll take about ten minutes. Maybe could you?"

"Sure," she said.

You will? "Uh..." I hesitated. "You know what my store is, right?"

"A video store, right?"

"Well, yeah, but most of what we have is adult movies. Is that going to be a problem?"

"I'm not going to be judging adult movies, am I?"

"Oh, no no no," I said. "The displays are kind of risqué and I don't want to offend you."

"I'll be fine," Ava said. "As long as it isn't too graphic."

"Not at all," I said. "You know where my store is?"

"I've got your address right here," pointing to the computer.

"You're a lifesaver."

"No problem," Ava replied. "I should be down there around five-thirty or so."

Hope you don't burn in hell for stepping inside a porn shop.

Ava walked in at quarter after five, wearing a long black coat and a cheerful smile. Slender, five eleven in flats, wavy blonde locks a couple inches past her shoulders.

You so don't belong here.

"Hi, Jon."

I introduced her to my manager and handed her the scoring sheet. "Thanks again for coming down. Lucy seriously hosed me."

"She can be a little ditzy," Ava said.

I led Ava around the store, showing her all the entries. *You don't look put off.*

I stood between the explicit movie covers and Ava as much as I could.

Finished, we returned to the front of the store.

"Who won?" my manager asked.

"Hold on," I said. "I really appreciate you taking the time to help me out, Ava."

"It was fun," she said. "Who did win, anyway?"

"I think I know," my manager said. "Unless you hated mine, I won."

"Was this yours?" Ava asked, pointing to the cut-out nudes on the counter that simulated intercourse by pulling a piece of paper.

"Yup."

"Then I think you won."

"Dammit," I said, looking up from the score sheets. "And I took second. Mine rocks."

My manager grinned. "But yours doesn't move. It's all about the motion. Pay up."

"You get cash prizes?" Ava asked.

"Yeah. Now I owe her a hundred bucks. But at least I'll save myself fifty with second place."

Ava laughed.

Shouldn't you be in a rush to get out of here?

"How long have you been with the bank, Ava?" my manager asked.

"Since December."

Noticed you the first day.

"How on earth did he convince you to come down here? You look so nice, I feel like I've got to go change."

"Me, too," I said.

Ava giggled. "This is a lot different than I was expecting. When Jon told me you guys had adult movies, I asked the other girls at the bank and they all laughed because they all knew what kind of store it was. And I thought it would be kind of dark and spooky, but it's not."

"Nope," I said. "Like a video store. With smut."

The three of us talked ten more minutes before Ava needed to go. "I'm sure I'll see you soon," I said.

"And good job picking the right winner," my manager added.

My manager turned to me. "She's really nice. And so pretty. How'd you convince her to come down here?"

"I asked."

"She's not a friend of yours?"

"Nope, one of the tellers at the bank. Didn't think she would once I told her we were a porn store. She's always struck me as uber-conservative, but apparently not."

"And she didn't run away as soon as she was done. Impressive."

Yeah, impressive. Nothing like Wren.

# # #

On my way to the bank Monday, I picked up a bouquet of carnations and a thank you card. As there weren't other customers there, I set the flowers on the counter at Ava's station. "Again, thank you so much for helping out on Friday."

"Thank you, Jon," Ava said. "That's so sweet. You didn't have to get me anything."

"And you didn't have to help me. But you did and I wanted you to know how much I appreciated it." I looked over to Lucy's desk. "Plus it'll piss Lucy off because she could have gotten flowers if she wouldn't've flaked on me. Be sure to rub it in, okay?"

"I don't think I'll need to," Ava said. Lucy looked over at us.

"These could have been yours," I called across the bank.

Lucy got up and came over. "He gave you these for being a judge?" Lucy asked Ava.

"Yup," I answered for her. "So the next time you choose your husband over a trip to a smut shop, you'll know what you're missing."

"If I would have known flowers were part of the deal..." Lucy returned to her desk.

December 1998 (Real World, Year 7)

Sunday, December 17th, Rebekah called. "What're you doing?" she asked.

"Watching football. What's up?"

"Can I come over there?"

We breaking up again?

"We need to talk."

"If we need to talk, you'd better then."

Twenty minutes later, Rebekah came upstairs to the living room and sat on the couch. "Who's playing?" she asked, nodding toward the television.

"I don't know," I said. "I'm hoping to go for a ride since it's not raining."

"I was over at my friend's again last night," she started.

And she convinced you to break this off?

"We'd got back from the Three B and this guy she'd been flirting with, that she knows from school, pulls up behind us as we're getting out of her car."

"Is this the same guy in her Biology class you've been telling me about?"

"Yeah, that guy. I forgot I told you about that. Anyway, he comes inside with us and we're talking about stuff and she's mixing drinks in the kitchen and I ask her if she wants me to take off so she can be alone and she's all like, 'No, stay. I don't think I like him anymore.' She brings him a drink and he stays there for another hour or so, looking like he wants me to leave. Finally, he gets up, says good night and takes off. Then he calls my friend this morning and asks if she wants to go to a party with him tonight."

I don't care. "Is she going to go?"

"She's not sure."

"Is he cute?" I asked.

"He's all right. She thinks he's kind of boring but he was pretty funny last night."

You want him now? What do you want to talk about?
"What's her problem?"

"There's this other guy she met at the bar last night who said he'd be down in Fairhaven tonight, and she wants to try to find him instead."

"Okay..."

Rebekah shifted on the couch, looking around my apartment. "Did the maids just come?"

"Friday," I replied.

"Can I take a bath? My tub is filthy, and I've been wanting a bath all week."

"Sure," I said. "You said we needed to talk. I can't imagine it's about your friend's boy troubles."

Rebekah got up from the couch and headed upstairs. "We do. Come talk to me."

She took off her pants. "Shit, I need to shave my legs. Can I take a shower instead?"

"Whatever," I replied.

She pulled the clear plastic shower curtain closed after she turned the water on. I sat on the toilet. "How do think things are with us?" she asked, while I watched her soap up her legs.

"The same," I replied. "Are you feeling different?"

"Yeah, I guess I am," she answered. "I've been hoping you'd have that mental connection you talked about, and it hasn't happened."

Not even close.

"I've been missing out on a lot of opportunities to meet people at school because of the time I've been spending with you. I don't think it's fair to me to keep seeing you if we're not moving toward something long-term."

Still enjoy your body.

"I really think it's about time for us to stop being a couple and move on with our lives."

Past time.

Silent, I watched her wash her hair.

"What do you think about what I'm saying, Jon?"

"I think it's bullshit that you'd come over, take off your clothes, get into the shower and break up with me. That's just fucking mean, Rebekah."

She turned off the water. I handed her a towel, then walked out of the bathroom.

Rebekah sat down on my bed. "I'm not trying to be mean, Jon."

"What would you think if I did the same thing to you. Came over, got naked and broke up with you, while I was naked. Give me a break. It's fucking cruel," I said.

Her eyes clouded. "I didn't think of it as being mean. I'm so comfortable with you and our relationship, I didn't think anything of it. I wanted to take a bath, you had a clean tub..."

"But you still came over here to dump me." I shook my head. "And you're still not dressed."

She went back into the bathroom, put her clothes on and returned to the bedroom. "Do you have anything to say about any of what I've said?"

"Like what?" I asked. "You're calling it off. You've obviously made up your mind, so I've got to accept it. What do you think I should say, Rebekah? I agree with you. You are missing out on shit by being with me. I don't feel we've made any connection. So you should break up with me. What else is there?" *Besides you're a bitch for doing it naked?*

"Well, it's almost Christmas," she said. "Do you think it'd be better to be done now or wait until after the holidays?"

"We'll spend New Year's Eve together and then we're done?" I asked.

"Yeah, I guess," Rebekah answered.

This is so stupid. But I love fucking you... "You're doing the breaking up, so it's kind of up to you..."

"Let's wait until after New Year's."

"Fine," I said. "I'm going for a ride." Rebekah walked downstairs behind me.

She hugged me in the carport. "Call me later."

Fat chance.

#   #   #

The next day I called Ezra. "While she was in the shower?" he asked.

"Can you believe that? Big fucking balls on her."

"Is she going to join you at Mary's for Christmas?" he asked.

"Naw, she's going down to Utah tomorrow to hang out with her folks until the twenty-ninth. She's coming to New Year's."

"That should be interesting."

"Well, we're not officially broken up until the next day, so..."

# # #

On the 21st, after dropping off the store's deposit, I returned to the flower shop around the corner from the bank. *If she's seeing someone, I can play it off as a Christmas present. Then why didn't I get anyone else at the bank flowers? Get some for Lucy as well. She's married, it won't be a big deal if they both get them from me. Don't get roses. Roses are always romantic. What kind of flowers do you get someone you want to ask out?*

Two bouquets to be delivered to the bank the next day; a moderate lily arrangement for Lucy and a bountiful orchid set for Ava. Both cards read the same:

Merry Christmas. Thanks for everything.

Jon

# # #

The next day Ava was with a customer, so I went straight to Lucy's desk. "Thanks Jon," Lucy said. "You didn't have to do that."

"You're welcome. Thanks for putting up with all my shit. I truly appreciate it."

"The flowers you got Ava are beautiful. You should've seen the expression on her face when she found out they were for her." Elbows on her desk, she whispered, "Do you have a thing for her?"

"Well, maybe," I replied. "Is she seeing anyone?"

"Not that I know of, but I'm not sure."

Dammit. "Well, I'm not going to ask her out if she's already involved with someone. Can you find out?"

"I'll see."

Finished with the customer, Ava brought a huge smile over to Lucy's desk. "Thank you so much, Jon," she said. "They are so pretty."

"No problem. Thanks for all your help," I stood up. "You both have a Merry Christmas."

"Thank you," Ava said again. "Merry Christmas."

# # #

In line at the bank on December 28th, I allowed a couple people to pass me in order to get to Ava's station. I handed her the deposit. "How was Christmas?" I asked.

"Wonderful," counting bills. "You?"

"Good. Down to Tacoma, spent the day with my mom and my cousin. Got more stuff than should be allowed, but that's what I get for being an only." *Ask her.* "Uh, would you like to get dinner sometime?"

She smiled. "Yeah."

Kick ass. "Oh, cool. Uh, I'm stuck at the store doing inventory the next couple days and I've got plans already for New Year's, so, um, what about the evening of the first?"

She thought a second. "Don't think I'm doing anything, so that should work. Can you call me so I can check my calendar at home?" She handed me her number.

So beautiful. So sweet. So out of my league.

# # #

"I got a beer," Ezra said. "Now what?"

"Quarters?" I suggested.

"I refuse to play Quarters with you," he replied. "I heard about the last time."

"I'll be nice," I replied.

"Uh uh. Not happening," Ezra said.

Rebekah said, "We could foos."

"Jon always wins," Jezzie said.

"I'll play with my left hand."

Sofia said, "It's not very fun when you play, Jon."

"Brewno?" I asked.

"Couldn't we do something without beer?" Jezzie inquired.

"You've never played," I said to her. "It's a good time."

The six of us circled the coffee table, with Sofia and me on the couch. I explained the rules as I dealt the cards.

After drinking on a Reverse, followed by a Skip after another Reverse plus a Wild Card all drink, Jezzie complained,

"This is stupid. Why are we even bothering with the cards? Let's finish our beers and do something else."

How about slap you?

"Yeah," Sofia said. "This isn't very fun."

"I've only got two cards left," Ezra added. "We can't quit now."

"Well, I'm done." Jezzie stood with a scowl to Ezra. And the game ended. Ezra challenged me to foosball. The two of us played without the rest of the creeps joining us.

At midnight, we mutilated Auld Ang Syne, joined in a group hug, then all save Rebekah left.

"How much have you had to drink?" Rebekah asked once we were alone.

"Three beers," I replied.

"You tired?"

"Not too tired." *Ring in the New Year getting some.*

Upstairs, naked, Rebekah hopped on me, stroking herself to a quick, quiet orgasm. *She's got to let me fuck her ass. It's our last time together.*

"I just came," Rebekah said, shifting away from my attempt to move south.

"Got to try," I said.

Into her pussy. *Ass in the morning.* I thrust again. *Last butt sex in who knows how long. Anal in the morning.* I came.

A six point five. Can do better alone.

January 1, 1999 (Real World, Year 7)

The morning sun woke me. *Going out with Ava tonight.* I looked right.

Why's she still here? I would of left in the middle of the night. Kind of like cheating on Ava to fuck her now. Shouldn't fuck her if we're officially broken up.

Rebekah appeared downstairs twenty minutes later, holding a bag. "You want some cereal?" I asked, lifting my bowl of Cheerios.

"Sure, yeah," she said. "So we're broken up now, huh?" she asked, from the kitchen.

"That's what I hear," I replied.

Rebekah on the opposite end of the couch from me, we finished our breakfast in silence, intently focused on the television. Rebekah stayed for another program. Then a third.

"I should probably take off," she said, shortly before one.

"Okay." *About time. Got to get ready.*

I walked her to the carport. She gave me a light peck. "Well, I'll see you," she said.

"Reckon so."

Her car pulled away.

Should've fucked her one more time. Ava would never know. Was that the right thing to do? Rebekah wasn't it. Wouldn't've let her go if she was. Did the same thing with Mallory. But I know. Rebekah isn't it.

Twelve:
August 17, 2001 (Real World, Year 9)

My hands clasped on the tall, marble-covered counter, mouth dry. A bead of sweat dawdled down my side. Ava came around the corner from the break room.

Such a beautiful girl.

"What do you think?" I asked, stepping away from the counter to display my tuxedo. "I clean up pretty nice."

"I totally forgot you had that auction tonight," Ava said. "You look nice."

Open your drawer.

"What time you going to be done?"

"Uh, sometime after ten, I suppose. Doesn't start until five."

Ava set her keys down on the counter. Lucy had left her desk, standing quietly at another teller's station, her eyes on Ava. A customer, who had overheard my discussion with Ezra in the coffee shop, waited in line behind me. The assistant manager had moved around her desk.

My heart skipped a beat, then another.

Ava turned back to me. "Call me when you get home. I want to know how it went."

Open your drawer. Am I pale? Can she see me sweating?

"Sure thing."

Her expression evolved from curious to excited as she pulled out the drawer.

"What's…"

While she opened the small black box, I asked, "Ava, will you marry me?"

Her eyes filled with tears and her face lit up. She leaned across the counter and hugged me.

As she pulled away, "Is that a yes?"

Smiling, nodding. "Yes."

Made in the USA
Monee, IL
12 September 2020

42114135R00157